Read SAP PRESS online also

With booksonline we offer you online access to leading SAP experts' knowledge. Whether you use it as a beneficial supplement or as an alternative to the printed book – with booksonline you can:

- Access any book at any time
- Quickly look up and find what you need
- Compile your own SAP library

Your advantage as the reader of this book

Register your book on our website and obtain an exclusive and free test access to its online version. You're convinced you like the online book? Then you can purchase it at a preferential price!

And here's how to make use of your advantage

1. Visit www.sap-press.com
2. Click on the link for SAP PRESS booksonline
3. Enter your free trial license key
4. Test-drive your online book with full access for a limited time!

Your personal **license key** for your test access including the preferential offer

h9kp-nix2-cmju-y8rs

SAP® Essentials

Expert SAP knowledge for your day-to-day work

Whether you wish to expand your SAP knowledge, deepen it, or master a use case, SAP Essentials provide you with targeted expert knowledge that helps support you in your day-to-day work. To the point, detailed, and ready to use.

SAP PRESS is a joint initiative of SAP and Galileo Press. The know-how offered by SAP specialists combined with the expertise of the Galileo Press publishing house offers the reader expert books in the field. SAP PRESS features first-hand information and expert advice, and provides useful skills for professional decision-making.

SAP PRESS offers a variety of books on technical and business related topics for the SAP user. For further information, please visit our website: *www.sap-press.com*.

André Faustmann, Michael Höding, Gunnar Klein, Ronny Zimmermann
SAP Database Administration with Oracle
2008, 818 pp.
ISBN 978-1-59229-120-5

Valentin Nicolescu, Katharina Klappert, Helmut Krcmar
SAP NetWeaver Portal
2008, 462 pp.
ISBN 978-1-59229-145-8

Frank Föse, Sigrid Hagemann, Liane Will
SAP NetWeaver ABAP System Administration
2008, 646 pp.
ISBN 978-1-59229-174-8

Thomas Schneider
SAP Performance Optimization Guide
2008, 638 pp.
ISBN 978-1-59229-202-8

Ingo Hilgefort

Integrating SAP® BusinessObjects XI 3.1 Tools with SAP NetWeaver®

Bonn • Boston

Galileo Press is named after the Italian physicist, mathematician and philosopher Galileo Galilei (1564–1642). He is known as one of the founders of modern science and an advocate of our contemporary, heliocentric worldview. His words Eppur si muove (And yet it moves) have become legendary. The Galileo Press logo depicts Jupiter orbited by the four Galilean moons, which were discovered by Galileo in 1610.

Editor Stefan Proksch, Maike Lübbers
Copy Editor Ruth Saavedra
Photo Credit GettyImages/Joe Drivas
Production Editor Iris Warkus
Cover Design Nadine Kohl
Layout Design Vera Brauner
Typesetting SatzPro, Krefeld (Germany)
Printed and bound in Canada

ISBN 978-1-59229-274-5

1st Edition 2009, 2nd Reprint 2010

Contents

Introduction

SAP® BusinessObjects™ (and former companies Crystal Decisions and Seagate Software) has been delivering an integration with SAP Enterprise Resource Planning (ERP) (R/3, R/3 Enterprise) and SAP NetWeaver® Business Warehouse (SAP NetWeaver BW) for over 10 years. When SAP acquired SAP BusinessObjects in 2008, the software started to reach a much higher amount of customers because SAP positioned SAP BusinessObjects as their business information solution on top of SAP NetWeaver Business Warehouse. The demand for good instructions on how to leverage the SAP BusinessObjects products in an SAP landscape increased, and customers were looking for simple product documentation explaining the usage and deployment of the SAP BusinessObjects software with the focus on SAP NetWeaver Business Warehouse and SAP ERP. Customers were looking for instructions on how to bridge their existing knowledge of SAP NetWeaver Business Warehouse into the SAP BusinessObjects world, and this is what I am aiming to achieve here.

I hope this book gives you a simple but technically detailed enough overview of what you can do today with the SAP BusinessObjects software in combination with your SAP landscape. I wrote this book from an SAP angle to show you how to leverage the existing knowledge and investment in your SAP system with SAP BusinessObjects on top.

Target Group

The book is written for those who are looking for simple instructions on how to use and deploy the SAP BusinessObjects software in combination with an SAP landscape. The book focuses on putting you in a position to leverage an SAP BusinessObjects system on top of your SAP system, to install and configure the software, and to create your first reports with tools such as Crystal Reports, SAP BusinessObjects Web Intelligence, SAP BusinessObjects Live Office, and Xcelsius software. The goal of this book is not to make you an SAP BusinessObjects expert or to explain every detailed aspect of the SAP BusinessObjects software, because several sources already fulfill such a need.

As a reader of this book you should have some previous knowledge of SAP NetWeaver Business Warehouse and SAP ERP. On the SAP BusinessObjects side I tried to keep the need for previous knowledge as minimal as possible, and you should be able to follow this book even without any SAP BusinessObjects knowledge, but you should consider further product documentation and training.

Technical Prerequisites

All steps and examples in this book are based on the SAP BusinessObjects XI 3.1 release in combination with an SAP NetWeaver Business Warehouse 7.x and SAP ERP 2005 system, but you can use previous releases from SAP NetWeaver Business Warehouse and SAP ERP as long as they are supported with the XI 3.1 release.

You can download the SAP BusinessObjects software from the SAP Service Marketplace or from the Download section at the Software Developer Network (SDN). The book is very practical, so I highly recommend you download the following components so you can follow all outlined steps:

- SAP BusinessObjects Enterprise XI 3.1
- Crystal Reports 2008
- Xcelsius 2008
- SAP BusinessObjects Live Office XI 3.1
- SAP BusinessObjects Integration for SAP Solutions XI 3.1

You should also ensure that you have access to an SAP NetWeaver Business Warehouse and SAP ERP system so that you can follow the examples. If you can't get access to an existing system, you can download a trial version from SAP NetWeaver via the Download section in SDN.

Structure of the Book

When this project started, I wasn't very sure if I would be able to explain the topic in enough detail and yet still keep this a simple and not overwhelming book. In each chapter I try to give you a very practical and step-by-step approach to use the software so you'll have very quick and early success with the software.

Here is a short overview on the content of the chapters.

Chapter 1 – SAP BusinessObjects Product Overview

This chapter introduces you to the SAP BusinessObjects Enterprise platform and the SAP BusinessObjects BI client tools that you will use in the following chapters. You will get a short overview of the main parts of the SAP BusinessObjects Enterprise components and take a quick look at the purpose of each of the SAP BusinessObjects BI solution client tools.

Chapter 2 – Installation and Configuration

In Chapter 2 you'll learn how to install and configure the SAP BusinessObjects server and client components. You'll receive step-by-step instructions on the installation of the software, the configuration steps on the SAP BusinessObjects side, and the configuration steps on the SAP NetWeaver side.

Chapters 3 to 7 – SAP BusinessObjects Clients

In Chapters 3 to 7 you'll receive an overview of how each of the SAP BusinessObjects client tools is able to connect to your SAP system and what the supported elements are for each of the client tools. In addition, each of these chapters includes step-by-step instructions on how you can use the client tool to create your first report, ad-hoc analysis, or dashboard on top of your SAP data.

Chapter 8 – Publications

Publications are the SAP BusinessObjects counterpart to the information broadcasting capabilities of SAP NetWeaver. In this chapter you'll receive the details on how to configure your SAP and SAP BusinessObjects system to leverage publications with your configured SAP authorizations and distribute reports and analytics to a large number of recipients.

Chapter 9 – Integration with SAP NetWeaver Portal

In this chapter you'll receive an overview and the necessary steps to integrate your SAP BusinessObjects system into the SAP NetWeaver Portal. You'll learn how to create iViews based on SAP BusinessObjects templates and how to integrate your SAP BusinessObjects system with the Knowledge Management component of your SAP NetWeaver Portal.

Chapter 10 – Troubleshooting and Tips

In this chapter you'll receive additional details on how to trace and troubleshoot your SAP BusinessObjects deployment. You'll also receive some tips on performance-related questions.

Chapter 11 – Outlook

This chapter provides a short outlook on topics that might be of interest for you and your deployment. These topics are part of the integration roadmap given out by SAP and SAP BusinessObjects but were technically not final at the point of writing this book.

Appendix

In the appendix you'll find information on how you can leverage Secure Network Communication (SNC) for a client authentication deployment, and you can find a list of the most recent correction notes for your SAP landscape that are important for the integration with the SAP BusinessObjects software.

Acknowledgments

There are a few people who have helped me over the years to become who I am today, and without them this book would have not been possible. I feel honored to work with these people and to be part of such a great team: Jacob Klein, Tim Lang, Whye Seng Hum, Falko Schneider, Stefan Sigg, Ingo Raasch, Peter Di Giulio, Grant Oltmann, Henrik Areskoug, Mike Seblani, Boris Kovacevic, and Erik Kwok.

Special thanks go to the team from SAP PRESS, who made it possible for me to focus on the writing and not to worry about style, layout, or publishing a book. Thank you, Maike Lübbers and Stefan Proksch; without you this would not have happened. I cannot forget here the SAP BusinessObjects Community team for explaining the meaning of SAP to me.

And finally many thanks to Gaby, Ronja, and Sally for giving me the time to write, but more importantly, for giving me great writing breaks.

In this chapter we'll take a quick look at the SAP NetWeaver Business Warehouse (BW) platform and the BusinessObjects client tools that we'll use during the exercises in this book. In the second half of this chapter you'll receive an overview of the components of SAP BusinessObjects Integration for SAP Solutions.

1 SAP BusinessObjects XI 3.1 and SAP NetWeaver

In this section we'll focus on the architecture of SAP BusinessObjects Enterprise to ensure that you understand the components that will be part of the installation.

The purpose of this section is not to give an in-depth overview on the SAP BusinessObjects Enterprise architecture; the intention is to provide an overview on the architecture with enough details so you can install, deploy, and configure the software. Figure 1.1 outlines the different tiers of SAP BusinessObjects Enterprise.

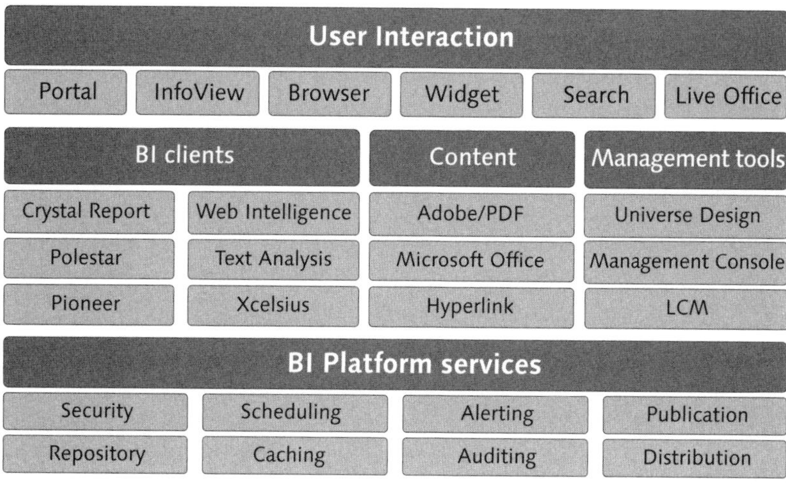

Figure 1.1 SAP BusinessObjects Enterprise Platform

User interaction

For user interaction, SAP BusinessObjects Enterprise includes a large set of tools and options. The most common user interface is InfoView. InfoView provides the user with the complete set of capabilities to leverage all of the features and functions of the BI client tools and delivers functionality such as viewing, scheduling, and broadcasting of reports and analytics to the end user.

SAP BusinessObjects Live Office is a plug-in for the Microsoft® Office environment that allows the user to use the BI client tools inside Microsoft Excel®, Word®, PowerPoint®, and Outlook®.

Part of the user interaction layer is also the integration into the different portal environments – including the SAP NetWeaver Portal. We'll discuss the different options and required steps to integrate SAP BusinessObjects Enterprise into the SAP NetWeaver Portal in Chapter 9, Integrating with the SAP NetWeaver Portal.

BI Tools and Clients

On the BI tools front, the platform supports all the different content types from SAP BusinessObjects such as Crystal Reports, SAP BusinessObjects Web Intelligence , SAP BusinessObjects Voyager, SAP BusinessObjects Polestar, and so on. All of the BI client tools are integrated with the platform to allow you to share your BI content in a secure and scalable platform. In addition, the platform also allows you to share content from other systems such as Microsoft Office or Adobe® Acrobat® and gives you the opportunity to use your BI platform to share different types of content in the same platform.

We'll go into more detail on the BI client tools in the next couple of chapters.

Management Tools

In the area of the management tools the BI platform delivers several options to manage the system itself and manage the integration with other system landscapes.

Central Management Console (CMC)

The Central Management Console (CMC) is a web-based tool that allows you to administrate and configure your SAP BusinessObjects Enterprise solutions. The following list represents some of the main tasks you can perform using the Central Management Console:

- Create, configure, and manage users and user groups
- Create, configure, and manage services of your platform
- Integrate with other user authentication providers, such as Lightweight Directory Access Protocol, Microsoft Active Directory, and SAP
- Assign object security to users and user groups
- Set up and configure scheduling and publications
- Administrate and manage your BI content and content categories

Central Configuration Manager

The Central Configuration Manager (CCM) provides the administrative functionality to configure and manage the services of your SAP BusinessObjects Enterprise system. You can use the Central Configuration Manager to start, stop, enable, or disable services and perform configuration steps on those services. In contrast to the Central Management Console, the Central Configuration Manager is available as a Windows client only.

Lifecycle Management Tool

SAP BusinessObjects delivers a Lifecycle Management tool that allows you to move content and dependent objects from your development environment to your test and quality environment and finally to your production environment. You can manage different versions, data connectivity, content dependencies, and the promotion of content objects between different systems.

Platform Service

The platform services deliver the core BI platform functionality to the end user and system administrator. The following is a brief explanation on the main components of the platform services.

Central Management Server (CMS)

The Central Management Server is the "heart" of the system and manages and controls all of the other services. In addition the Central Management Server manages access to the system database. The system database contains all information about the users, groups, server configurations, available content, available services, and so on. The main tasks of the Central Management Server are:

- Maintaining security by managing users and user groups and the associated groups configured in the SAP BusinessObjects platform.
- Managing objects by keeping track of all objects hosted in the platform and managing the physical location of those objects and the object definition by using the system database.
- Managing services by constantly validating the status of each service and the overall list of available services. In addition, the Central Management Server is able to handle load balancing to allow for enhanced scalability and better usage of hardware.
- Auditing by keeping track of any event inside the platform and thus allowing the administrator to base further deployment considerations on actual information from the usage of the system.

File Repository Services

Each deployment of the SAP BusinessObjects Enterprise platform has an input and an output file repository service. The input service is responsible for storing the content available in the platform, except instances (scheduled reports), which are managed by the output file repository service.

Processing Tier

The processing tier of the SAP BusinessObjects Enterprise platform includes (along with other components) the following main components:

- **Job processing services**
  The job processing services are responsible for fulfilling requests from the Central Management Server to execute a prescheduled job for a specific report. To be able to run the job successfully, these services require access to the underlying data sources.
- **Cache services**
  The cache services are used in combination with the processing services. When a request from a user can be fulfilled with cached information, there is no need to use the processing service. Otherwise, the cache services hand over the request to the processing services.

- **Viewing processing services**
  The viewing processing services are responsible for retrieving the content objects from the file repository services, executing the content against the data source, and showing the actual content to the end user via the different viewer types.

Server Intelligence Agent (SIA)

The Server Intelligence Agent (SIA) allows you to simplify some administrative tasks such as adding or removing services or starting and stopping services. For example, you could assign all of the processing services to a specific SIA, which then allows you to start and stop all those service with a single command.

Publication and Publishing Services

Part of the SAP BusinessObjects XI Release 3.1 platform is the ability to create a publication for Crystal Reports, SAP BusinessObjects Web Intelligence, or SAP BusinessObjects Desktop Intelligence. Publication on the SAP BusinessObjects platform is the counterpart to information broadcasting on the SAP NetWeaver platform. It allows you to set up a scheduling process for document types that will send out the personalized result set to a large set of users. We'll take a closer look at this functionality in combination with your configured SAP data-level security in Chapter 8, Publications with SAP Security.

1.1 SAP BusinessObjects BI Client Tools

In this section we'll briefly cover the BI client tools that we'll use later in combination with your SAP system. The main purpose of this section is to give you a brief introduction to each of the tools and to explain the main use for each of the tools.

1.1.1 Crystal Reports

Crystal Reports is a tool that allows you to create a broad range of reports. You can create legal or form-based reports such as an actual tax report or a customer invoice. Crystal Reports also provides you the flexibility to create very complex reports, for example, financial reports involving hierarchies.

By using features like crosstabs and the strong formatting capabilities, you can easily create financial reports, as shown in Figure 1.2.

Actual vs Budget with Variances

12/18/2008 6:24:55PM

Actual vs Budget with Variances

For the Months Ending 03/31/2005

	March					YTD				
	Actual	Budget	Act vs Bud Variance	Last Year	Curr vs Last Year	Actual	Budget	Act vs Bud Variance	Last Year	Curr vs Last Year Variance
Revenue										
Sales Revenue										
Bike Sales - Competition	$183,342.03	$141,284.73	($42,057.30)	$94,572.06	$88,769.97	$530,577.42	$466,006.26	($64,571.16)	$444,161.41	$86,416.01
Bike Sales - Hybrid	$35,258.67	$25,972.11	($9,286.56)	$15,799.35	$19,459.32	$58,835.00	$27,717.17	($31,117.83)	$54,999.16	$3,835.84
Bike Sales - Kids	$10,575.30	$7,449.72	($3,125.58)	$5,020.80	$5,554.50	$13,483.19	$15,896.47	$2,413.28	$11,690.43	$1,792.76
Bike Sales - Mountain	$117,392.84	$81,079.78	($36,313.06)	$62,599.69	$54,793.15	$127,030.57	$144,175.75	$17,145.18	$108,284.64	$18,745.93
Sales Gloves	$1,101.50	$990.77	($110.73)	$442.21	$659.29	$2,046.05	$1,667.94	($378.11)	$2,036.64	$9.41
Sales Helmets	$5,347.12	$6,054.00	$706.88	$1,634.82	$3,712.30	$9,600.78	$14,840.39	$5,239.61	$7,831.41	$1,769.37
Sales Locks	$631.75	$107.99	($523.76)	$366.83	$264.92	$1,435.23	$2,118.56	$683.33	$1,220.53	$214.70
Sales Returns	$5,351.02	$3,504.21	($1,846.81)	$5,351.02	$0.00	$17,757.85	$7,645.52	($14,253.64)	$15,416.63	($2,341.22)
Sales Saddles	$1,116.13	$204.78	($911.35)	$532.13	$584.00	$2,263.16	$1,351.67	($911.49)	$2,375.62	($112.46)
Net Sales	$349,414.32	$259,639.68	($89,774.64)	$175,616.87	$173,797.45	$727,513.55	$666,128.70	($61,384.85)	$617,183.21	$110,330.34

Figure 1.2 Crystal Reports Sample Financial Report

In Figure 1.3 you can see that Crystal Reports also provides the functionality to create reports with charts and other visualization elements and includes user interactivity such as drill down and interactive filtering.

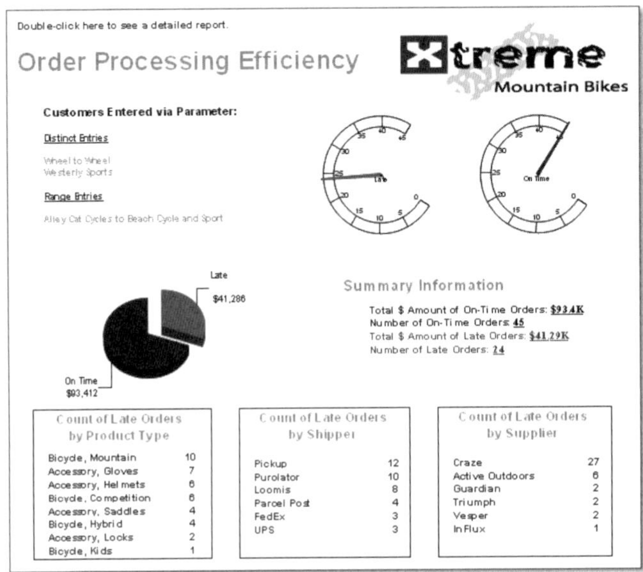

Figure 1.3 Crystal Reports Sample Report

Overall, Crystal Reports is the industry leader for enterprise reporting, allowing you to create highly formatted reports but also provide interactive reports to your end users.

1.1.2 Web Intelligence

SAP BusinessObjects Web Intelligence is a BI tool focusing on the concept of self-service reporting and providing the end user the ability to create ad hoc new reports or change existing reports based on new business requirements. SAP BusinessObjects Web Intelligence empowers the end user to answer business questions using a very simple and intuitive user interface (UI) and typically providing access to a broader range of data.

SAP BusinessObjects Web Intelligence allows the end user to dynamically create data-relevant queries; apply filters to the data; sort, slice, and dice through data; drill down; find exceptions; and create calculations.

Using SAP BusinessObjects Web Intelligence, you can easily create a simple sales report showing revenue broken down by several dimensions, as shown in Figure 1.4.

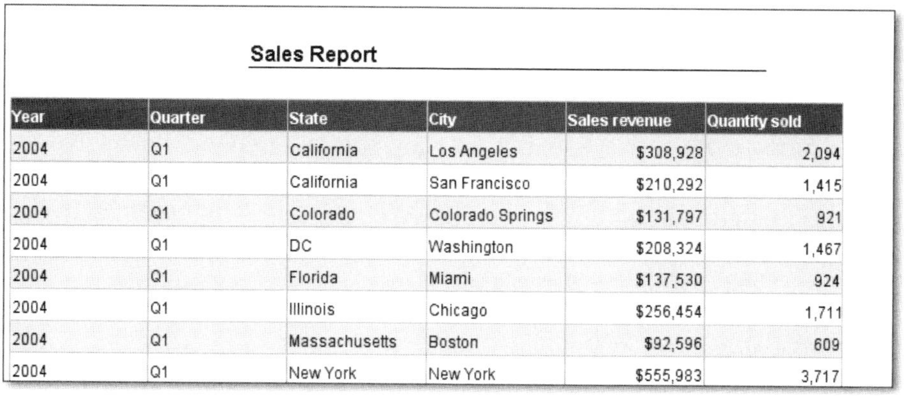

Sales Report

Year	Quarter	State	City	Sales revenue	Quantity sold
2004	Q1	California	Los Angeles	$308,928	2,094
2004	Q1	California	San Francisco	$210,292	1,415
2004	Q1	Colorado	Colorado Springs	$131,797	921
2004	Q1	DC	Washington	$208,324	1,467
2004	Q1	Florida	Miami	$137,530	924
2004	Q1	Illinois	Chicago	$256,454	1,711
2004	Q1	Massachusetts	Boston	$92,596	609
2004	Q1	New York	New York	$555,983	3,717

Figure 1.4 Simple SAP BusinessObjects Web Intelligence Report

More importantly, with a few clicks you'll be able to change the report to a sales report showing the top 10 states based on revenue with a chart showing the top 10 cities based on revenue (see Figure 1.5)

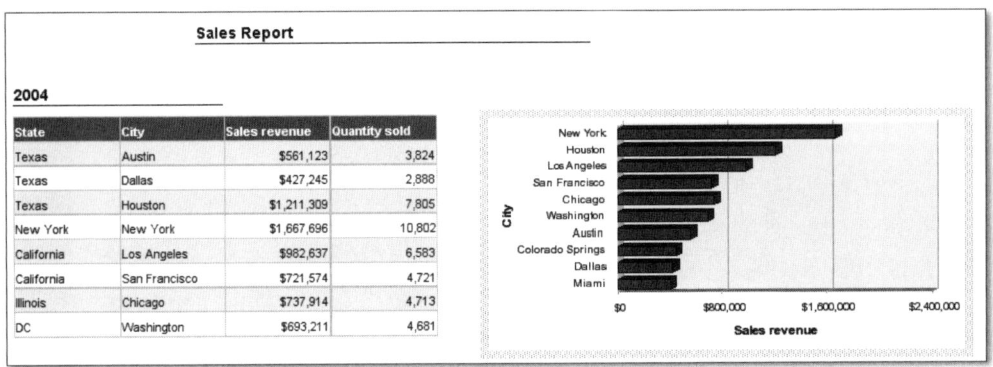

Sales Report

2004

State	City	Sales revenue	Quantity sold
Texas	Austin	$561,123	3,824
Texas	Dallas	$427,245	2,888
Texas	Houston	$1,211,309	7,805
New York	New York	$1,667,696	10,802
California	Los Angeles	$982,637	6,583
California	San Francisco	$721,574	4,721
Illinois	Chicago	$737,914	4,713
DC	Washington	$693,211	4,681

Figure 1.5 SAP BusinessObjects Web Intelligence Report with Chart

SAP BusinessObjects Web Intelligence allows you to reduce your IT department's workload of creating or changing reports and provide your end users with a real self-service reporting environment.

1.1.3 Universe Designer

The Universe Designer allows you to create connections to your data sources and to create universes that you can then provide to business users to analyze the data in a more user-friendly way. A universe provides an easy to understand and non-technical interface for your users so they can focus on analyzing and sharing the data by using common business terms.

The Universe Designer provides you with a graphical interface allowing you to define connections to relational databases (RDBMS) and multidimensional data structures (online analytical processing [OLAP]) and define the business semantics on top of the data source.

1.1.4 Xcelsius

Xcelsius is a product that allows you to transform your data into stunning visualization models that will allow your end users to monitor key performance indicators (KPIs) and identify critical data in a very simple and intuitive way. Xcelsius provides the ability to create a simple dashboard such as a single gauge up to a complex what-if scenario based on a broad range of data. Xcelsius is designed to put you in a position to develop simple to complex dashboards in days instead of months. You can share the dashboards with your end users via Microsoft Office, Adobe PDF, or a page in your corporate portal.

Figure 1.6 shows a simple Xcelsius dashboard providing you access to three different views in the form of charts and allowing you to use a slider as a navigation element to change the value of the sales growth for your forecast.

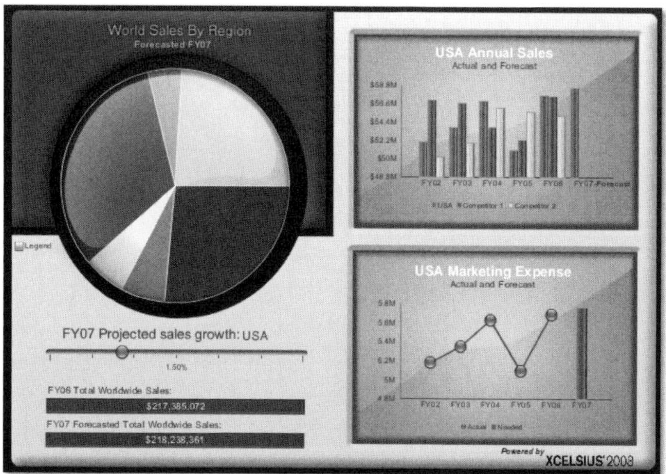

Figure 1.6 Xcelsius Sample of a Sales Dashboard

Figure 1.7 shows a more complex dashboard that allows you to perform a complete profitability analysis by changing multiple factors such as growth rate and expenses. The Xcelsius dashboard shows immediately the impact on overall net income.

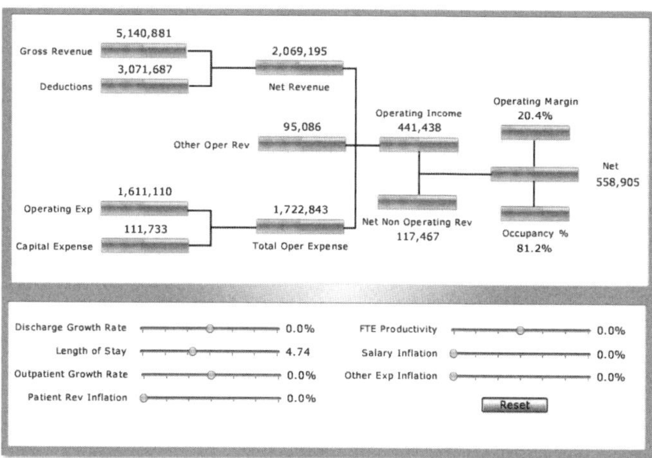

Figure 1.7 Xcelsius sample – What-if Analysis

1.1.5 Other BI Client Tools

SAP BusinessObjects offers other BI client tools such as SAP BusinessObjects Voyager and SAP BusinessObjects Polestar that are available in the XI 3.1 release and work with SAP systems, but the focus of this book is to give you a great start with the overall solution; explaining each of the tools would go beyond the scope of this book. The focus here is to give you all the information you need to deploy and configure the SAP BusinessObjects platform with your SAP system, and if you follow all the steps, you should have no problems using any of the BI client tools offered for the XI 3.1 platform.

1.2 SAP BusinessObjects Integration for SAP Solutions

SAP BusinessObjects Integration for SAP Solutions is an add-on product for your SAP BusinessObjects XI 3.1 platform that allows you to use the BI client tools and the platform features in combination with your SAP NetWeaver Business Warehouse or SAP Enterprise Resource Planning (ERP) system. The following is a short description of the components that are included in SAP BusinessObjects Integration for SAP Solutions:

- **Data Connectivity**
  You can use a broad range of data connectivity in combination with your SAP system. The data connectivity elements shown in Table 1.1 are part of the SAP BusinessObjects Integration for SAP Solutions.

Data Connectivity	Usage
BW MDX	You can use this connectivity with Crystal Reports and connect to your SAP NetWeaver Business Warehouse system.
BW Query	This is the predecessor of the BW MDX connectivity.
ODS	You can use this connectivity to connect with Crystal Reports directly (without the need for a BW query) to the Operational Data Source (ODS) layer in your SAP NetWeaver Business Warehouse system.

Table 1.1 Integration for SAP Solutions – Data Connectivity

Data Connectivity	Usage
InfoSet	You can use this connectivity with Crystal Reports and use classic InfoSets (not to be confused with InfoSets from SAP NetWeaver Business Warehouse) and SAP queries from your SAP ERP system.
Open SQL	You can use this connectivity with Crystal Reports to connect to tables, Advanced Business Application Programming (ABAP) functions, and data clusters in your SAP NetWeaver Business Warehouse or SAP ERP system.
OLAP BAPI	This is the connectivity that you can use with SAP BusinessObjects Voyager and SAP BusinessObjects Web Intelligence to connect to your SAP NetWeaver Business Warehouse system.

Table 1.1 Integration for SAP Solutions – Data Connectivity (cont.)

- **SAP Authentication**
  The SAP authentication component allows you to integrate your SAP roles and users with your SAP BusinessObjects Enterprise system. You can import the SAP roles and users and use them as standard user groups and users in your SAP BusinessObjects server. In addition, the component allows you to use single-sign-on functionality.
- **BW Publisher**
  The BW Publisher allows you to take a Crystal Reports object from the SAP NetWeaver Business Warehouse system and publish it (save it to) to the SAP BusinessObjects Enterprise system.
- **Content Administration Workbench**
  The Content Administration Workbench gives you the functionality to set up, configure, and administrate the integration of your SAP BusinessObjects Enterprise system with your SAP NetWeaver Business Warehouse system. The tool is available as a standard SAP transaction, and it allows you to publish, delete, and synchronize your Crystal Reports content in the SAP NetWeaver Business Warehouse system with your SAP BusinessObjects Enterprise system.
- **Web content**
  The web content that is available to you during the installation represents SAP-specific features that are available in InfoView and the Central Management Console, for example, the My Roles navigation option in InfoView.

- **SAP NetWeaver Portal – Knowledge Management**
  You can integrate the complete repository of your SAP BusinessObjects system into the SAP NetWeaver Portal and provide functionality such as feedback, ranking, and collaboration on top of your SAP BusinessObjects system by using the features from the Knowledge Management component.
- **SAP NetWeaver Portal – iView template and sample iViews**
  The SAP BusinessObjects Integration for SAP Solutions also delivers a specific iView template that you can use to integrate BI content into the SAP NetWeaver Portal. The iView template offers functionalities such as defining a viewer or selecting between a last instance and on-demand reporting of a particular report.

In the next sections you'll learn the necessary steps to install and deploy the SAP BusinessObjects server and client components in combination with the SAP BusinessObjects Integration for SAP Solutions.

2 Installation and Configuration

The installation and configuration of the SAP BusinessObjects server and client components consists of four main areas:

1. Installation of the server-side components of SAP BusinessObjects Enterprise and SAP BusinessObjects Integration for SAP Solutions (see Section 2.1, SAP BusinessObjects – Server-Side Installation)
2. Installation of the client-side components from the BI client tools (Crystal Reports, Xcelsius, Universe Designer) and the SAP BusinessObjects Integration for SAP Solutions (see Section 2.2, SAP BusinessObjects – Client-Side Installation)
3. Preparing the SAP server landscape to work in combination with the SAP BusinessObjects software (see Section 2.3, SAP NetWeaver – Server-Side Configuration)
4. Configure the integration between SAP NetWeaver and the SAP BusinessObjects solutions (see Section 2.4, Integrating SAP BusinessObjects and SAP NetWeaver)

Installation and Deployment

In the following sections the installation and configuration is broken down into the installation of the server-side software and the client-side software. If you are following all of these steps with a single hardware system available to you, you can install the server and client components from SAP BusinessObjects on a single system.

The recommended approach for this situation is to install the software in the following order:

- SAP BusinessObjects Enterprise
- SAP BusinessObjects client tools
- SAP BusinessObjects Integration for SAP Solutions (client and server components)

2.1 SAP BusinessObjects – Server-Side Installation

In this chapter we'll concentrate on the server side of the landscape and provide an overview of SAP BusinessObjects Enterprise. We'll then install the server landscape and install SAP BusinessObjects Integration for SAP Solutions in combination with SAP BusinessObjects Enterprise.

2.1.1 Installation of SAP BusinessObjects Enterprise

In this section you'll install and configure the SAP BusinessObjects Enterprise software. The focus here is to enable you to deploy a simple SAP BusinessObjects platform scenario. SAP BusinessObjects Enterprise is a BI platform that can be deployed and scaled to fit your requirements. Further details on complex deployment scenarios and detailed installation material can be downloaded from *http://service.sap.com/bosap-instguides* (for accessing the service marketplace you require a logon account that can be requested on the main page, *http://service.sap.com*).

Technical Prerequisites

Before you start the actual installation of SAP BusinessObjects Enterprise please ensure that the following requirements are met:

- Validate the exact details of the supported platforms and ensure that this matches you environment. You can review the list of supported platforms at *http://service.sap.com/bosap-support*.
- Check that your account for the operating system has administrative privileges.
- If you are planning to deploy on a distributed system, you need to have access to all machines via TCP/IP.
- You must have administrative access to the application server. Supported application servers are Jboss, Tomcat, Oracle, WebLogic, WebSphere, and SAP J2EE.
- You require access to a database system to install the system database for SAP BusinessObjects Enterprise. Supported database systems are IBM DB2, MySQL, Microsoft SQL Server, Oracle, and Sybase.

SAP BusinessObjects Enterprise – Default Installation

The default installation of SAP BusinessObjects Enterprise includes the Java application server Tomcat and MySQL for your system database.

For details on how to deploy the software using a different database system or a different supported application server including SAP J2EE, you can download the following documentation at *http://service.sap.com/bosap-instguides:*

- SAP BusinessObjects Enterprise XI 3.1 Deployment Planning Guide
- SAP BusinessObjects Enterprise XI 3.1 Installation Guide for Windows
- SAP BusinessObjects Enterprise XI 3.1 Installation Guide for Unix
- Web Application Deployment Guide for Windows
- Web Application Deployment Guide for Unix

Installation Routine

For the installation routine we'll assume a single-server deployment scenario and we'll use Tomcat as the Java application server and MySQL for the system database. Table 2.1 shows the information for the environment that we'll use to give you more details on the values that will be entered in the configuration screens.

Description	Value
Server name	VMWSAP12
SAP application server	CIMTDC00.WDF.SAP.CORP
SAP system ID	CIM
SAP client number	003
System number	00

Table 2.1 System Information

If you want to leverage a logon group of your system, you need to have the details of the message server and the logon group of your system, which then replaces the values for the application server and the system number.

Based on the situation of performing a single-server deployment, the server name (VMWSAP12) will also become the name for our SAP BusinessObjects Enterprise system.

1. After you started the installation routine you'll be asked to select a language for the installation routine itself. This does not influence the language for the actual deployment of the software. In our example we'll select English as the setup language.
2. In the next two screens you'll be asked to accept the license agreement and enter the license keycode that you obtained. After this step, you have the choice of language packs (Figure 2.1). This time the selection influences the availability of the software in different languages. For our installation we will select English.

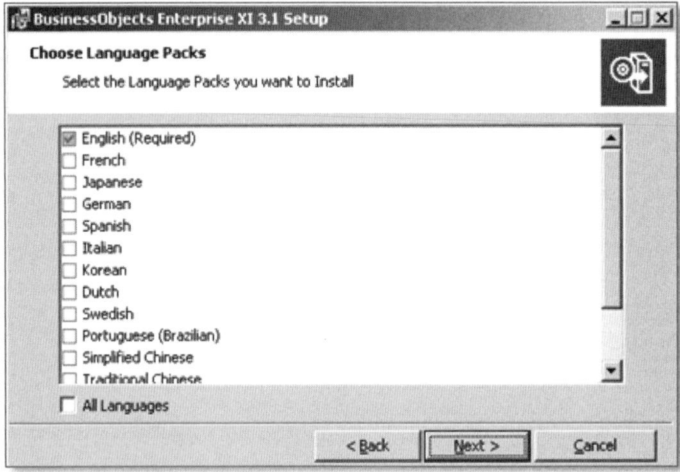

Figure 2.1 SAP BusinessObjects Enterprise – Language Packs

3. Next you select the type of installation you want to perform (see Figure 2.2). You can select a new installation, which is the easiest way to deploy a standard SAP BusinessObjects system. You should select CUSTOM OR EXPAND INSTALL when you want to select specific components and WEB TIER when you need to deploy the web applications. In our scenario we'll select NEW. When you select INSTALL MYSQL DATABASE SERVER, the installation process will also install a MySQL database and populate the system database into this database system.

   The option ENABLE SERVERS UPON INSTALLATION is selected by default and ensures that all installed components are activated after the installation is finished.

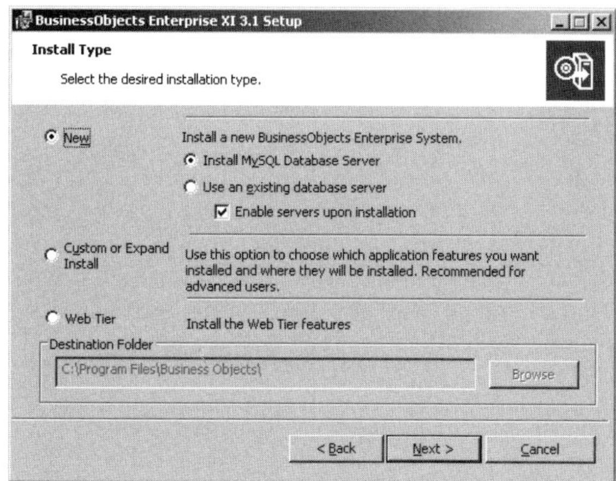

Figure 2.2 SAP BusinessObjects Enterprise – Installation Type

4. You use the next screen (see Figure 2.3) to configure the port for your Central Management Server and the password for the administrator account. We'll accept the default port 6400 and define a password for the administrator.

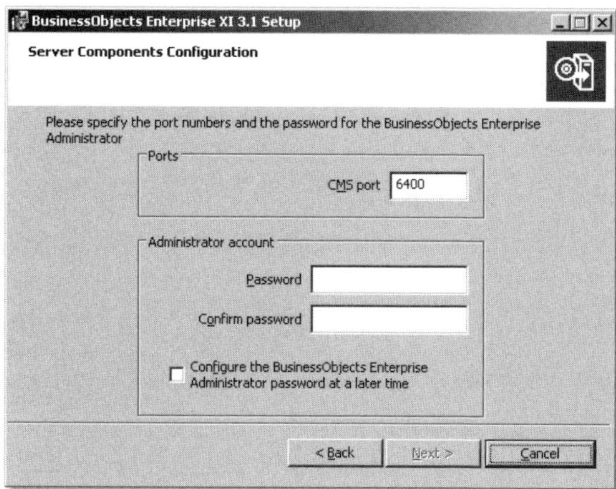

Figure 2.3 SAP BusinessObjects Enterprise – Server Components Configuration

5. Next the installation routine sets up your Server Intelligence Agent (see Figure 2.4). By default, the node name will match your machine name, but you can also assign an alias here. In addition, you can configure the port that the Server Intelligence Agent will use. We'll use the machine name as the node name and accept the default port (VMWSAP12:6410).

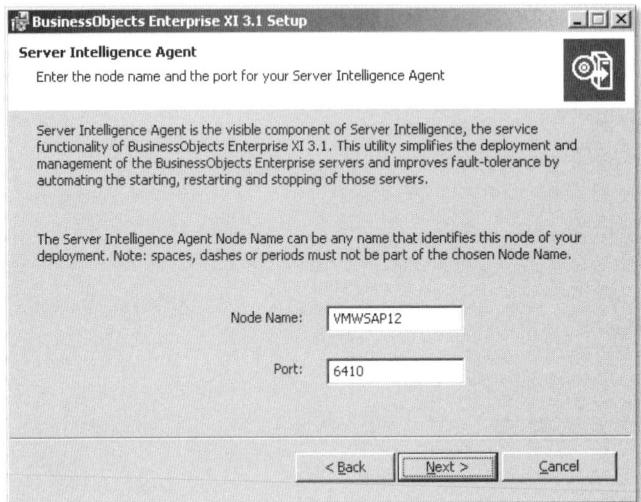

Figure 2.4 SAP BusinessObjects Enterprise – Server Intelligence Agent

6. Because we installed MySQL for the system database, in the next step the database configuration screen comes up (see Figure 2.5). Which screen you see depends on the database system you select.

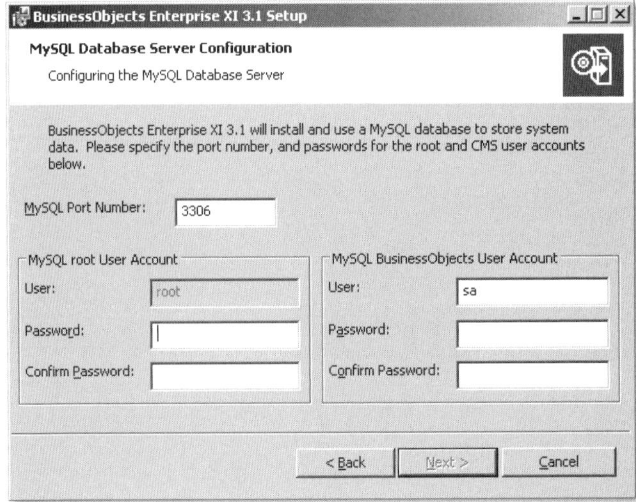

Figure 2.5 SAP BusinessObjects Enterprise – Database Server Configuration

You need to specify the port number used by MySQL and provide a password for the two accounts that will be generated as part of the installation routine. The installation routine will set up one MySQL root user account and a MySQL SAP BusinessObjects user account.

7. In the next screen you can select the type of application server for your landscape, and you need to select the server type for Java or the website for the IIS deployment (see Figure 2.6). The installation allows you to select one option or both. In our example we'll select the option to install Tomcat as the Java application server.

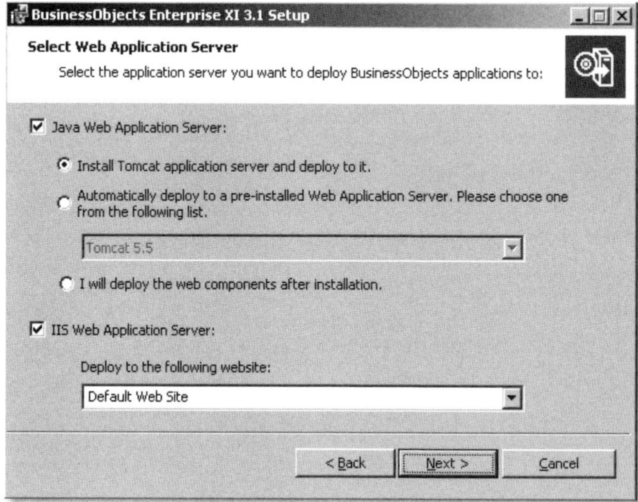

Figure 2.6 SAP BusinessObjects Enterprise – Web Application Server

8. Based on your selection in the previous screen, you're now asked to configure the ports for the Java application server (Figure 2.7).

Java Application Server vs. Internet Information Server (IIS)

If you're considering a deployment with the IIS, you still need to have a Java application server deployment for the deployment of the Central Management Console (CMC) and the Web services because those elements are not natively supported on IIS in the XI 3.1 release.

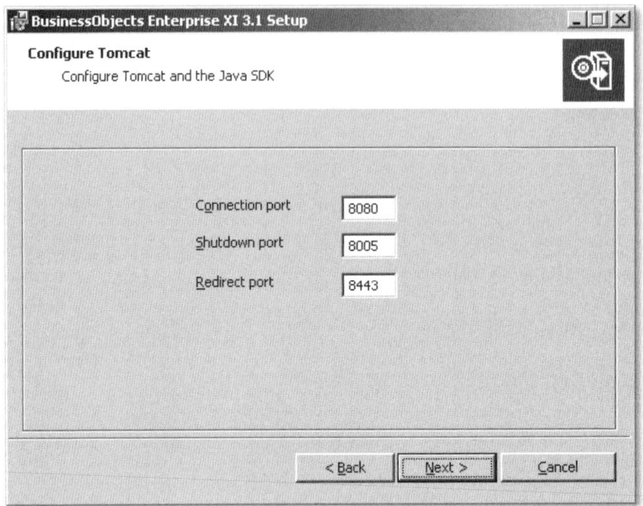

Figure 2.7 SAP BusinessObjects Enterprise – Application Server Details

In our example we accept the default ports for the Tomcat application server that the installation process recommends and continue to the next screen, where you can start the actual installation routine. If you selected an existing application server, you need to enter the ports from your custom deployment. Depending on your hardware, you should be able to finish the installation routine relatively quickly and see the final screen giving you the opportunity to launch the Central Management Console for administrative purposes.

2.1.2 SAP BusinessObjects Integration for SAP Solutions – Server-Side Installation

In this section we'll focus on the prerequisites and installation of SAP BusinessObjects Integration for SAP Solutions on the server side.

Technical Prerequisites

After you have finished the installation of the SAP BusinessObjects Enterprise landscape, you start the installation of SAP BusinessObjects Integration for SAP Solutions. Before you start the actual setup routine, some technical prerequisites need to be met:

- The file *saplogon.ini* needs to be installed on all data-access-related components.
- If load balanced logon will be part of the deployment, the following entry must appear in the services file (found in *%windir%\system32\drivers\etc*) on any SAP BusinessObjects Enterprise machines running a Central Management Server or data processing server component (for example, Crystal Reports Job Server): `sapms [SAP System ID] [SAP tcp port number]/tcp`
- The file *librfc32.dll* (or the Unix equivalent, depending on your platform) needs to be deployed on the SAP BusinessObjects Enterprise system:
  - For the Windows environment copy *librfc32.dll* to the *%windir%\system32* folder.
  - For Unix environments copy the file *librfccm* to the folder *business-objects_root/enterprise120/PLATFORM* and add the location to the library path. The *PLATFORM* placeholder depends on your selected platform (solaris_sparc for an installation on Solaris).
- Components from the SAP Java Connector (Version 2.1.8) need to be deployed on the SAP BusinessObjects Enterprise server:
  - The file *sapjco.jar* needs to be available as part of the shared library path for the Java application server from SAP BusinessObjects Enterprise. For example, for a Tomcat installation on Windows you need to copy the file *sapjco.jar* to the folder *\Program Files\Business Objects\Tomcat55\shared\lib*, where you might have to create the folder *shared* with the subfolder *lib*. For Unix you need to place the file in the application server shared *lib* directory. For other Java application servers you need to specify the path to the file via the CLASSPATH.
  - For Windows environments deploy the file *sapjcorfc.dll* to the *%windir%\system32* folder.
  - For Unix environments copy the file *libsapjcorfc* to the folder *business-objects_root/enterprise120/PLATFORM* and add the location to the library path. The *PLATFORM* placeholder depends on your selected platform (solaris_sparc for an installation on Solaris).
- If you're planning to use a message server with a logon group, the entry `sapms[SID] [port]/tcp` must appear in the *services* file on the SAP BusinessObjects Enterprise system.

You can replace `[SID]` with the system ID of your SAP system, and replace `[port]` with the port number of the message server that SAP BusinessObjects Enterprise will log onto (for example, `sapmsCIM 3600/tcp`).

SAP Java Connector

The SAP Java Connector can be downloaded from the SAP Service Marketplace (*http://service.sap.com/connectors*). Please ensure that you download the 32-bit version based on the platform you choose to install for SAP BusinessObjects Enterprise because SAP BusinessObjects XI Release 3.1 does not support a native 64-bit version of the SAP Java Connector.

Prerequisites for Crystal Reports Publishing

SAP BusinessObjects Integration for SAP Solutions provides you with the capability to store a Crystal Reports object into the SAP NetWeaver Business Warehouse repository and from there to publish the report to the SAP BusinessObjects Enterprise server. This integration can be implemented with a BW Report Publishing Service, which is delivered as part of SAP BusinessObjects Integration for SAP Solutions or with an SAP Gateway. Both of these options have advantages and disadvantages as shown in Table 2.2.

	BW Report Publishing Service	SAP Gateway
Installation	▸ Easy installation and configuration	▸ More complex installation and configuration
Scalability	▸ New publishing instances are created when needed	▸ Uses local resources more efficiently than the publishing service
Administration	▸ Each publishing service can only connect to a single SAP NetWeaver Business Warehouse system ▸ Publishing services are not automatically stopped if they are not needed anymore ▸ Changes to the configuration require changes to the registry	▸ Capable of handling multiple SAP NetWeaver Business Warehouse systems with a single gateway

Table 2.2 Comparison of BW Report Publishing Service and SAP Gateway

Based on your system landscape and your requirements, you can select your type of deployment. We'll discuss the publishing process in more detail in Section 2.4.2, Setting up the Publishing Process for Crystal Reports. For now, this is a decision about the installation of SAP BusinessObjects Integration for SAP solutions.

If you're not sure which deployment option you want to select, it is recommend that you start with the BW Report Publishing Service, which is easier to install and configure, and you can decide later on to move to an SAP Gateway configuration.

Installation Routine

In this section we go through the installation routine of SAP BusinessObjects Integration for SAP Solutions step by step.

1. After you have met the technical prerequisites, you can start the installation of SAP BusinessObjects Integration for SAP Solutions. In the first screen of the installation routine you'll be asked which language you prefer for the UI of the installation. The choice you make here does not influence the languages for SAP BusinessObjects Integration for SAP Solutions. You'll be asked to list the languages to be installed at a later stage of the process.
2. In the next two screens you'll be asked to accept the license agreement, and you'll have to enter the license keycode for the product. After these two steps you'll be presented with a list of languages. This time the language refers to the language of the SAP BusinessObjects software that you're installing.
3. Next you'll be asked if you want to install the client components or the server components (see Figure 2.8), or if you want to make a custom selection of the components. The options CLIENT and SERVER represent preconfigured options that only install the required components. The option CUSTOM allows you to select from the list of all components those that you explicitly want to install. You can select CUSTOM to see all available options in the next screen. (The screenshots included in this book always show the default screen where you still have to make your choice.)
4. Figure 2.9 shows all components that are included in SAP BusinessObjects Integration for SAP Solutions. The list includes all components for the server side and the client side, and you can find a description of all of the components in Section 1.2, SAP BusinessObjects Integration for SAP Solutions.

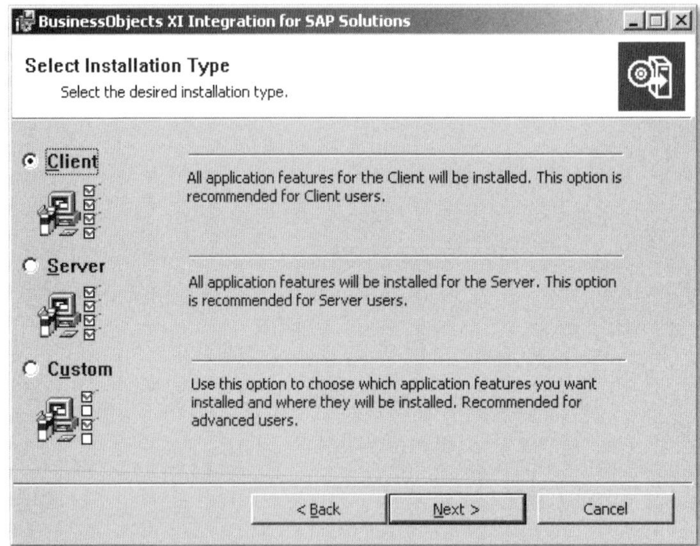

Figure 2.8 Integration for SAP Solutions – Installation Type

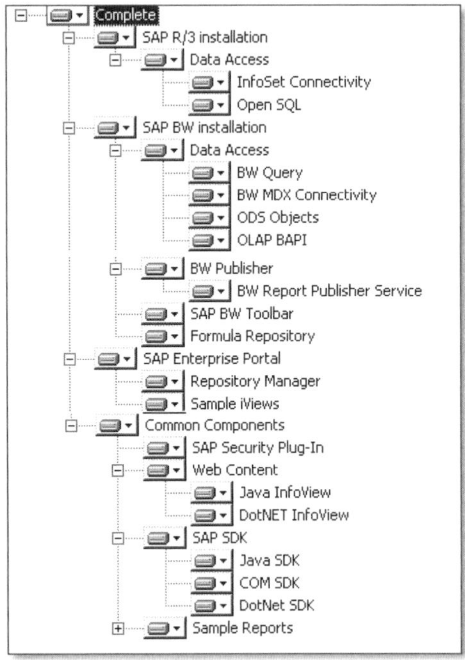

Figure 2.9 Integration for SAP Solutions – All Components

You can now select all of the required components for the SAP BusinessObjects Enterprise server landscape as shown in Table 2.3.

Installation Area	Installation Component	Detailed Selection
SAP R/3 installation	Data Access	InfoSet Connectivity
	Data Access	Open SQL
SAP BW installation	Data Access	BW MDX Connectivity
	Data Access	ODS Objects
	Data Access	OLAP BAPI
	BW Publisher	BW Report Publishing Service
SAP Enterprise Portal	Repository Manager	
	Sample iViews	
Common Components	SAP Security Plug-in	
	Web Content	
	SAP SDK	Java SDK

Table 2.3 SAP BusinessObjects Integration for SAP Solutions – Server-Side Components

5. After you have selected the items and moved to the next step, you'll be asked to provide credentials to log on to the SAP BusinessObjects Enterprise Central Management Server. These credentials are required so that the installation routine can make the necessary changes to the underlying system database for SAP BusinessObjects Enterprise.

   As you can see in Figure 2.10, you need to provide the name of your Central Management Server and the password for the administrative account. The name of your Central Management Server will match the name of your server if you have followed our steps so far.

6. In the next screen (see Figure 2.11) you need to configure the details for the BW Report Publishing Service. You can enter the details based on the descriptions in Table 2.4. The value for the program ID can be freely selected, but remember that the value is case sensitive.

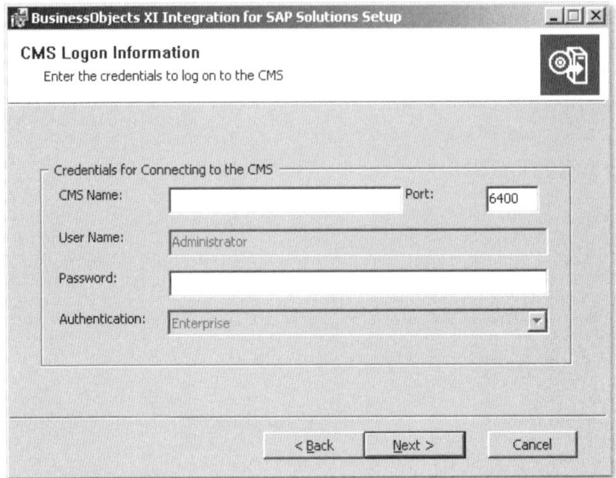

Figure 2.10 Integration for SAP Solutions – Central Management Server Logon

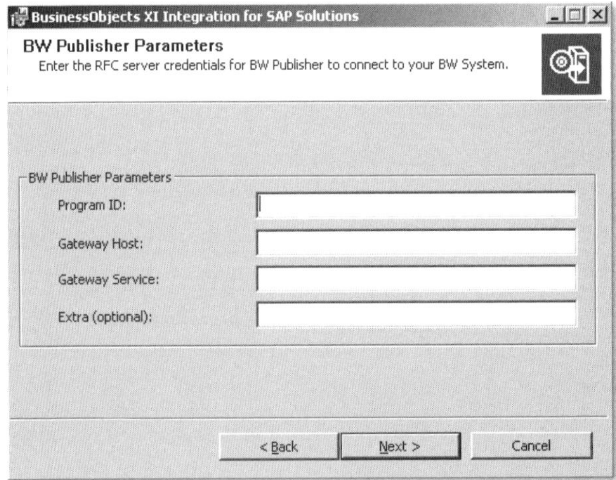

Figure 2.11 Integration for SAP Solutions – BW Publisher Parameters

Parameter Name	Description
Program ID	Enter a name for the BW Report Publishing Service. This program ID will identify the service. You cannot enter any spaces in the name, and the name is case sensitive. Example: BW_PUBLISHING_VMWSAP12

Table 2.4 Parameter Options for the BW Report Publishing Service

Parameter Name	Description
Gateway Host	Enter the fully qualified name of your SAP server. If you're using an SAP cluster environment, you should enter the name of the central instance here. Example: CIMTDC00.WDF.SAP.CORP
Gateway Service	Enter the port number that the gateway host is listening on. Example: 3300
Extra (optional)	If you're planning to use Secure Network communication (SNC) between your SAP and SAP BusinessObjects systems, you can enter additional flags in the field.

Table 2.4 Parameter Options for the BW Report Publishing Service (cont.)

7. In the next steps you can decide if you want to deploy the Java applications as part of the installation or if you'll deploy them manually afterwards (see Figure 2.12).

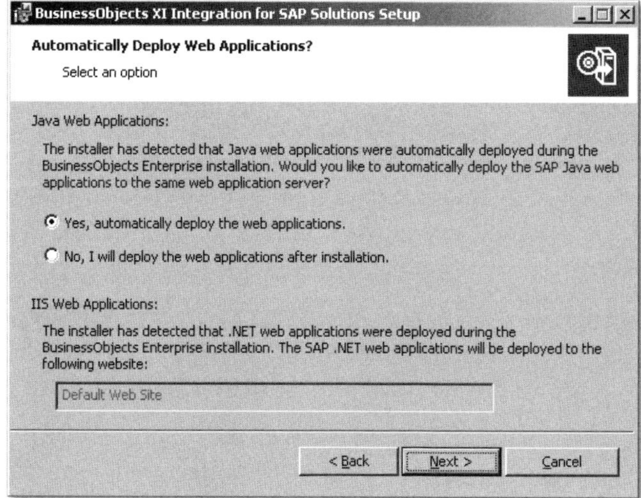

Figure 2.12 Integration for SAP Solutions – Web Application Deployment

If you decide to deploy the applications automatically, the system will ask for the application server details in the next screen. For our installation we'll select the option to deploy the web applications automatically.

Automatic Deployment During Installation

The supported application servers for automatic deployment during the installation are Tomcat, WebLogic, Websphere, and Oracle Application Server.

For the exact versions of the supported application server, please refer to the supported platforms of SAP BusinessObjects Enterprise XI Release 3.1 (*http://service.sap.com/bosap-support*).

For details on how to deploy the web application tier manually using a different supported application server including SAP J2EE, you can download the following documentation at *http://service.sap.com/bosap-instguides:*

- Web Application Deployment Guide for Windows
- Web Application Deployment Guide for Unix

After this step the installation will start and deploy the necessary components. When the installation has finished, you should be able to perform the following steps:

- You should be able to open InfoView, and the SAP authentication should be listed as one of the available authentication options as shown in Figure 2.13.

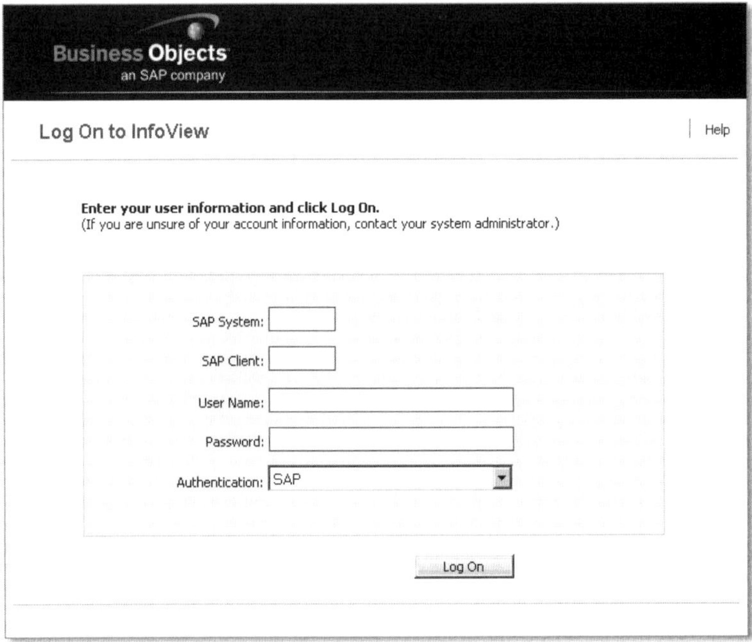

Figure 2.13 InfoView Logon Screen

- You should be able to open the Central Management Console (CMC), and SAP should be listed as one of the available authentication options.
- You should be able to log on to the Central Management Console and navigate to the Authentication area, where you'll see SAP as a separate available authentication provider.
- The BW Report Publishing Service should start and keep running.

You now have installed your SAP BusinessObjects Enterprise system in combination with SAP BusinessObjects Integration for SAP Solutions. In the next section we'll continue with the installation of the SAP BusinessObjects client tools and the client-side parts of SAP BusinessObjects Integration for SAP Solutions.

2.2 SAP BusinessObjects – Client-Side Installation

In this section we'll cover the installation of the SAP BusinessObjects client tools and the installation of the SAP BusinessObjects Integration for SAP Solutions for those clients. A more detailed technical overview of how each of those client tools can be used in combination with your SAP system will be done in the following chapters.

2.2.1 Installation of SAP BusinessObjects BI Client Tools

In this section we'll go through the installation of the client tools: Crystal Reports, Xcelsius, SAP BusinessObjects Live Office, and Universe Designer. In an actual production environment it is not necessary to deploy the client tools on the server environment, but for now we are working on the assumption that this is a single-server deployment. If you have separate hardware available to you, you should have no problem following the steps to install the client tools on the additional system.

Crystal Reports

1. Just like the installation routine for SAP BusinessObjects Enterprise, you first can select the setup language for the installation routine.
2. In the next steps you need to accept the license agreement and enter the license keycode for the product. Then you can select the language packs you want to install for Crystal Reports. In our installation we select English.

3. In the next screen (see Figure 2.14) you can select the installation type. The option TYPICAL installs Crystal Reports with the most common elements, and the option CUSTOM allows you to select the components you want to install. If you're not sure which option to select, I recommend selecting CUSTOM.

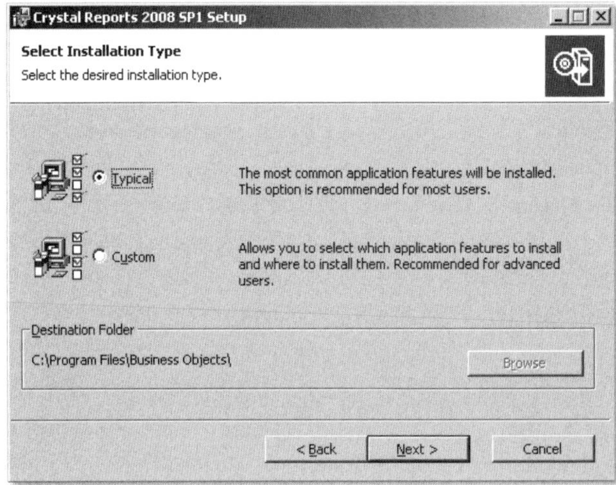

Figure 2.14 Crystal Reports – Installation Type

4. For the custom installation type (see Figure 2.15), you can select the exact components that you want to install on your client.

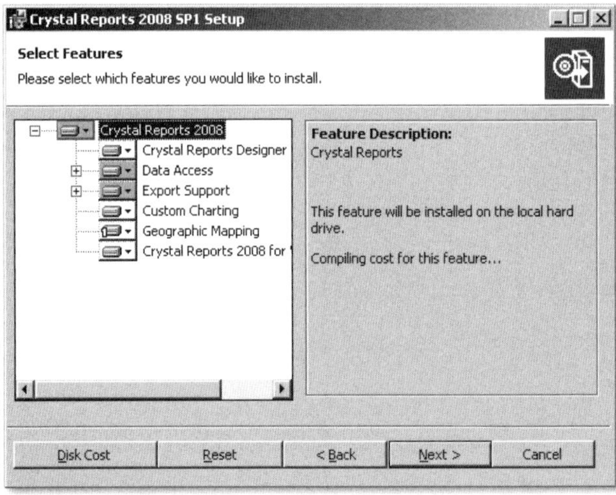

Figure 2.15 Crystal Reports – Installation Components

5. In the next step of the installation process you can configure the option to update your Crystal Reports installation automatically.
6. In the final step you can start the actual installation routine for Crystal Reports.
7. Next the installation of Crystal Reports will start, and you should be able to use Crystal Reports after a short time.

Xcelsius

1. Just like the installation routine for Crystal Reports, you'll be asked here as well to select a setup language.
2. After you have accepted the license agreement and provided the license keycode, you can select the languages for the software. In our installation we select English.
3. You can then select the folder for your Xcelsius installation (see Figure 2.16). If Xcelsius is not the first SAP BusinessObjects product that you install on the system, the suggested path will be the path from your other SAP BusinessObjects products.

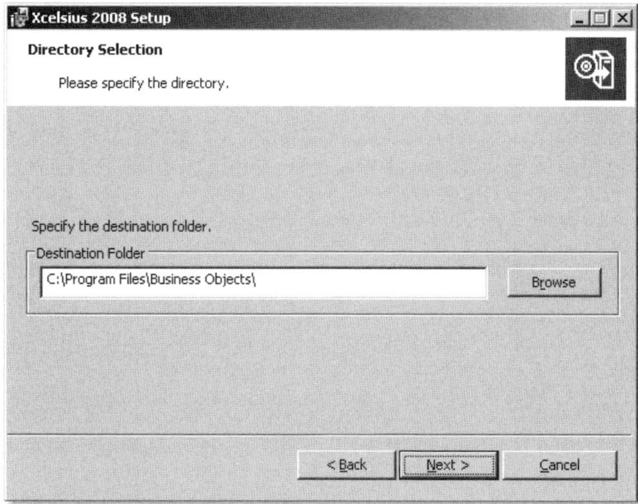

Figure 2.16 Xcelsius – Directory Selection

4. After you have confirmed the folder for the installation, you can move to the next screen, which allows you to start the actual installation routine.

5. After this screen the installation will start, and you can use Xcelsius after a short period of time.

Xcelsius and SAP BusinessObjects Live Office

If you install SAP BusinessObjects Live Office and Xcelsius on the same system, Xcelsius will ask you to configure the SAP BusinessObjects Live Office compatibility on the first start of Xcelsius.

You can configure the compatibility in the menu path FILE • PREFERENCES • EXCEL OPTIONS.

If you prefer to work with SAP BusinessObjects Live Office inside Xcelsius, then you need to activate the compatibility mode. If you disable the compatibility mode, you'll need to work with SAP BusinessObjects Live Office outside Xcelsius in a separate Microsoft Excel spreadsheet.

SAP BusinessObjects Live Office

1. Just like the previous installation routines, the first step in the SAP BusinessObjects Live Office installation routine is the selection of the setup language.
2. After you have accepted the license agreement, you can select the language packs for your SAP BusinessObjects Live Office deployment. In our installation we select English.
3. In the next screen you can set the destination folder for the installation (see Figure 2.17). Use the BROWSE button to specify the location for the installation or accept the default path. If SAP BusinessObjects Live Office is not the first SAP BusinessObjects product that you are installing, the installation will suggest the path that you used for the other SAP BusinessObjects products on your client system.
4. After confirming the folder location, you can start the actual installation routine in the next screen.
5. After this step the installation routine will start, and you should be able to use the SAP BusinessObjects Live Office functionality in Microsoft Excel, PowerPoint, and Word as soon as the installation is finished.

SAP BusinessObjects Live Office License Keys

Notice that the client-side installation routine of SAP BusinessObjects Live Office does not ask for a license key. The reason is that the license key has to be entered on the SAP BusinessObjects Enterprise system. To do so you can log on to the Central Management Console, navigate to the License Keys area, and enter the keycode for SAP BusinessObjects Live Office.

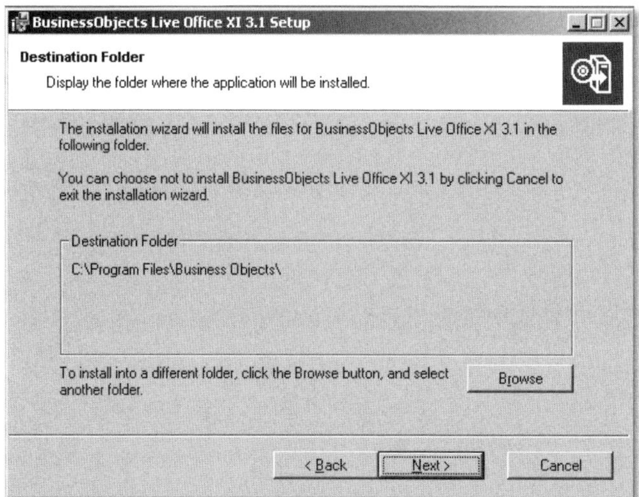

Figure 2.17 SAP BusinessObjects Live Office – Destination Folder

Universe Designer

The following is a list of SAP BusinessObjects client tools that are delivered to you with the SAP BusinessObjects Enterprise platform:

- Web Intelligence Rich client
- Desktop Intelligence
- Data Source Migration Wizard
- Import Wizard
- Publishing Wizard
- Query as a Web Service
- Business View Manager
- Universe Designer

For our purposes in this book, we need the Universe Designer and the Query as a Web Service tool.

You have two options to install the SAP BusinessObjects client tools available to you. You can either use the separate available SAP BusinessObjects client tools installation routine, which requires the SAP BusinessObjects Client DVD or the equivalent download of the SAP BusinessObjects client tools setup, or you can use the SAP BusinessObjects Enterprise installation routine that we used previously for the server-side installation and perform a custom installation that will only include the client components.

1. If you decide to use the SAP BusinessObjects Enterprise installation routine, you need to select the option CUSTOM OR EXPAND INSTALL (see Figure 2.18) so that you can select only the client components and ensure that the server components are not installed.

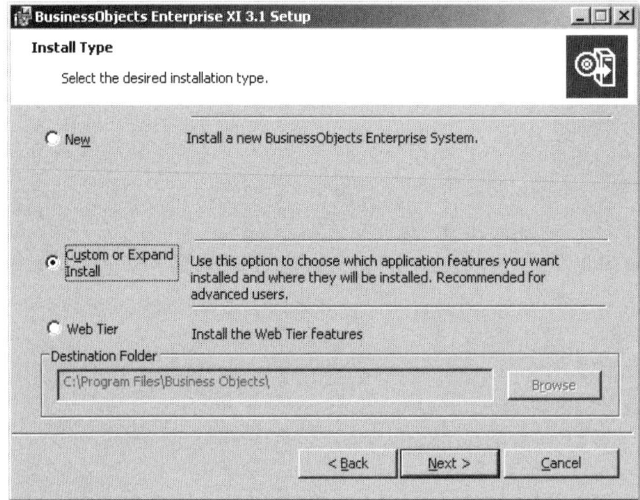

Figure 2.18 SAP BusinessObjects Enterprise – Install Type

2. Next you can select the client components from SAP BusinessObjects Enterprise, as shown in Figure 2.19. You can deselect all other components, and in that way you will only install the client features from SAP BusinessObjects Enterprise on your system that includes the Universe Designer and the Query as a Web Service tool.
3. When using the SAP BusinessObjects-specific client setup, you'll recognize that the steps are very similar to the custom setup option from SAP BusinessObjects Enterprise, with the main difference being that only the client components are available to you.

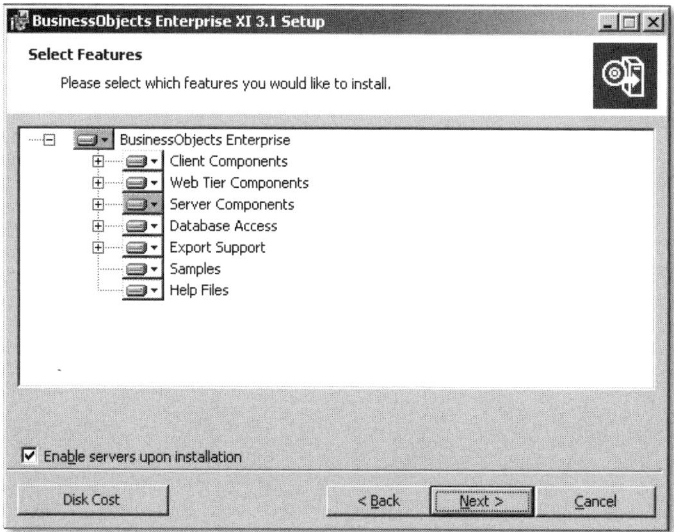

Figure 2.19 SAP BusinessObjects Enterprise – Components

2.2.2 SAP BusinessObjects Integration for SAP Solutions – Client-Side Installation

After you have finished the installation of the server-side components, you continue with the installation of the BI clients in combination with SAP BusinessObjects Integration for SAP Solutions.

For the communication between the BI clients and the SAP system, you need to install the SAP system frontend on each of the clients that will use the SAP BusinessObjects design tools.

Technical Prerequisites

You need to ensure that the following components of the SAP system frontend are available on the client:

- SAP GUI Suite
- SAP BW Add-On for BW 3.5 components
- SAP Business Explorer for SAP NetWeaver Business Warehouse (BW) 7.x systems

Business Explorer 3.5 Components

Even if you are using SAP NetWeaver Business Warehouse 7.x, you still have to install the BW 3.5 Add-On components from the SAP system frontend because Crystal Reports uses UI components from the BW 3.5 Add-on.

This is a prerequisite for the SAP BusinessObjects XI Release 3.1 products and might change in future releases.

Installation Routine

1. After you have installed the SAP system frontend with the BW Add-On BW 3.x and SAP NetWeaver BW 7.x components, you can start the installation of SAP BusinessObjects Integration for SAP Solutions. In the first screen of the installation routine you'll be asked which language you prefer for the UI of the installation.
2. In the next two screens you'll be asked to accept the license agreement, and you'll have to enter the license keycode for the product. After these two steps you'll be presented with a list of language packs, and this time the language refers to the language of the SAP BusinessObjects software you're installing. For our installation we'll select English.
3. Next you'll be asked if you want to install the client components or the server components (see Figure 2.20) or if you want to make a custom selection of the components.

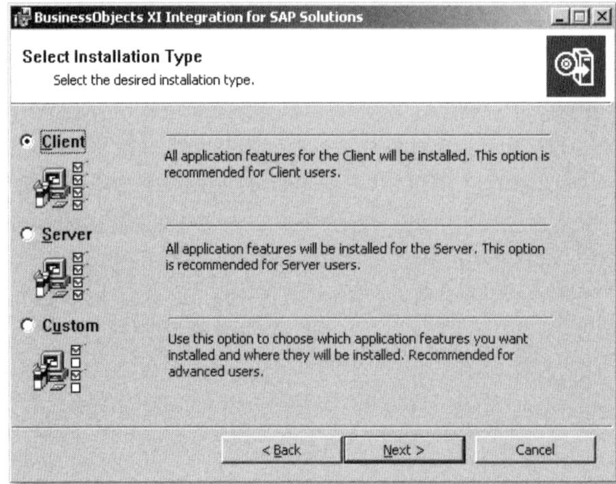

Figure 2.20 Integration for SAP Solutions – Installation Type

4. You can select CUSTOM to see all available options (see Figure 2.9).
5. You can now select all of the necessary components for the client-side installation as shown in Table 2.5. The components listed in Table 2.5 are those that are needed to use the SAP BusinessObjects client tools with SAP BusinessObjects Integration for SAP Solutions.

BW Query vs. BW MDX Connectivity

Notice that the Integration for SAP Solutions includes a BW Query connectivity and a BW MDX connectivity. It is highly recommended that you use the BW MDX connectivity. The BW MDX connectivity is a much more enhanced connectivity to your SAP NetWeaver BW system and in comparison to the BW Query connectivity, the BW MDX connectivity provides support for display attributes and BW queries with multiple structures.

Installation Area	Installation Component	Detailed Selection
SAP R/3 Installation	Data Access	InfoSet Connectivity
	Data Access	Open SQL
SAP BW Installation	Data Access	BW MDX Connectivity
	Data Access	ODS Objects
	Data Access	OLAP BAPI
	SAP BW Toolbar	
Common Components	SAP Security plug-in	
	Sample Reports	BW Query Sample Reports
	Sample Reports	InfoSet Sample Reports
	Sample Reports	Open SQL Sample Reports

Table 2.5 Integration for SAP Solutions – Client-Side Components

2.3 SAP NetWeaver – Server-Side Configuration

In the previous sections we installed and configured the SAP BusinessObjects Enterprise system and the BI client tools. In the next couple of sections we'll configure the SAP NetWeaver system to work in combination with the SAP Business-

Objects system. The following is a list of activities that need to be performed on the SAP system server side to ensure that you can move forward with the installation and configuration of the two systems.

2.3.1 Server Patch Level

SAP BusinessObjects Integration for SAP Solutions requires a minimum patch level of the SAP system. You need to ensure that your SAP system meets those requirements. You can verify the patch level of your SAP system by logging onto to your SAP system and following the menu path System • Status (see Figure 2.21).

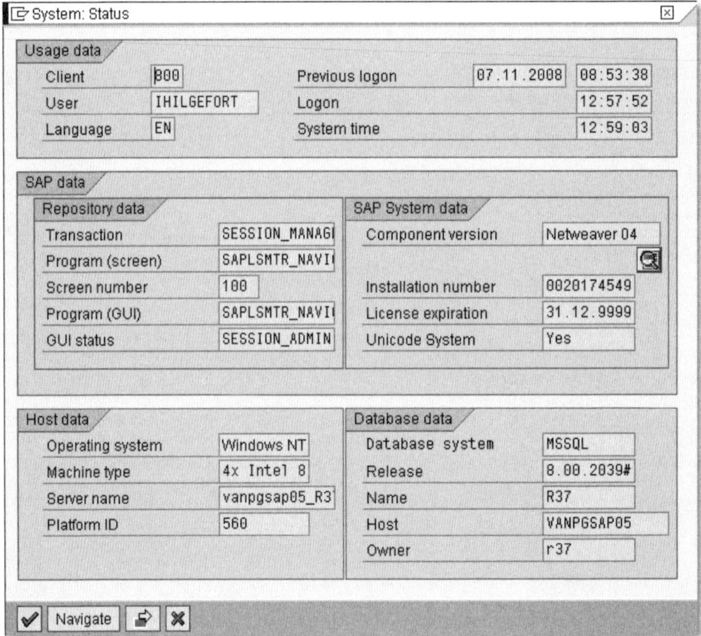

Figure 2.21 SAP System Status

Selecting the magnifying glass next to the component version will take you to a detailed list of patch levels of your SAP system (see Figure 2.22), and you can compare the patch level and version of your system with the supported systems for SAP BusinessObjects Integration for SAP Solutions. You can find the most recent list of supported versions for the SAP BusinessObjects portfolio at *http://service.sap.com/bosap-support*.

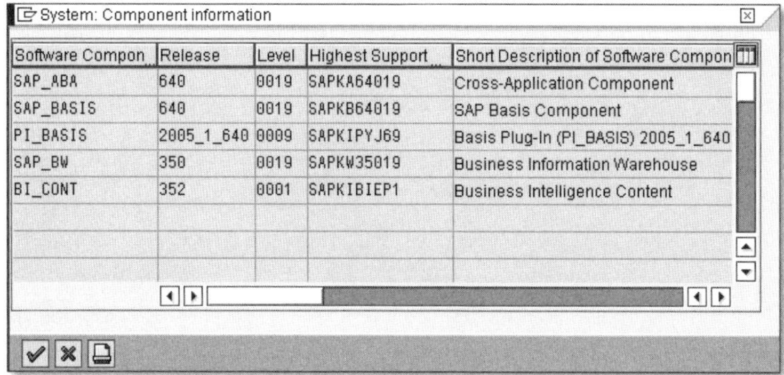

System: Component information

Software Compon	Release	Level	Highest Support	Short Description of Software Compon
SAP_ABA	640	0019	SAPKA64019	Cross-Application Component
SAP_BASIS	640	0019	SAPKB64019	SAP Basis Component
PI_BASIS	2005_1_640	0009	SAPKIPYJ69	Basis Plug-In (PI_BASIS) 2005_1_640
SAP_BW	350	0019	SAPKW35019	Business Information Warehouse
BI_CONT	352	0001	SAPKIBIEP1	Business Intelligence Content

Figure 2.22 SAP System Component Information

2.3.2 Supported Platforms

The list of supported platforms for SAP BusinessObjects Integration for SAP Solutions can be downloaded from *http://service.sap.com/bosap-support.*

Ensure that you also pay attention to the list of additional notes that are mentioned in the list of supported platforms because here SAP BusinessObjects also mentions very recent SAP notes that will help you improve the overall solution or that will fix known issues.

2.3.3 ABAP Transports

Parts of SAP BusinessObjects Integration for SAP Solutions require ABAP transports to be imported into your SAP system. These ABAP transports enable the functionality required to use the components. The following list represents components that require an ABAP transport to be imported into the SAP system. Most of the ABAP transports are required for the connectivity when you use Crystal Reports, but the SAP authentication is required for all of the client tools and your SAP authentication on the SAP BusinessObjects Enterprise system.

The ABAP transports are not part of the actual installation routine for SAP BusinessObjects Integration for SAP Solutions. You can find the ABAP transports directly on the source media (download from service marketplace or DVD) in a folder called TRANSPORTS:

- Open SQL connectivity
- InfoSet connectivity

- BW MDX Driver connectivity
- BW ODS connectivity
- Row-level Security Definition editor
- Cluster Definition editor
- SAP authentication
- Content Administration Workbench
- BW Query parameter personalization

ABAP Transports

You can find the details on the ABAP transports and the objects that are created in the Appendix of the Installation Guide for SAP BusinessObjects Integration for SAP Solutions. The installation guide can be downloaded from *https://service.sap.com/bosap-instguides*.

Ensure that you also verify if future service packs for the SAP BusinessObjects software do contain updates to those transports.

2.3.4 Single Sign-On

To be able to use Single Sign-On between the SAP NetWeaver system and SAP BusinessObjects Enterprise you need to configure the SAP system to accept Single Sign-On logon tickets and to create them. This involves setting parameter values in the profile (see Table 2.6) of your SAP system via Transaction RZ10; setting or changing those values requires a restart of the system.

Profile Parameter	Value	Comment
`login/create_sso2_ticket`	1 or 2	Use the value 1 if the server possesses a public key certificate signed by the SAP CA (*SAP Certification Authority*). Use the value 2 if the certificate is self-signed. If you are not sure, then use the value 2.
`login/accept_sso2_ticket`	1	Use the value 1 so that the system will also accept logon tickets.

Table 2.6 Single Sign-On Profile Parameters

2.3.5 User Authorizations

Depending on the SAP BusinessObjects client tool and the connectivity you use for your SAP system, the SAP users will require specific authorizations to be able to create, edit, or simply view the content created with the SAP BusinessObjects tools.

A detailed list of required authorizations is available in the chapter "Authorizations" in the Installation & Administration Guide for the Integration for SAP Solutions, which is available for download at *https://service.sap.com/bosap-instguides.*

In addition to the standard authorizations to perform tasks such as viewing a BW query in the case of a SAP NetWeaver Business Warehouse system, SAP BusinessObjects Integration for SAP Solutions also includes a specific authorization class ZSSI. This class includes authorization objects that allow you to specify authorizations for specific tasks such as creating a new report or changing a server definition in the Content Administration Workbench.

2.4 Integrating SAP BusinessObjects and SAP NetWeaver

In this section we'll focus on configuring the integration between the SAP BusinessObjects Enterprise server landscape and our SAP NetWeaver system. The main tasks we will cover are:

- Configuring the SAP authentication for SAP BusinessObjects Enterprise (see Section 2.4.1, Configuration of SAP Authentication)
- Setting up the publishing process for Crystal Reports (see Section 2.4.2, Setting up the Publishing Process for Crystal Reports)
- Configuring the viewing of reports as part of the SAP system frontend (see Section 2.4.3, Viewing Reports within the SAP System Frontend)

2.4.1 Configuration of SAP Authentication

After the installation of the SAP BusinessObjects Integration for SAP Solutions, the SAP BusinessObjects Enterprise server offers you the SAP authentication mechanism as an additional option. The SAP authentication provides the capability to use the existing SAP roles and assigned users and the functionality to use Single Sign-On for the reports that the end users will consume.

1. To start the configuration of the SAP authentication you need to log on to the Central Management Console with an administrative account. You can use the authentication method Enterprise and the account Administrator that was created during the installation.
2. After a successful authentication you'll be presented with the main screen (see Figure 2.23) of the Central Management Console, which provides two main navigation elements. On the top is a drop-down box that you can use to navigate directly to the configuration areas. In addition, you can use the toolbar on the left-hand side.

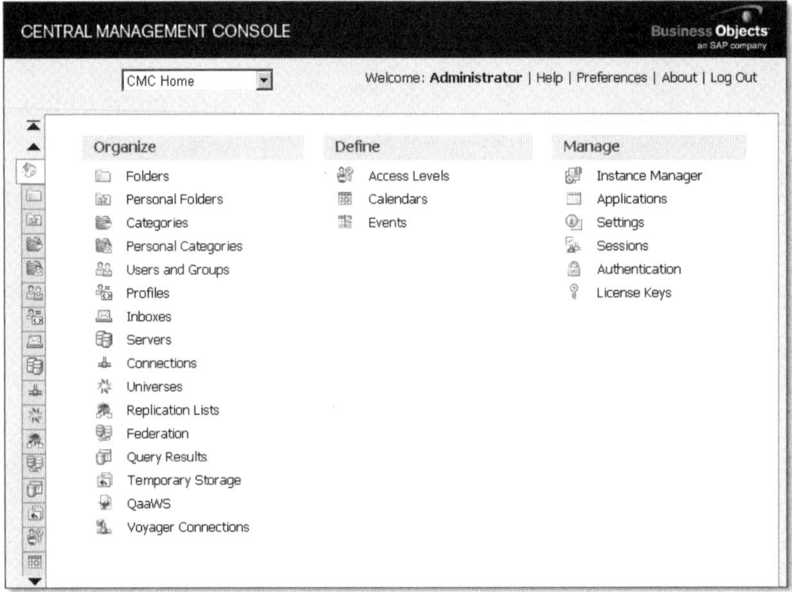

Figure 2.23 Central Management Console – Start Screen

3. To configure the SAP authentication details, you select AUTHENTICATION, and the system then presents the list of available authentication providers (see Figure 2.24).
4. You can now double click the SAP authentication provider, and the system will present you with the screen shown in Figure 2.25 so that you can create a new SAP system entry. In this first step of the configuration you can identify the SAP systems that you want to use in combination with the SAP BusinessObjects Enterprise system. Only systems that are configured during this step can use the full functionality of the SAP BusinessObjects landscape.

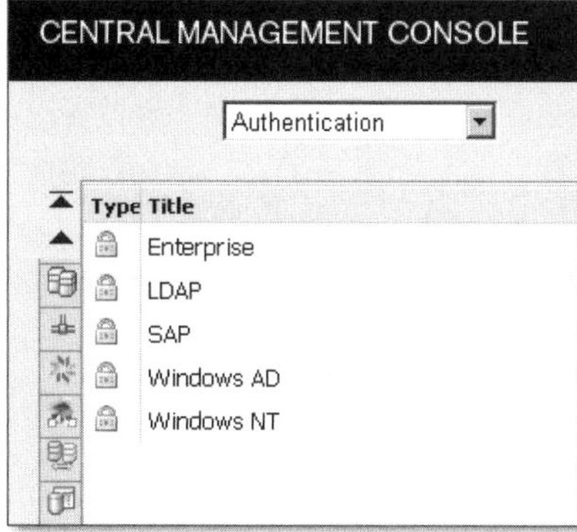

Figure 2.24 Central Management Console – List of Authentication Providers

The configuration screen allows you to configure your system based on an application server with a system number or a message server with a logon group. Start by entering the system ID of your SAP system and the client number; then enter either a combination of message server with a logon group or application server with a system number (see Figure 2.25). When you're finished with the configuration, your system will appear in the LOGICAL SYSTEM NAME field so that you can select any of the configured systems later on.

Entitlement Systems
Entitlement Systems | Role Import | SNC Settings | Options
Logical system name CIMCLNT003
System CIM Client 003
Disabled
Load balancing
Message Server
Logon Group
Application host
Application Server CIMTDC00.WDF.SAF
System Number 00
Username DEMO
Password ••••••••••
Language en
New Delete Update

Figure 2.25 SAP Authentication – Entitlement System

The user account that is requested here is used only for administrative tasks, such as reading the users and roles from the SAP system or validating role membership of users authenticating against the system. The user account requires only a bare minimum of authorizations on the SAP side (see Table 2.7 for details). Enter the user credentials from the SAP account that you created based on those authorizations and the language code, and click the UPDATE button to save your entries.

Table 2.7 lists all necessary authorization objects and authorization values that need to be assigned to the user credentials that are being leveraged in the SAP Authentication configuration dialog.

Authorization Object	Authorization Field	Value
S_DATASET	ACTVT	33,34
	FILENAME	*
	PROGRAM	*
S_RFC	ACTVT	16
	RFC_NAME	BDCH, STPA, SUSO, SUUS, SU_USER, SYST, SUNI, PRGN_J2EE, /CRYSTAL/SECURITY
	RFC_TYPE	FUGR
S_USER_GROUP	ACTVT	3
	CLASS	* For security reasons you can also list user groups that have access to SAP BusinessObjects Enterprise.

Table 2.7 Authorizations for SAP Authentication Configuration

5. Navigate to the OPTIONS tab of the SAP authentication (see Figure 2.26). This dialog allows you to configure the behavior of the SAP authentication for your SAP BusinessObjects Enterprise server. All configurations you perform in this step will apply to all of the SAP entitlement systems. A detailed explanation of all possible options is shown in Table 2.8.

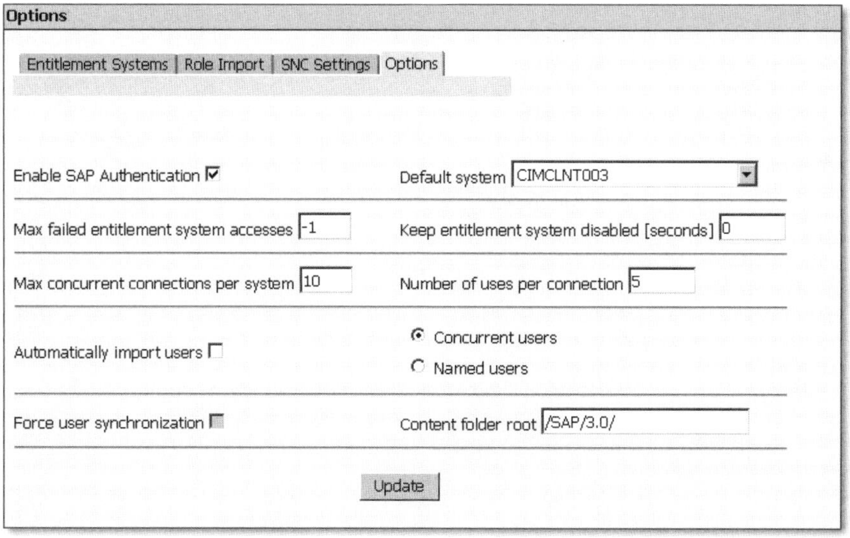

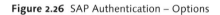

Figure 2.26 SAP Authentication – Options

Configuration Option	Description
Enable SAP Authentication	You can use this checkbox to disable SAP authentication for the SAP BusinessObjects system. If you want to disable only a single entitlement SAP system, you can do that on the Entitlement Systems tab.
Default System	The default system is used when a user is trying to authenticate SAP credentials without specifying the SAP system. A common scenario is a user navigating from the SAP NetWeaver Portal to the SAP BusinessObjects Enterprise system without specifying for which SAP system the authentication should be performed. In such a scenario the default system will be used as a fallback, and the SAP BusinessObjects Enterprise system will try to authenticate the user against the default system.
Max failed entitlement system accesses	You can use this setting to configure how many attempts the SAP BusinessObjects server should make to connect to an SAP system that is temporarily not available. The value –1 is used for an unlimited number; the value 0 is used for one attempt, and values larger than 0 represent the actual numeric value.

Table 2.8 Available Configuration Options

Configuration Option	Description
Keep entitlement system disabled (seconds)	This setting is used in combination with the option above to configure the time in seconds that the SAP BusinessObjects Enterprise server will wait before trying to access an SAP system again that previously had reached the maximum number of failed attempts.
Max concurrent connections per system	Here you can configure the maximum number of concurrent connections that SAP BusinessObjects Enterprise can keep open towards the SAP entitlement system.
Number of uses per connection	Here you can specify the number of operations that can be performed on a single connection. For example, setting the value to 5 will result in the connection being closed after 5 operations or logons on this connection.
Automatically import users	This checkbox allows you to enable the import of SAP users that are assigned to the roles that have been imported for the SAP entitlement system. If you deselect this option, the actual user account will be created during the authentication process of each account.
Concurrent users Named users	These options allow you to configure the user type for the SAP user accounts that are being created as part of the SAP authentication. Select these options carefully and ensure that this fits your installed license model of the SAP BusinessObjects Enterprise system.
Force user synchronization	If you enable this option, each update in the Role Import tab will also result in a synchronization of the assigned SAP users with the corresponding user accounts on your SAP BusinessObjects Enterprise system.
Content folder root	This setting is used for the publishing process for Crystal Reports objects. The path entered here specifies the starting folder for replicating the SAP role structure during the publishing process. This value has to be identical to the value entered in the Content Administration Workbench.

Table 2.8 Available Configuration Options (cont.)

6. After configuring the options for the SAP authentication, you can navigate to the Role Import tab (see Figure 2.27) to use the SAP roles and users for your SAP BusinessObjects Enterprise system. The screen allows you to select one

system from the list of SAP entitlement systems you created and provides a list of available SAP roles. Each of these roles can be imported by adding it to the IMPORTED ROLES field. As soon as you click the UPDATE button, each of the SAP roles will become a user group in your SAP BusinessObjects system and, if you configured to automatically import the users, the assigned users will become users in your system.

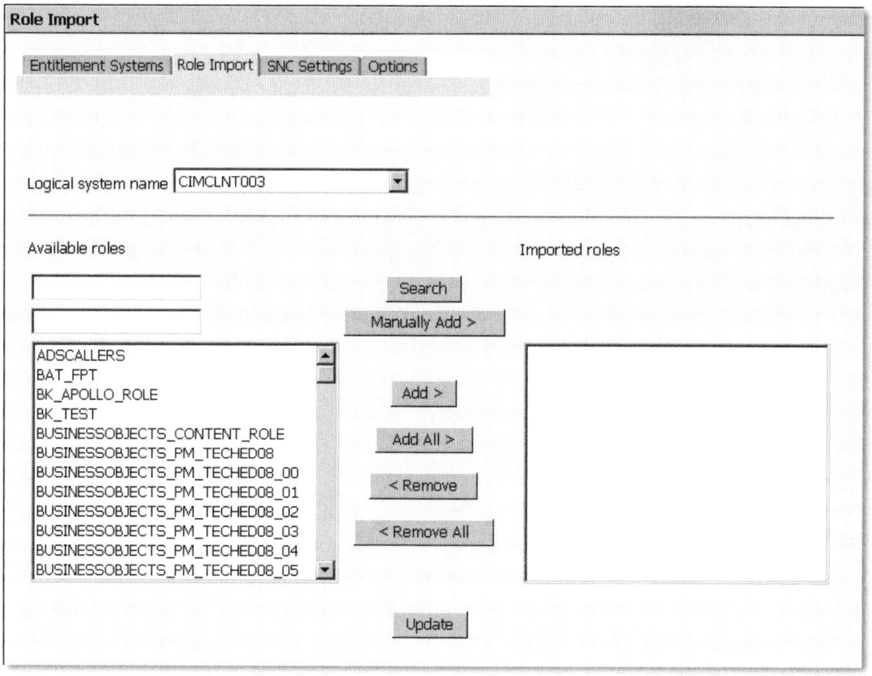

Figure 2.27 SAP Authentication – Role Import

For each of the imported SAP roles, the system generates an SAP BusinessObjects user group based on the following logic:

```
[SAP System ID] ~ [SAP client number]@[SAP role]
```

Example:

```
CIM~003@BUSINESSOBJECTS_CONTENT_ROLE
```

Each imported user follows the syntax:

```
[SAP System ID] ~ [SAP client number]/[SAP user]
```

Example:

```
CIM~003/DEMO_USER
```

Role Import and Authentication with SAP Credentials

The Role import option only offers those SAP roles that have users assigned to them. SAP roles with no user assignment will not be shown as available roles for the import.

After you imported the SAP roles, each of the generated user groups has no assigned rights in the SAP BusinessObjects system. Those resulting user groups are only assigned to the standard SAP BusinessObjects user group *Everyone*.

If you want to continue in a very simple way and configure the correct rights assignment of all of your user groups later on, you can add those user groups to the *Administrator* group for now by navigating to the User and Groups area, selecting the imported roles, and right-clicking to select Join Group and join them to the user group *Administrators*.

SAP Authentication and SAP BusinessObjects Client Tools

Not all client tools from the SAP BusinessObjects XI 3.1 release offer a complete SAP authentication logon dialog. SAP BusinessObjects Live Office, Query as a Web Service, Universe Designer, and Xcelsius 2008 only offer input boxes for user name and password. In those cases you can use the above-described syntax to authenticate with your SAP credentials.

After you imported the SAP roles and users from your entitlement system, you should be able to use your SAP credentials and authenticate against the SAP BusinessObjects Enterprise server and log on with those credentials to InfoView or the Central Management Console using the SAP authentication.

2.4.2 Setting up the Publishing Process for Crystal Reports

The publishing process for Crystal Reports allows storing of Crystal Reports objects into the SAP NetWeaver Business Warehouse repository and then synchronizing them with your SAP BusinessObjects Enterprise system. This task can be done from within the Crystal Reports designer tool or via the Content Administration Workbench as an administrative task. The main benefit of the publishing integration with SAP NetWeaver Business Warehouse is the integration of the Crystal Reports objects into lifecycle management and translation integration with your SAP system. When stored in the SAP NetWeaver Business Warehouse system, the Crystal Reports object becomes an object that can be transported between SAP systems. In addition, all translation-relevant objects are pushed into the translation-relevant tables as part of the publishing process.

Crystal Reports Publishing

The publishing integration with the SAP NetWeaver Business Warehouse system described here is only available for Crystal Reports at the time of writing this book (not for Web Intelligence or Xcelsius).

The actual publishing process consists of multiple steps (see Figure 2.28):

1. If the user creates a new report object with the Crystal Reports designer and then saves this report into the SAP NetWeaver Business Warehouse repository, the publishing process identifies the SAP BusinessObjects Enterprise system that is assigned to the SAP role used as the location for the report object. During this step the configuration details, such as the actual TCP/IP destination configured in transaction SM59, and the assigned languages are read from the configuration details set in the Content Administration Workbench.
2. The SAP NetWeaver Business Warehouse system then sends the Crystal Reports content object (rpt file), the name of the Central Management Server, the translated strings, and the actual publishing command via RFC to the SAP NetWeaver Business Warehouse publishing service.
3. In the last step the Crystal Reports object is added to the repository of the SAP BusinessObjects Enterprise system. Each language configured in the Content Administration Workbench results in a single report object.

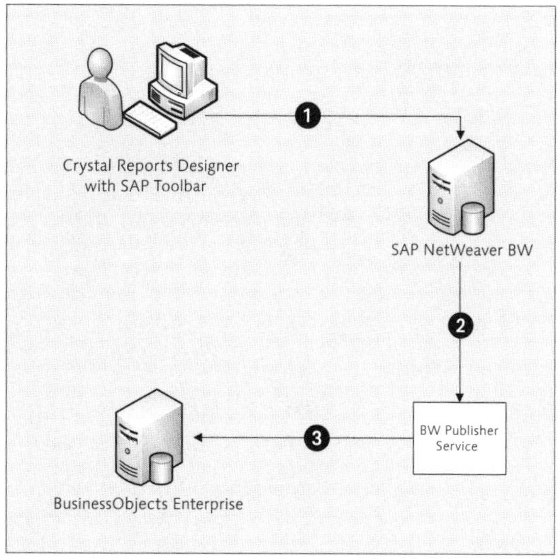

Figure 2.28 Publishing Process

The actual location of the Crystal Reports content can be configured based on a base folder in the Content Administration Workbench. Below the base folder the Crystal Reports objects will be stored in a folder structure based on the following logic (see also Figure 2.29):

- Below the configured based folder, a folder with the logical system name of your SAP system is created (for example, CIMCLNT003 for the System ID CIM and client 003).
- Below the folder for the logical system name, a folder for each of the roles containing Crystal Reports content is created. The folder is created based on the technical name and description of the SAP role.
- For each language configured in the Content Administration Workbench, a Crystal Reports object is stored in the role folder.

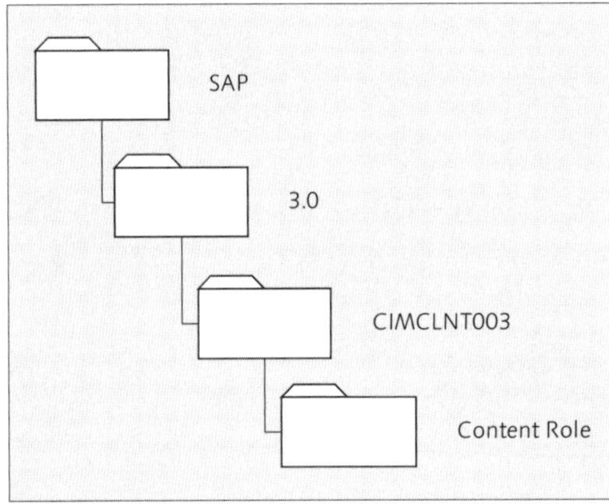

Figure 2.29 Publishing – Role Structure Example

The overall configuration of the publishing process consists of five main steps that will be explained in detail in the following sections:

1. Configuration of the publishing service
2. Creation of an RFC destination
3. Creation of an SAP BusinessObjects Enterprise server entry in the Content Administration Workbench
4. Configuration of the BW source parameters for the publishing process
5. Configuration of the necessary rights for the SAP BusinessObjects user groups and users

Configuration of the Publishing Service

On a Windows installation the BW publishing service is configured via settings in the registry. These values are set as part of the installation but can be changed in the registry afterwards. The path in the registry is *HKEY_LOCAL_MACHINE\SOFTWARE\Business Objects\Suite 12.0\SAP\BW Publisher Service* as shown in Figure 2.30.

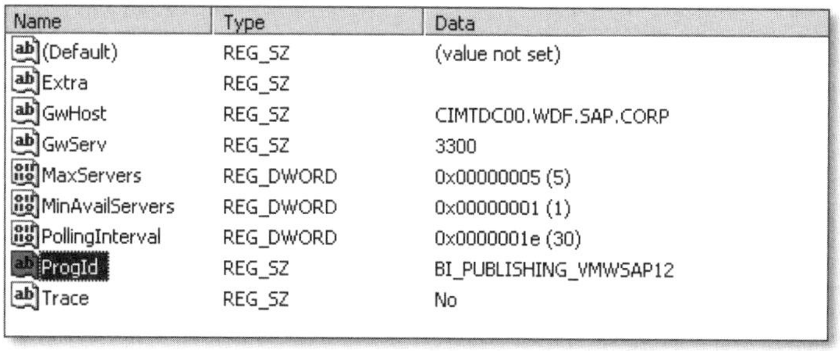

Name	Type	Data
(Default)	REG_SZ	(value not set)
Extra	REG_SZ	
GwHost	REG_SZ	CIMTDC00.WDF.SAP.CORP
GwServ	REG_SZ	3300
MaxServers	REG_DWORD	0x00000005 (5)
MinAvailServers	REG_DWORD	0x00000001 (1)
PollingInterval	REG_DWORD	0x0000001e (30)
ProgId	REG_SZ	BI_PUBLISHING_VMWSAP12
Trace	REG_SZ	No

Figure 2.30 BW Report Publishing Service Configuration

1. You can enter the details based on the descriptions shown in Table 2.9:

Parameter Name	Description
Program ID	Enter a name for the BW Report Publishing Service. This program ID identifies the service. You cannot enter any spaces in the name, and the name is case sensitive. Example: BW_PUBLISHING_VMWSAP12
Gateway Host	Enter the fully qualified name of your SAP server. If you are using an SAP cluster environment, you should enter the name of the central instance here. Example: CIMTDC00.WDF.SAP.CORP
Gateway Service	Enter the port number on which the gateway host is listening. Example: 3300

Table 2.9 Parameter Options for the BW Report Publishing Service

2. After you configured the values, you can start the BW publishing service via the Central Configuration Manager.

   On a Unix deployment you can run the following script to start a publishing service instance:

SAP BusinessObjects/bwcepub.sh num -aPROGID -gGWHOST –Xgwservice

- *SAP BusinessObjects* is the root directory of your SAP BusinessObjects Enterprise installation.
- *num* is the number of publishing service instances to start.
- Regarding *PROGID*, *GWHOST*, and *GWSERVICE* refer to Table 2.9 for further details.

Creation of an RFC Destination

The second step is to set up an RFC destination that will use the BW publishing service. This RFC destination is used for the SAP NetWeaver Business Warehouse system to communicate with the BW publishing service. If you're looking to set up multiple BW publishing services for fault tolerance or you're looking to configure a single SAP NetWeaver Business Warehouse system to publish content to multiple SAP BusinessObjects Enterprise systems, you need to create separate RFC destinations for each BW publishing service.

1. To create the new RFC destination log on to the SAP NetWeaver Business Warehouse system and start Transaction SM59 (see Figure 2.31).

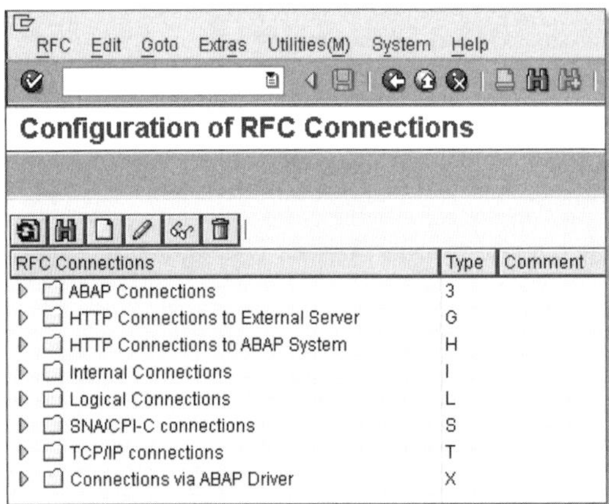

Figure 2.31 RFC Destination

2. Follow the menu path EDIT • CREATE to start a new RFC destination. You need to enter a name for the RFC destination and select a type (see Figure 2.32). For our configuration we'll use the name BI_PUBLISHING and the type TCP/IP for the RFC destination.

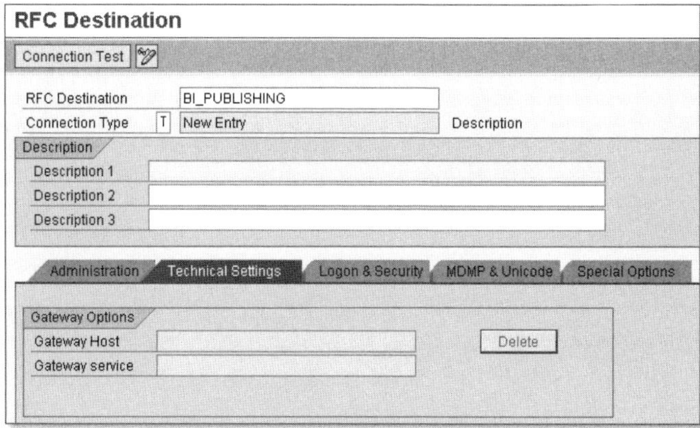

Figure 2.32 RFC Destination – Connection Type

3. Click SAVE (alternatively, you can follow the menu path CONNECTION • SAVE), and the screen will get updated (see Figure 2.33). You can now enter the details from the previously configured publishing service.

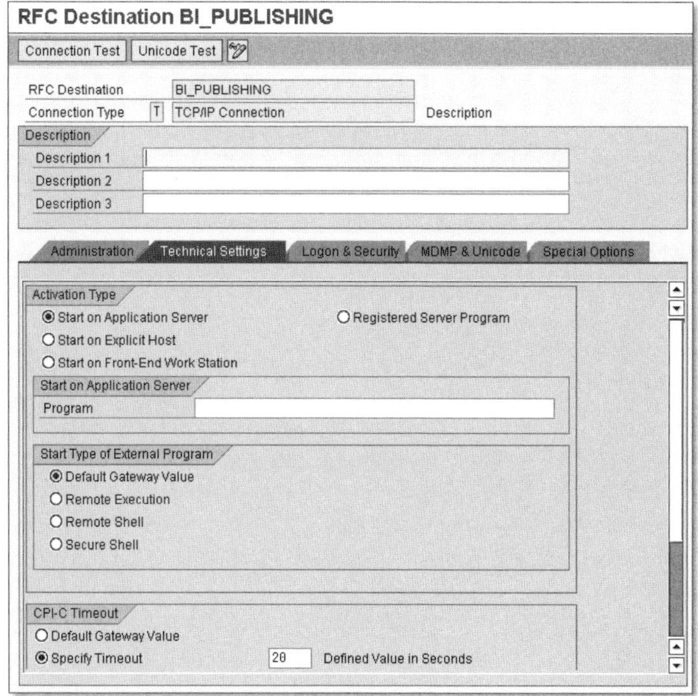

Figure 2.33 RFC Destination – Details

In Table 2.10 you can see the configuration values you need to enter for your RFC destination.

Value	Description
Application type	Registered server program
Program	The program ID you entered for the BW publishing service (case sensitive) Example: BW_PUBLISHING_VMWSAP12
Start Type of External Program	Default gateway value
CPI-C Timeout	Default gateway value
Gateway Host	Enter the fully qualified name of your SAP server. If you're using an SAP cluster environment, you should enter the name of the central instance here. Example: CIMTDC00.WDF.SAP.CORP
Gateway Service	Enter the port number on which the gateway host is listening. Example: 3300

Table 2.10 Values for the RFC Destination

If you're planning to use an SAP Gateway instead of the BW publishing service, then you need to configure your RFC destination according to Table 2.11.

Value	Description
Application type	Start on explicit host
Program	Enter the full path to the executable BWCEPUB.exe. If you installed the software with the default settings, you would enter the following: *C:\Progra~1\Busine~1\Busine~1.0\win32_x86\ bwcepub.exe* The path needs to be entered in an MS-DOS style.
Target Host	Enter the full qualified name of the server that contains the executable. Example: VMWSAP12.WDF.SAP.CORP

Table 2.11 Values for the RFC Destination (SAP Gateway)

Value	Description
Gateway Host	Enter the fully qualified name of your SAP server. If you're using an SAP cluster environment, you should enter the name of the central instance here. Example: CIMTDC00.WDF.SAP.CORP
Gateway Service	Enter the port number on which the gateway host is listening. Example: 3300

Table 2.11 Values for the RFC Destination (SAP Gateway) (cont.)

4. You can now save your newly created RFC destination and test the connection. If you're using the BW publishing service, ensure that the service is up and running (via the Central Configuration Manager) before testing the connection. If the RFC destination works well, you should receive an overview on the response time (see Figure 2.34).

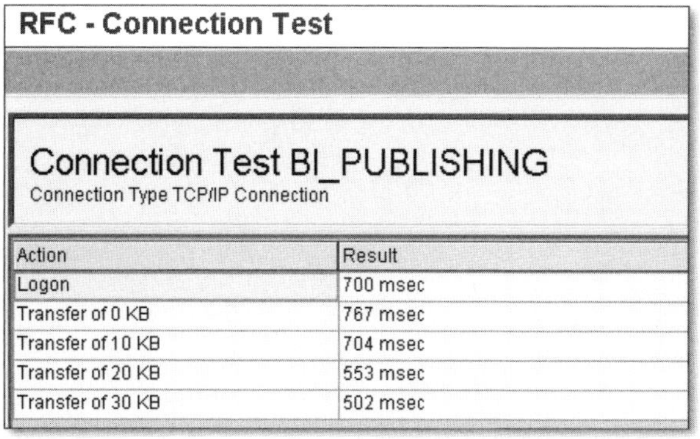

RFC - Connection Test

Connection Test BI_PUBLISHING

Connection Type TCP/IP Connection

Action	Result
Logon	700 msec
Transfer of 0 KB	767 msec
Transfer of 10 KB	704 msec
Transfer of 20 KB	553 msec
Transfer of 30 KB	502 msec

Figure 2.34 RFC Destination – Connection Test

SAP BusinessObjects Enterprise Server Definition

After you have configured the BW publishing service and the RFC destination, you can define your SAP BusinessObjects Enterprise system and put the separate parts together into your server definition. The SAP BusinessObjects Integration for SAP Solutions delivers the Content Administration Workbench, which allows you to define and administrate the SAP BusinessObjects systems that you want to use in combination with the SAP NetWeaver Business Warehouse system.

1. Before accessing the Content Administration Workbench, you need to ensure that the SAP account you'll be using has the authorization objects listed in Table 2.12.

Authorization Object	Authorization Field	Value
S_RFC	RFC_TYPE	FUGR
	RFC_NAME	/CRYSTAL/CE_SYNCH, SH3A, SUNI
	ACTVT	16
S_TCODE	TCD	/CRYSTAL/RPTADMIN, RSCR_MAINT_PUBLISH
S_TABU_CLI	CLIIDMAINT	X
S_TABU_DIS	ACTVT	02, 03
	DICBERCLS	&NC&
S_BTCH_JOB	JOBACTION	DELE, RELE
	JOBGROUP	''
S_RS_ADMWB	ACTVT	16
	RSADMWBOBJ	WORKBENCH
ZCNTADMCES	ACTVT	01, 02, 03, 06
ZCNTADMJOB	ACTVT	01, 06
ZCNTADMRPT	ACTVT	02, 03, 06, 07, 23, 39

Table 2.12 Authorizations for Content Administration Workbench

Detailed Authorizations

The authorizations listed in Table 2.12 are authorizations for an administrative user. You can find a detailed list of authorization for administrators, publishers, and consumers in the Installation Guide for the SAP BusinessObjects Integration for SAP Solutions, which is available at *https://service.sap.com/bosap-instguides.*

2. You can access the Content Administration Workbench by starting Transaction /CRYSTAL/RPTADMIN (see Figure 2.35). The Content Administration Workbench is part of the ABAP transports of the SAP BusinessObjects Integration for

SAP Solutions and allows you to configure your SAP BusinessObjects Enterprise system in combination with the SAP NetWeaver Business Warehouse system.

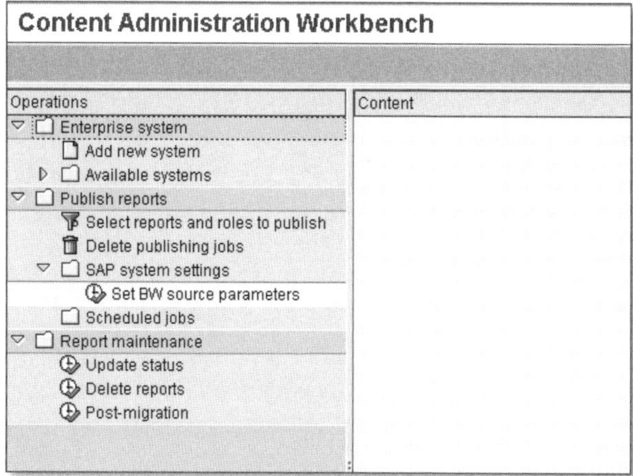

Figure 2.35 Content Administration Workbench – Start Screen

3. Double-click the item ADD NEW SYSTEM to start the process of creating your own SAP BusinessObjects Enterprise server definition. First, you'll be shown the SYSTEM tab of your server definition (see Figure 2.36).

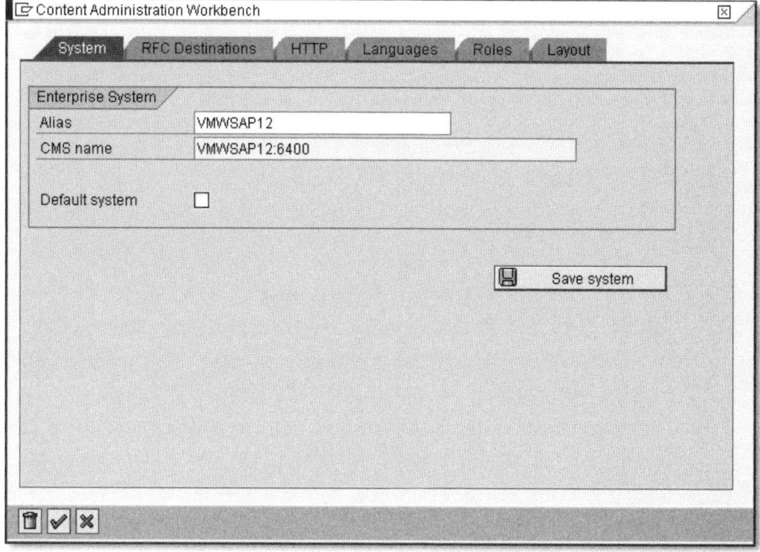

Figure 2.36 SAP BusinessObjects Enterprise System Definition – System

4. You can enter an alias for your system, and then you need to enter the full qualified name of the Central Management Server of your SAP BusinessObjects system. If you're using the default port (6400), then there's no need to enter it in addition to the name of your Central Management Server, but if you configured a different port, you need to enter the port as part of your Central Management Server name. The DEFAULT SYSTEM checkbox allows you to set up one SAP BusinessObjects Enterprise as the default system for your SAP NetWeaver Business Warehouse system. Those reports stored in SAP roles that have not been assigned explicitly to an SAP BusinessObjects Enterprise system will then be published to the default system.

   In our example the value for the Central Management Server name is VMWSAP12:6400.

5. You can now move to the RFC DESTINATIONS tab (see Figure 2.37). Here you can add the RFC destination that you created in the previous section. If you created multiple destinations to use fault tolerance, you can add all of them here.

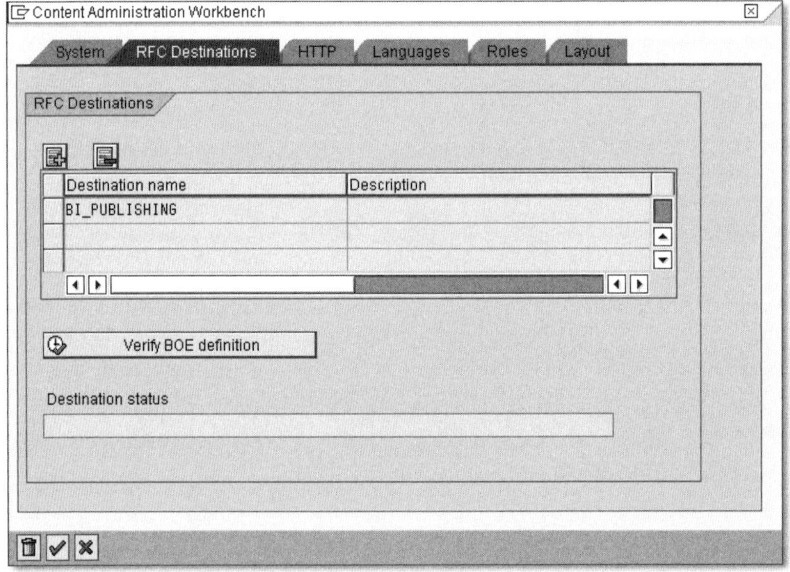

Figure 2.37 SAP BusinessObjects Enterprise System Definition – RFC Destination

6. The VERIFY BOE DEFINITION button allows you — as soon as you have finished the configurations — to verify if all of the communication between the SAP NetWeaver Business Warehouse system and your SAP BusinessObjects Enter-

prise system is working. This function does not run an actual publishing process; it validates all communication steps between all involved components.

7. The HTTP tab (see Figure 2.38) allows you to configure the necessary entries so that your end users will be able to view Crystal Reports objects from the SAP GUI.

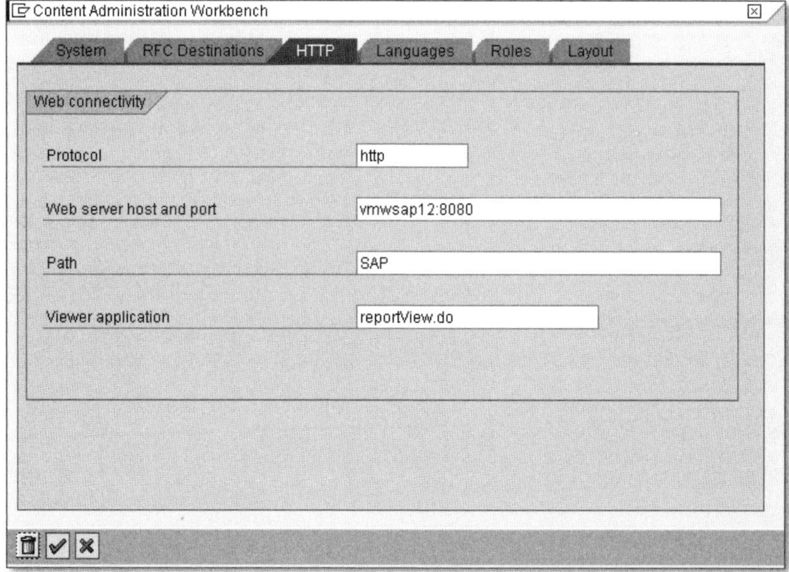

Figure 2.38 SAP BusinessObjects Enterprise System Definition – HTTP

You can use Table 2.13 to see the values that you need to enter in this dialog.

Value	Description
Protocol	You can enter either http or https as the protocol for viewing reports here.
Web server host and port	Enter the fully qualified name of the server that hosts the web applications of your SAP Business-Objects Enterprise system. If you're using a Java application server, you also need to include the port for the application server. Example: VMWSAP12:8080

Table 2.13 SAP BusinessObjects Enterprise System Definition – HTTP Values

Value	Description
Path	Enter the virtual path from your application server that contains the viewing application. For the default installation this value is "SAP". There is no need to include a forward slash in the dialog.
Viewer application	Enter the name of the actual application being used to open the report. The default value is reportView.do. The application reportview.do is technically a wrapper around the standard application OpenDocument that is able to use SSO in an SAP landscape.

Table 2.13 SAP BusinessObjects Enterprise System Definition – HTTP Values (cont.)

8. On the LANGUAGES tab (see Figure 2.39) you can configure the list of languages that will be used for the translation of Crystal Reports objects. For each language configured in this screen, the publishing process will create one Crystal Reports object so that you can, after translating the strings, view a report in multiple languages. With the ADD ALL LANGUAGES button you can add all of the languages configured for your SAP NetWeaver Business Warehouse system to the list.

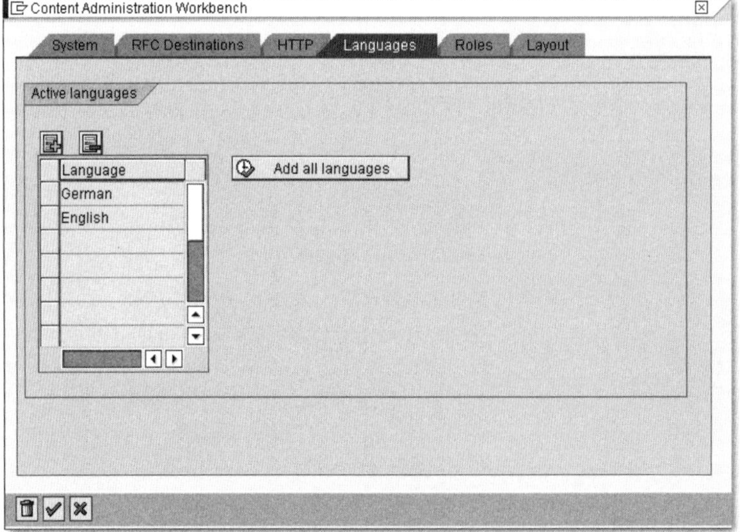

Figure 2.39 SAP BusinessObjects Enterprise System Definition – Languages

Publishing and Translation

Part of the actual publishing process is the extraction of strings into the translation system. The list of languages you configure here (see Figure 2.39) also represents the list of available languages for the report. When saving a Crystal Report into the SAP system, you can decide to prepare the report object for translation, which results in the strings being pushed into the translation system, and you can use Transaction SE63 for translation purposes.

9. On the ROLES tab (see Figure 2.40) you need to select those roles that will be assigned to your SAP BusinessObjects Enterprise system. Any Crystal Reports object stored in the assigned roles will then be published to your SAP BusinessObjects Enterprise system. With the INSERT ROW icon you can select roles from your SAP NetWeaver Business Warehouse system and assign them to your SAP BusinessObjects Enterprise server definition. Click the REASSIGN ROLES button to select roles that have already been assigned to another SAP BusinessObjects Enterprise system definition. Those roles will then be removed from their current assigned server definition and will be assigned to your SAP BusinessObjects Enterprise system.

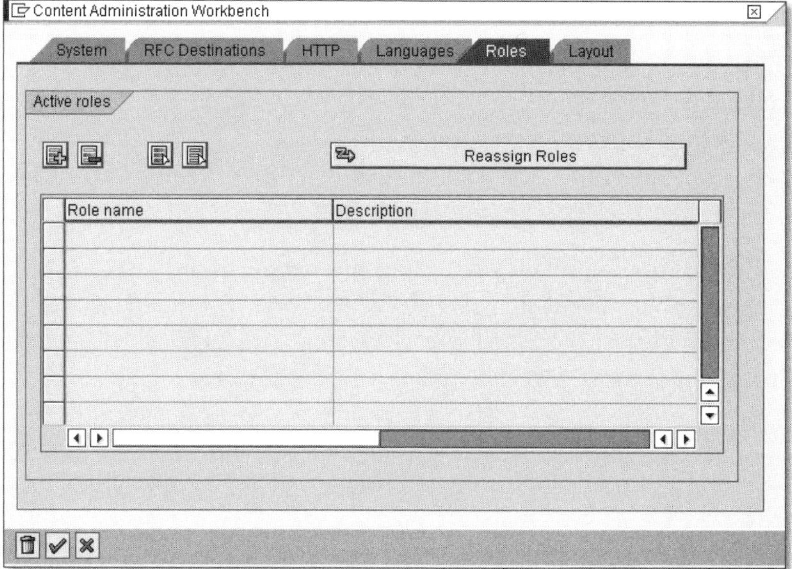

Figure 2.40 SAP BusinessObjects Enterprise System Definition – Roles

SAP BusinessObjects Enterprise – Role Assignment

Based on the ability to assign an SAP BusinessObjects Enterprise system to a subset of SAP NetWeaver Business Warehouse roles, you can easily connect a single SAP NetWeaver Business Warehouse system to multiple SAP BusinessObjects Enterprise systems, for example, using one SAP BusinessObjects system for your HR department and another system for all other departments.

10. On the LAYOUT tab (see Figure 2.41) you can configure the base folder that will be used for the publishing. The role replication occurs underneath the base folder (see Figure 2.29).

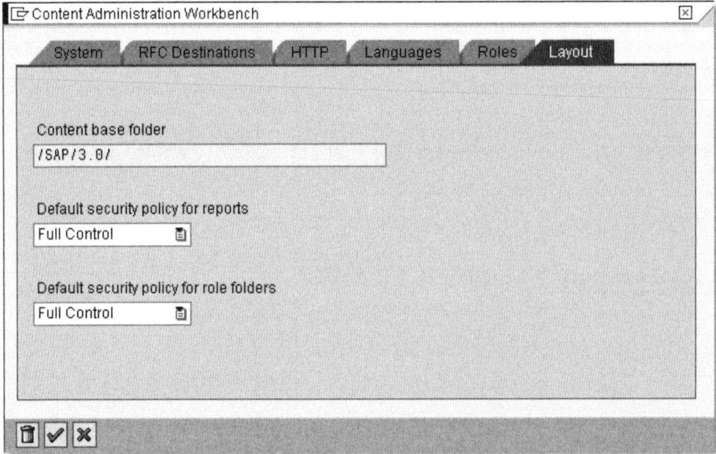

Figure 2.41 SAP BusinessObjects Enterprise System Definition – Layout

Two additional options allow you to specify a default security setting for the role folders and the Crystal Reports objects that will be created as a result of the publishing process. You can leave the default settings for now because we will discuss the security assignment later in this chapter.

Content Base Folder

The folder listed as part of the SAP BusinessObjects Enterprise definition (see Figure 2.41) needs to match the CONTENT BASE FOLDER configured in the OPTIONS tab of the SAP authentication (see Figure 2.26).

11. After you have finished all of the settings, you can confirm your SAP BusinessObjects Enterprise system. You should now re-open your system definition

(by double-clicking it) and navigate to the RFC DESTINATION tab. You can use the VERIFY BOE DESTINATION button to validate that all involved components can communicate with each other. Keep in mind that this test is not performing an actual publishing, it is only testing the communication.

Configuring BW Source Parameters

During the publishing process the SAP NetWeaver Business Warehouse system creates Crystal Reports objects in the SAP BusinessObjects Enterprise system. Part of this process is the configuration of the connection to the underlying SAP system, and you need to configure those values inside the Content Administration Workbench.

1. Log onto the SAP server and start Transaction /CRYSTAL/RPTADMIN for the Content Administration Workbench.
2. Follow the menu path PUBLISH REPORTS • SAP SYSTEM SETTINGS (see Figure 2.42).

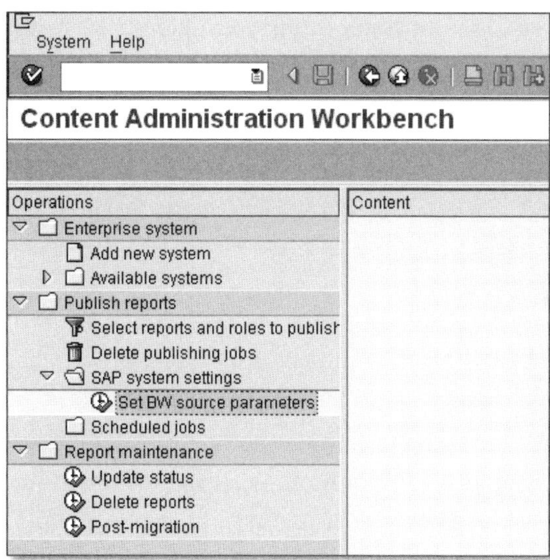

Figure 2.42 BW Source Parameters

3. Double-click the entry SET BW SOURCE PARAMETERS to bring up the screen shown in Figure 2.42.
4. Click the CHANGE icon [icon] to allow changes to the table (or you can follow the menu path TABLE VIEW • DISPLAY • CHANGE).

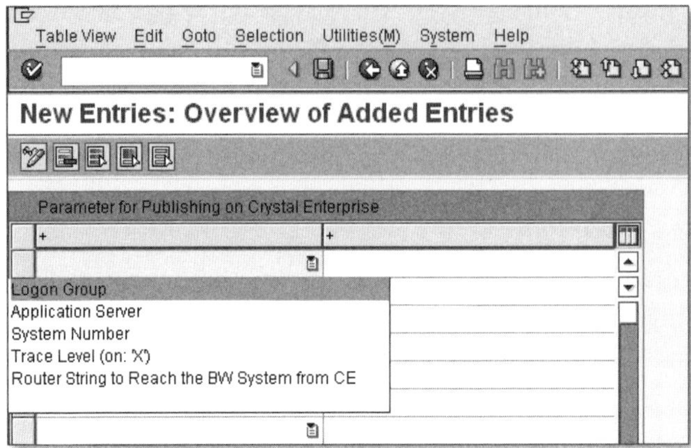

Figure 2.43 BW Source Parameter Start Screen

5. You can now click the NEW ENTRIES button to create new entries. Depending on your system landscape, you need to enter either a combination of application server and system number or a combination of application server (which then represents a message server) and logon group. In our example we'll enter the values shown in Table 2.14.

Property	Value
Application Server	CIMTDC00.WDF.SAP.CORP
System number	00

Table 2.14 Values for BW Source Parameters

Assignment of Necessary Rights

So far you've configured your SAP BusinessObjects Enterprise and SAP system to be able to publish Crystal Reports objects. The only step missing to complete the configuration is the assignment of security rights to those user groups in SAP BusinessObjects Enterprise — in our scenario the imported SAP roles — that will view or publish content.

The following is only a recommendation for splitting users based on the functional aspects. There are lots of different ways to implement the user and user group rights, and the following is only meant to convey the concepts.

Overall it is recommended that you split the SAP users into three main roles:

- **SAP BusinessObjects Enterprise administrators**
  Users with this role will be able to configure the publishing and perform administrative tasks in your SAP BusinessObjects Enterprise system such as importing other SAP roles and users or assigning security rights to folders and objects.
- **SAP BusinessObjects content publisher**
  Users with this role will be able to publish content in the assigned roles. These users can create, edit, and publish content. The reason for creating such a role explicitly is to be able to differentiate these users from the next group of users — role members.
- **Role members**
  A role member is a user assigned to a role in the SAP system that has been imported into your SAP BusinessObjects Enterprise system. These members have the necessary security rights to view the content that is assigned to their role, but they cannot create, edit, or publish the content.

The overall recommendation is to set up these role definitions and the user assignments in your SAP system, and you can then use those configurations by importing the SAP roles and users into SAP BusinessObjects Enterprise during the configuration of the SAP authentication.

Assigning the necessary rights is possible in two main areas. You can use the Content Administration Workbench to assign a set of default rights to the role members, and you need to use the Central Management Console to assign the necessary rights to the content publisher roles in the SAP BusinessObjects User Group area.

Content Administration Workbench

1. To configure the default security settings for the role members you need to log on to your SAP system and start Transaction /CRYSTAL/RPTADMIN for the Content Administration Workbench.
2. Open the list of SAP BusinessObjects Enterprise systems and select your previously defined system.
3. Navigate to the Layout tab. Here you can configure the recommended default security values for the role members. It is recommended that you use View for the default policy for the report objects and use the value View on Demand for

the default policy on the folder level. These settings represent the standard definitions available in your SAP BusinessObjects Enterprise systems and will allow these users to view the published reports on demand. If you also want to allow your role members to schedule reports, you can set the default policy to the SCHEDULE option.

Central Management Console

For our example we'll assume that we have the following SAP roles:

- **CONTENT_ADMINISTRATOR**
  We'll use this role to configure users that are able to publish and administrate content for our configured entitlement system CIM.
- **BUSINESSOBJECTS_CONTENT_ROLE**
  This is the role that contains the actual content. Users with this role will be able to view the content but not publish new or change existing content.

The following steps outline how to assign the necessary rights in the SAP BusinessObjects Enterprise system to the imported SAP roles:

1. Log on to the Central Management Console to configure the necessary rights for the content publisher role. Ensure that you log on with an administrator account and that the content publisher role you want to use is imported into your SAP BusinessObjects Enterprise system using the configuration of the SAP authentication.
2. Select the FOLDERS area in the top left of the Central Management Console (see Figure 2.44).

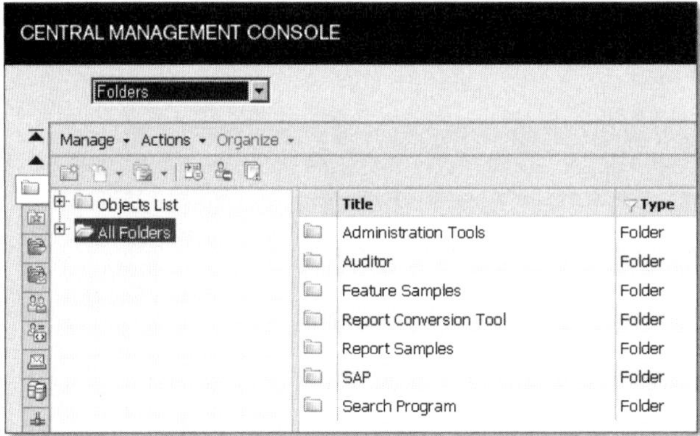

Figure 2.44 Central Management Console – Folders

3. You can now open the list of folders from your SAP BusinessObjects Enterprise system and navigate down to the folder structure for your SAP system. In our example — based on the default configuration — you should find a folder SAP and underneath it a folder called 3.0. Below that you will find a folder named for your SAP system ID and the client number (see Figure 2.45). This folder structure represents the default configuration that you created in the previous steps during the configuration of the publishing up to this point.

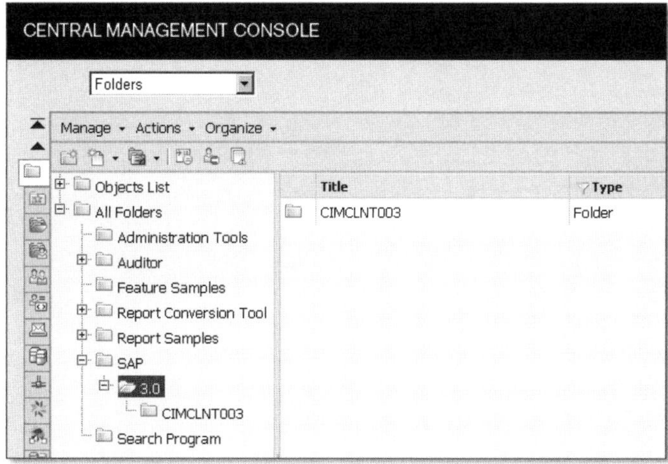

Figure 2.45 Central Management Console – Folder Structure

4. Now you can select the folder and open the menu MANAGE • USER SECURITY (see Figure 2.46).

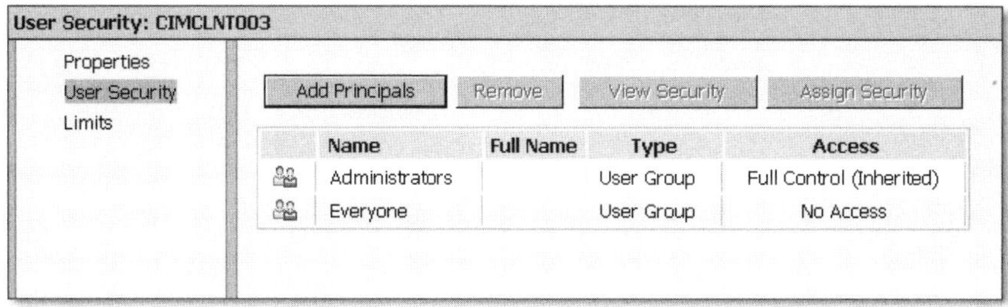

Figure 2.46 User Security

5. You can then use the ADD PRINCIPALS function and can select the groups you want to use for the assignment of security rights on this folder (see Figure 2.47).

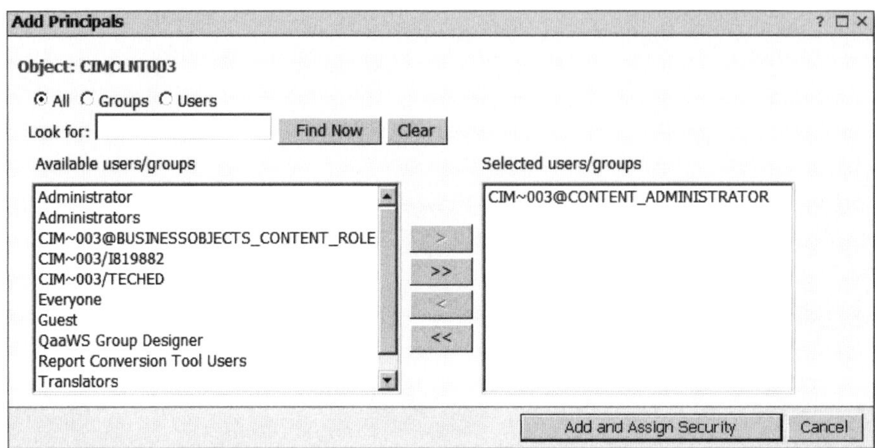

Figure 2.47 Add Principals

In our example we're adding the role CIM~003@CONTENT_ADMINISTRATOR. After you added the role to the list of selected users/groups, you can click the Add and Assign Security button (see Figure 2.47).

Figure 2.48 Assign Security

6. Navigate to the Advanced tab (see Figure 2.48) and click the link Add/Remove Rights to see a detailed list of security rights that you can assign to the role (see Figure 2.49).

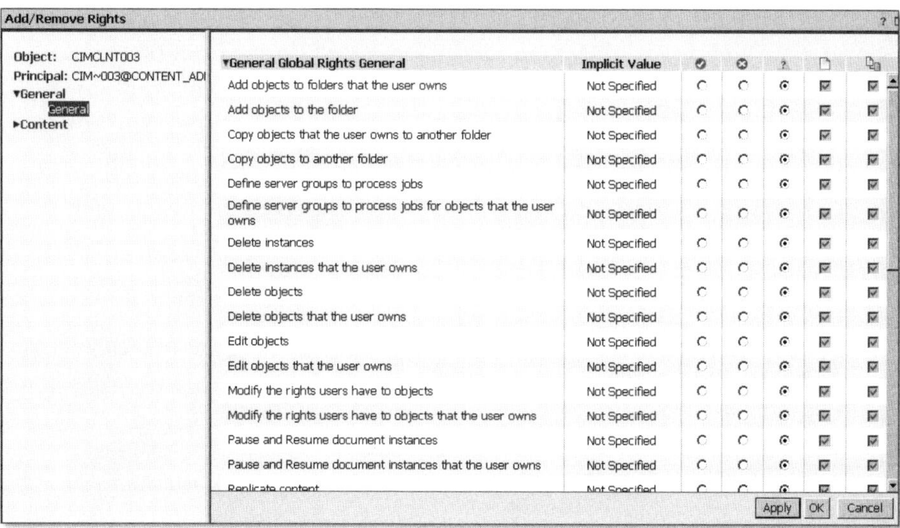

Figure 2.49 Add/Remove Rights

7. By using the Add/Remove Rights option you can now grant the following rights to the selected role:
   - Add objects to the folder that the user owns
   - Add objects to the folder
   - Copy objects to another folder that the user owns
   - Copy objects to another folder
   - Delete objects that the user owns
   - Delete objects
   - Edit objects
   - Edit objects that the user owns
   - Modify the rights users have to objects
   - View objects
   - View objects that the user owns

You can use the three columns to either grant, deny, or inherit the security authorization for the role. In our example we'll explicitly grant the rights listed above.

Based on the listed security rights, the user role will be able to publish, update, and delete content in the folder. Based on the level that you selected to assign the security rights, this can mean the role is able to perform those tasks only for a single role, for all roles for a single entitled SAP system, for multiple entitled SAP systems, or even for all entitled SAP system.

8. Confirm the changes and confirm the assignments in the next screen.
9. After you confirmed the assigned security, navigate to the USERS AND GROUPS area in the Central Management Console (see Figure 2.50).

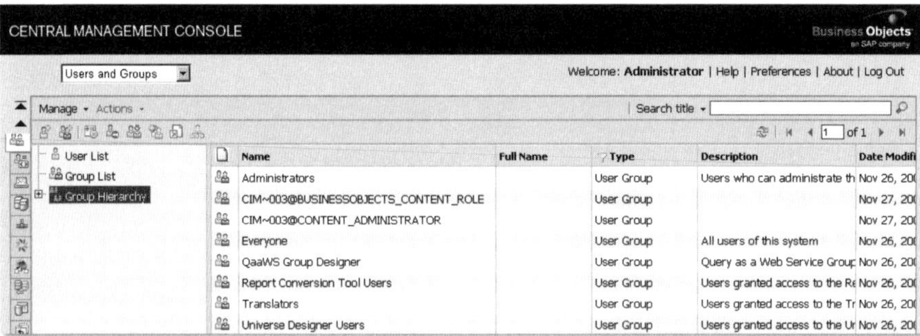

Figure 2.50 Users and Groups

10. Select the content-containing role — in our example CIM~003@BUSINESS-OBJECTS_CONTENT_ROLE — and select the menu MANAGE • USER SECURITY (see Figure 2.51).

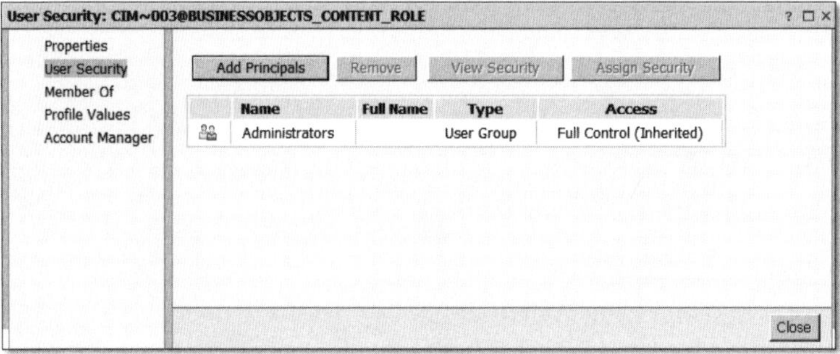

Figure 2.51 User Security

11. Click the ADD PRINCIPALS button and add the content administrator role — in our example CIM~003@CONTENT_ADMINISTRATOR — as principal to the role (see Figure 2.52).

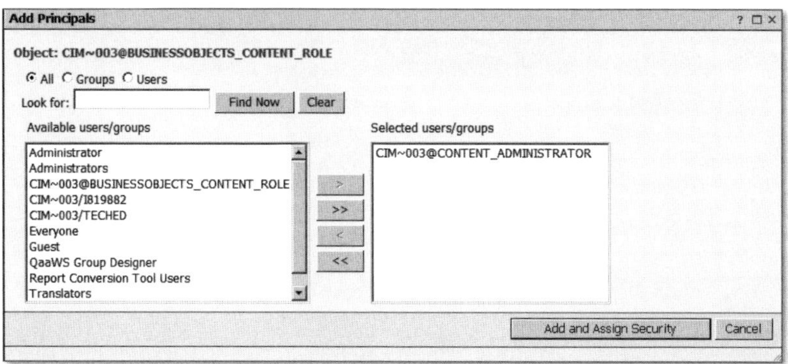

Figure 2.52 Add Principals

12. Click the Add and Assign Security button to assign the list of rights:
    - Add objects to the folder that the user owns
    - Add objects to the folder
    - Copy objects to another folder that the user owns
    - Copy objects to another folder
    - Delete objects that the user owns
    - Delete objects
    - Edit objects
    - Edit objects that the user owns
    - Modify the rights users have to objects
    - View objects
    - View objects that the user owns

    You can use the three columns to either grant, deny, or inherit the security authorization for the role. In our example we'll explicitly grant the rights listed above.

    Based on the listed security rights, the content administrator role will be able to add, edit, or change the assignment of rights for the content-containing role.
13. Confirm your changes and the assignment of the content administrator role as principal for the content containing role.
14. After you confirmed the changes, navigate to the Access Levels area in the Central Management Console (see Figure 2.53).

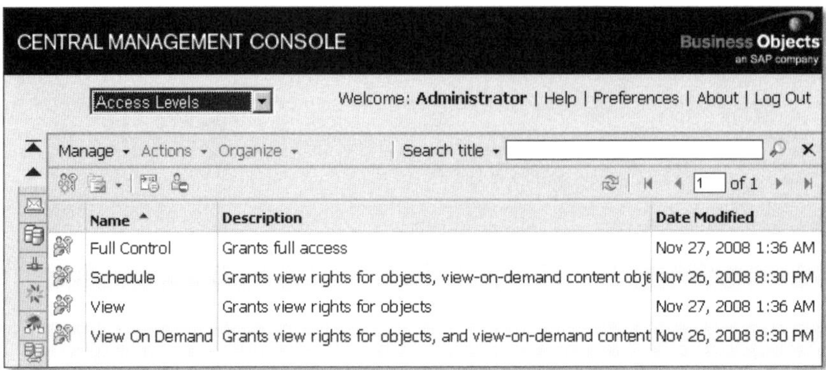

Figure 2.53 Access Levels

15. Follow the menu path MANAGE • SECURITY • ALL ACCESS LEVELS.
16. Select ADD PRINCIPALS and add the content administrator role (CIM~003@ CONTENT_ADMINISTRATOR).
17. Use the functionality ADD AND ASSIGN SECURITY to specify the rights for the role. Add the following rights:
    - View objects
    - View objects that the user owns
    - Edit objects
    - Edit objects that the user owns
    - Use access level for security assignment
18. Confirm the changes.

Assigned Security for the Content Administrator

The need for the content administrator to be able to modify the role and folder assigned rights is based on the content administrator role needing to be able to use the settings from the LAYOUT tab (see Figure 2.41) to specify the security according to those settings.

2.4.3 Viewing Reports within the SAP System Frontend

Because you can store Crystal Reports objects in the SAP role menu, your users can also view these objects directly from their role menu. During the process of storing the Crystal Reports object in the SAP system, a role entry is created that can be used to view the Crystal Reports object on demand. To enable viewing of reports via the role menu, you need to configure an http request handler that is included as part of the Crystal Content Administration Workbench transport.

1. Log on to your SAP system and start Transaction SICF (see Figure 2.54).

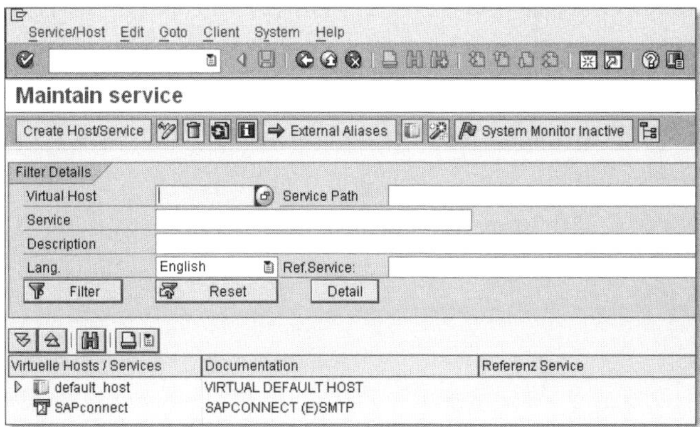

Figure 2.54 Maintain Services

2. Navigate to the folder *default_host/SAP/BW* and open the entry "ce_url". There you can navigate to the HANDLER LIST tab (see Figure 2.55).

   The entry /CRYSTAL/CL_BW_HTTP_HANDLER, as shown in Figure 2.55, needs to be your top entry in the handler list.

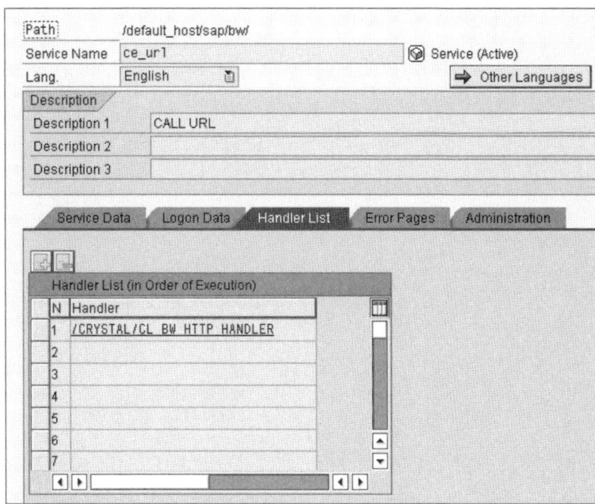

Figure 2.55 Handler List

2.4.4 Publishing Summary

At this point, as part of the publishing configuration, you have:

- Configured the SAP authentication and imported SAP roles and users in the Central Management Console
- Configured the publishing service on your SAP BusinessObjects Enterprise system
- Created an RFC destination in Transaction SM59 for communication between your SAP system and your SAP BusinessObjects Enterprise publishing service
- Created an SAP BusinessObjects Server definition in Transaction /CRYSTAL/RPTADMIN and assigned SAP roles to your SAP BusinessObjects Enterprise system
- Assigned the necessary rights to the SAP roles in your SAP BusinessObjects Enterprise system

Based on those steps you are now able to:

- Publish a Crystal Reports object from the Crystal Reports designer via an SAP role to your SAP BusinessObjects Enterprise system
- View a Crystal Reports object via the role menu of your SAP system frontend

In this chapter we will take a look at how you can leverage Crystal Reports in combination with SAP NetWeaver Business Warehouse and SAP ERP and how you can leverage the existing information in these systems.

3 Crystal Reports and SAP NetWeaver

3.1 Crystal Reports and SAP NetWeaver Business Warehouse

In the following sections we'll go into more detail using Crystal Reports on top of SAP NetWeaver Business Warehouse. The sections will outline the connectivity between Crystal Reports and your SAP system, and you'll learn how to build your first report using Crystal Reports.

3.1.1 Data Connectivity Overview

In Figure 3.1 you can see an overview of the Crystal Reports capabilities to connect to your SAP NetWeaver Business Warehouse (SAP NetWeaver BW) system. Crystal Reports offers three separate connectivities:

- **BW MDX connectivity**
  This is the most recent and enhanced data connectivity to use for Crystal Reports. The BW MDX connectivity is an enhanced version of the BW Query connectivity, and it delivers support for free characteristics and multiple structures in the BW queries. The BW MDX connectivity is able to connect to an SAP NetWeaver Business Warehouse query and an SAP NetWeaver Business Warehouse InfoProvider.
- **BW Query connectivity**
  The BW Query connectivity is the original data connectivity developed during the partnership between SAP and Crystal Decisions (later BusinessObjects). This connectivity has not been further enhanced for several releases, and it is highly recommended that you use the successor connectivity — BW MDX connectivity.

- **ODS/DSO connectivity**
  The ODS/DSO (operational data store) connectivity allows you to use a direct connectivity (via BAPI functions) to the ODS objects in your SAP NetWeaver Business Warehouse system. By using this connectivity, you can use the ODS layer for reporting without the need to create a BW query on top.

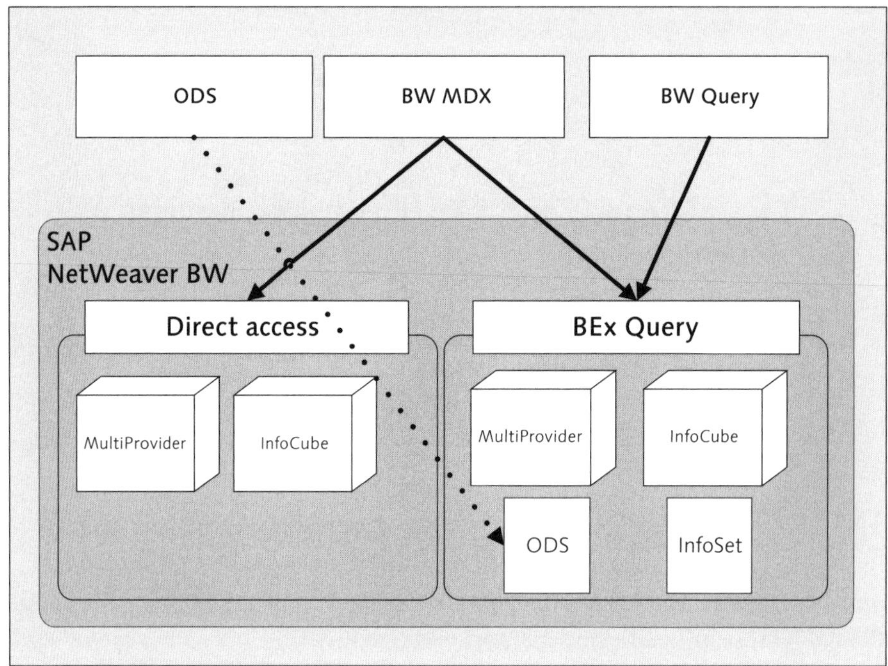

Figure 3.1 Crystal Reports Connectivity for SAP NetWeaver Business Warehouse

In the following sections when I refer to SAP NetWeaver Business Warehouse connectivity, I always refer to the BW MDX connectivity in Crystal Reports.

3.1.2 Supported and Unsupported SAP NetWeaver Business Warehouse Elements

Table 3.1 shows the supported and unsupported features of Crystal Reports on top of SAP NetWeaver Business Warehouse queries. The table represents the level of support for the release XI 3.1.

	BW Query Driver	BW MDX Driver
InfoProvider		
Direct access to InfoCube and MultiProvider	No	Yes
Access to BW queries	Yes	Yes
Characteristic Values		
Key	Yes	Yes
Short description	Yes	Yes
Medium and long description	No	Yes
BW Query Features		
Support for hierarchies	Yes	Yes
Support for free characteristics	No	Yes
Support for calculated and restricted keyfigures	Yes	Yes
Support for currencies and units	Yes	Yes
Support for multiple structures	No	Yes
Support for formulas and selections	Yes	Yes
Support for filter	Yes	Yes
Support for display and navigational attributes	Yes	Yes
Support for conditions and exceptions	No	No
Data Types		
Support for type CHAR (characteristics)	Yes	Yes
Support for type NUMC (characteristics)	Yes	Yes
Support for type DATS (characteristics)	No	No
Support for type TIMS (characteristics)	No	No
Support for type Date (keyfigures)	Yes	Yes
Support for type Time (keyfigures)	Yes	Yes

Table 3.1 Supported and Unsupported BW Query Features for Crystal Reports

	BW Query Driver	BW MDX Driver
SAP Variable – Processing Type		
User Input	Yes	Yes
Authorization	Yes	Yes
Replacement Path	Yes	Yes
SAP Exit/Custom Exit	Yes	Yes
Precalculated Value Set	Yes	Yes
General Features for Variables		
Support for optional and mandatory variables	Yes	Yes
Support for keydate dependencies	Yes	Yes
Support for default values	Yes	Yes
Support for personalized values	Yes	Yes
SAP Variables – Variable Type		
Single value	Yes	Yes
Multiple single value	Yes	Yes
Range value	Yes	Yes
Complex selection	Yes	Yes
Formula variable	Yes	Yes
Hierarchy variable	Yes	Yes
Hierarchy node variable	Yes	Yes
Text variable	No	No
Keydate variable	No	Yes
Currency variable	Yes	Yes
Hierarchy version variable	No	No

Table 3.1 Supported and Unsupported BW Query Features for Crystal Reports (cont.)

Supported and Unsupported Features

As you can see, Crystal Reports doesn't use the features of conditions and exceptions inside a BW query. You can easily create exceptions in Crystal Reports by using the highlighting capabilities, and you can create conditions in your report using the Group Expert in combination with options such as a TopN or BottomN group. Keep in mind that a BW query with a condition will transfer all of its records to Crystal Reports based on the missing support — not just the records that meet the condition in the BW query.

In the area of supported data types for the characteristics and keyfigures of your BW query you will recognize that some data types are not supported by Crystal Reports. This does not mean you won't be able to use the characteristic. Instead, it means the characteristics are supported with a standard data type such as a string (for example, a characteristic of data type DATS (date/time) will be treated as a field of type String in Crystal Reports).

"Keydate dependency" refers to the functionality of identifying the usage of a keydate in the underlying BW query and the possibility that other elements require an update after the keydate has changed (for example, a list of hierarchy nodes might require a refresh after the keydate has changed). For Crystal Reports this dependency is only supported when you view reports via SAP BusinessObjects Enterprise, but not in the Crystal Reports designer itself.

An often-asked question concerns the difference between accessing a BW query and accessing an InfoCube directly. Table 3.2 shows the supported elements when accessing the BW query or InfoCube level with the SAP BusinessObjects XI 3.x product suite.

SAP NetWeaver Business Warehouse Metadata Element	SAP OLAP BAPI Support Level
Characteristics (including time and unit)	InfoCube and BW Query
Hierarchies	InfoCube and BW Query
Basic key figures	InfoCube and BW Query
Navigational attributes	BW Query only
Display attributes	InfoCube and BW Query
Calculated keyfigures/Formulas	BW Query only
Restricted keyfigures	BW Query only

Table 3.2 SAP NetWeaver Business Warehouse Metadata Support via OLAP BAPI

SAP NetWeaver Business Warehouse Metadata Element	SAP OLAP BAPI Support Level
Custom structures	BW Query only
Variables	BW Query only

Table 3.2 SAP NetWeaver Business Warehouse Metadata Support via OLAP BAPI (cont.)

InfoCube Access

In addition to the differences shown in Table 3.2, you also should consider the fact that when accessing the InfoCube directly, you do not have the functionality to create authorization variables that will filter the data based on the user authorizations. There are always options to solve such a situation, but this is an important topic to consider in your deployment.

In Table 3.3 you can see how Crystal Reports uses the elements from the BW query.

BW Query Element	Crystal Reports Designer Element
Characteristic	For each characteristic you'll receive a field representing the key value and a field for the description.
Hierarchy	A hierarchy is represented by a parent-child relationship.
Keyfigure	Each keyfigure can have up to three elements: numeric value, unit, and formatted value. The formatted value is based on the user preferences configured in the SAP system.
Calculated and restricted keyfigures	Each calculated and restricted keyfigure is treated like a keyfigure. The user does not have access to the underlying definition in the Crystal Reports designer.
Filter	Filters are applied to the underlying query but are not visible in the Crystal Reports designer.

Table 3.3 SAP NetWeaver Business Warehouse Metadata Mapping for Crystal Reports

BW Query Element	Crystal Reports Designer Element
Navigational attribute	Navigational attributes are treated the same way as characteristics.
Display attribute	Display attributes become standard fields in the Field Explorer and are grouped as subordinates of the linked characteristic.
SAP variables	Each variable with the property "Ready for Input" results in a parameter field in Crystal Reports.

Table 3.3 SAP NetWeaver Business Warehouse Metadata Mapping for Crystal Reports (cont.)

3.1.3 Creating Your First Crystal Report with SAP NetWeaver Business Warehouse

We will now use the knowledge we've gained from the previous sections and create our first report with Crystal Reports on top of the SAP NetWeaver Business Warehouse system. When you create a new report with Crystal Reports on top of SAP NetWeaver Business Warehouse, you can do so using the SAP Toolbar or you can use the standard menu in Crystal Reports (File • New • Standard Report • SAP BW MDX connectivity). The benefits of using the SAP Toolbar are as follows:

- You'll be presented with the familiar SAP UI for selecting queries and opening and saving objects.
- Crystal Reports will automatically prepare a list of values for each parameter field created for each SAP variable.

It is highly recommended that you use the SAP Toolbar for creating reports in an SAP NetWeaver Business Warehouse landscape.

SAP Toolbar vs. File • New

You can use the SAP Toolbar to create a report on top of your SAP NetWeaver Business Warehouse system, and you can use the menu path File • New and the select the proper SAP connectivity. It is important that if you start to create a report with the SAP Toolbar, you publish the report to your SAP BusinessObjects Enterprise system (and do not use the menu path File • Save), because otherwise the report object will have incomplete information and a Single Sign-On will not be possible.

In this example for creating a new Crystal Reports report, we'll use a BW query created on top of the SAP Demo cube (0D_SD_C03) with the following elements:

- Calendar Month/Year (0CALMONTH) and Sold-to Party (0D_SOLD_TO) in the rows
- Material (0D_MATERIAL) in the free characteristics
- Open Orders (0D_OORVALSC), Open Orders Quantity (0D_OORQTYBM), Costs (0D_COSTVALS) and Net sales (0D_NETVAL_S) in the columns
- A optional range variable for the Calendar Month/Year characteristics in the filter area

Allows External Access (Release for ODBO)

For BW queries to be used in Crystal Reports, you need to set the property ALLOW EXTERNAL ACCESS (in SAP NetWeaver Business Warehouse 3.x it's called RELEASED FOR ODBO). This property can be set in the BW Query Designer.

Based on this BW query, we'll now create a new Crystal Reports object that will show the value of our open orders per month and provide the capability to perform a drill-down to the customer level.

1. After you have installed Crystal Reports and the client components from SAP BusinessObjects Integration for SAP Solutions, you'll recognize an SAP-specific toolbar (see Figure 3.2) and menu in Crystal Reports.

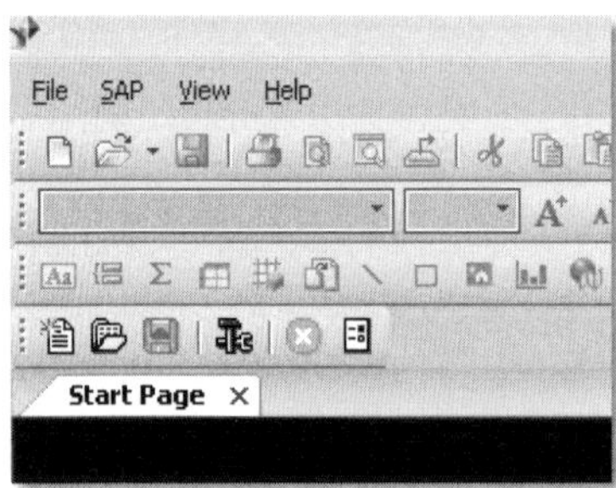

Figure 3.2 SAP Toolbar in Crystal Reports Designer

2. Select SETTINGS from the SAP menu and select the option USE MDX DRIVER WITH SUPPORT FOR MULTIPLE STRUCTURE. When you activate this option, the SAP toolbar will always leverage the BW MDX connectivity instead of the older BW query connectivity.

3. Select CREATE NEW REPORT FROM A QUERY from the SAP menu.
4. The SAP logon pad will come up, and you can select your SAP system from the list. After you selected the system, you need to provide the client number, your SAP credentials, and the logon language.
5. Next Crystal Reports will use the familiar UI from the Business Explorer for selecting a BW query.
6. Select your BW query, and Crystal Reports will create a new empty report for you with the BW query connected as a data source.
7. Follow the menu path VIEW • FIELD EXPLORER and ensure that the Field Explorer is shown. The Field Explorer offers you all of the elements from the BW query and offers a tree control to show the structure of the retrieved metadata (see Figure 3.3).

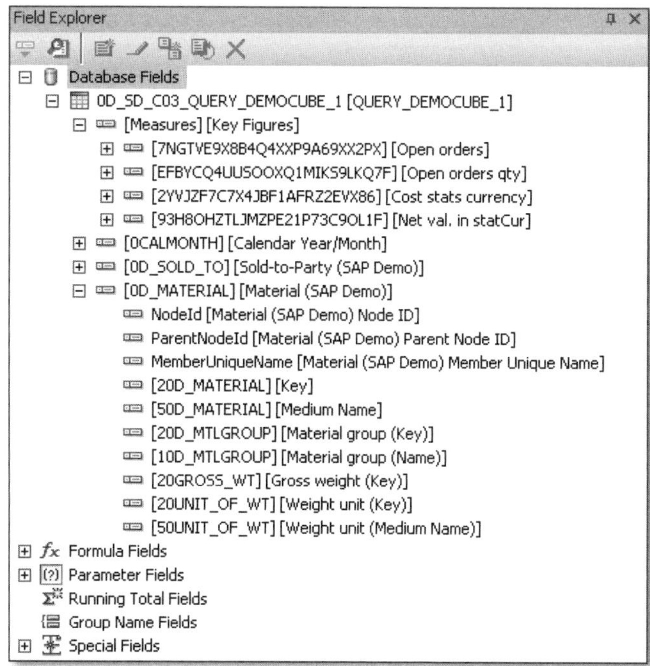

Figure 3.3 Field Explorer in Crystal Reports

8. At this point you can use the full functionality of Crystal Reports Designer to create a new report. The following steps show only some basic steps to illustrate how easily you can create a report with Crystal Reports.

9. Enter the characteristics SOLD-TO PARTY and MATERIAL and the keyfigures OPEN ORDERS VALUE and OPEN ORDER QUANTITY in the detail section of your report.
10. Select the menu path VIEW • PRINT PREVIEW. Because the underlying BW query contains a variable, Crystal Reports will prompt for values (see Figure 3.4).

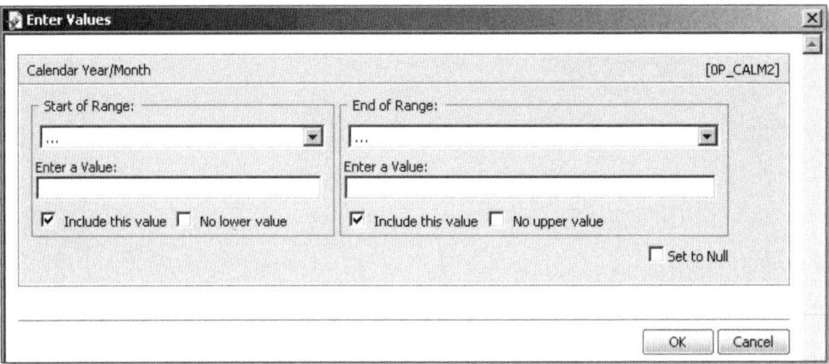

Figure 3.4 Variable Screen

11. Select a set of values from the list and click OK to run the report. Because the underlying variable is optional, you can also select the SET TO NULL checkbox so that no filter is set. Crystal Reports will then retrieve the data and show a preview of your report (see Figure 3.5).

Optional Variables

If the underlying variable in the BW query is configured to be an optional variable, Crystal Reports will offer the SET TO NULL checkbox, which removes the variable from the actual data retrieval to ensure that all records are considered.

12. Select the menu path INSERT • GROUP and insert a group for the Calendar Year/ Month key value.
13. Select the first keyfigure in your report, select the menu path INSERT • SUMMARY, and select the previously created group as the summary location.
14. Follow the menu path REPORT • SECTION EXPERT and select the HIDE (DRILL-DOWN OK) checkbox for the detail section (see Figure 3.6).
15. Select the menu path INSERT • CHART and place the chart "Placeholder" in the REPORT HEADER. Because the report already contains a group and summaries for the keyfigures, Crystal Reports picks up this information and creates a chart based on the keyfigure and the grouping for the Calendar Year/Month.

Figure 3.5 Preview in Crystal Reports

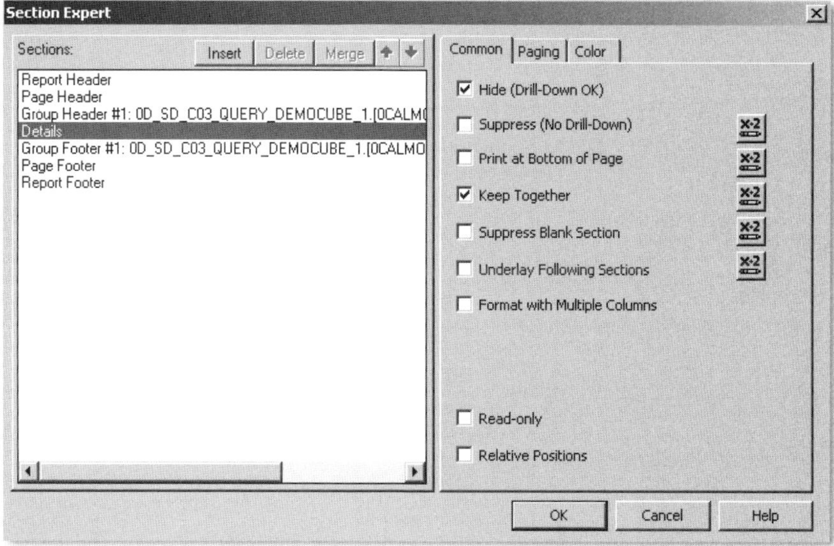

Figure 3.6 Section Expert

16. Select the menu path View • Print Preview. Your report should look similar to Figure 3.7

17. Select the menu path SAP • Save Report. Crystal Reports will offer you the typical SAP UI showing the assigned roles, and you can store the Crystal Reports object in the SAP NetWeaver BW system.

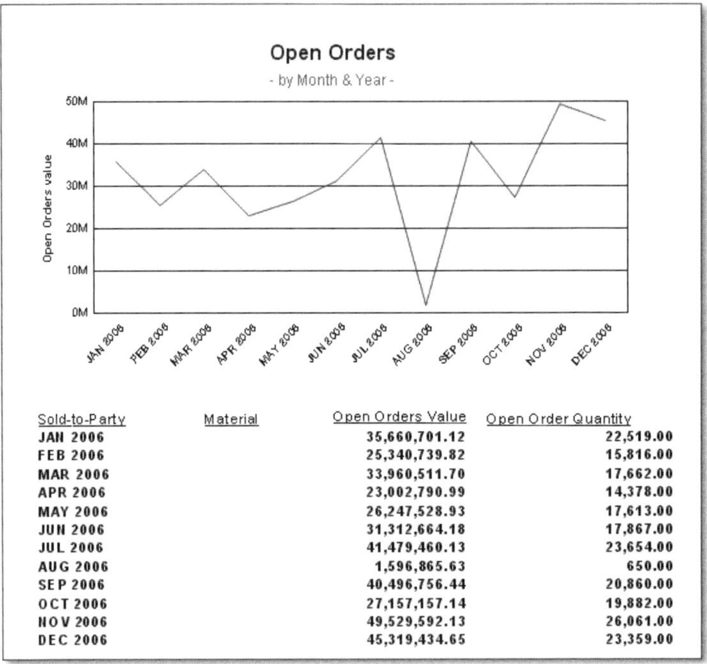

Sold-to-Party	Material	Open Orders Value	Open Order Quantity
JAN 2006		35,660,701.12	22,519.00
FEB 2006		25,340,739.82	15,816.00
MAR 2006		33,960,511.70	17,662.00
APR 2006		23,002,790.99	14,378.00
MAY 2006		26,247,528.93	17,613.00
JUN 2006		31,312,664.18	17,867.00
JUL 2006		41,479,460.13	23,654.00
AUG 2006		1,596,865.63	650.00
SEP 2006		40,496,756.44	20,860.00
OCT 2006		27,157,157.14	19,882.00
NOV 2006		49,529,592.13	26,061.00
DEC 2006		45,319,434.65	23,359.00

Figure 3.7 Crystal Reports Preview

18. In the SAVE dialog select a role for your report and enter a name in the description field. After clicking SAVE you'll be asked if you want to publish the Crystal Reports object to your SAP BusinessObjects Enterprise system (see Figure 3.8).

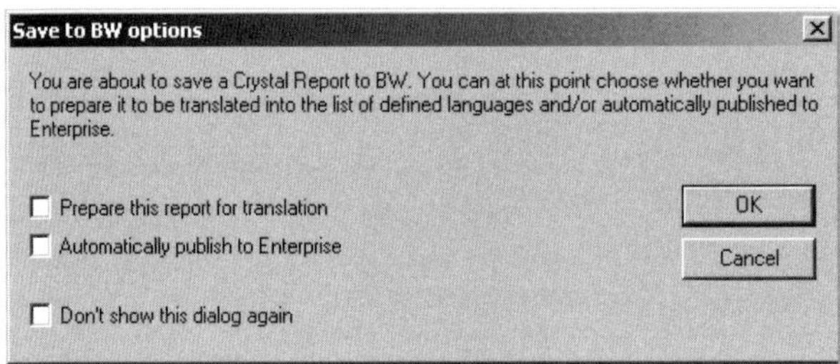

Figure 3.8 Save to BW Options Dialog

19. You can publish the Crystal Reports object to SAP BusinessObjects Enterprise, and based on the configuration during the installation, the report will be published from the SAP NetWeaver Business Warehouse system to your SAP Busi-

nessObjects Enterprise server (see Section 2.4.2, Setting up the Publishing Process for Crystal Reports).

Selecting the option PREPARE THIS REPORT FOR TRANSLATION results in all strings being extracted to the SAP translation system, and you'll be able to translate all strings in Transaction SE63. After the translation and a republishing of the report, you can use the report in multiple languages.

20. After you published the report, you should receive a success message and should now be able to view the report either using InfoView or from the role menu in the SAP NetWeaver Business Warehouse system.
21. When logging on to InfoView with your SAP credentials, you'll see that below the entry PUBLIC FOLDERS is a shortcut called MY ROLES, which allows you to navigate directly to all of the roles to which you have access.

3.2 Crystal Reports and SAP ERP

Crystal Reports is not only able to use the data in your SAP NetWeaver Business Warehouse system, but it can connect directly to your SAP ERP system. In the following sections I'll uncover the options available to you for such data connectivity.

3.2.1 Data Connectivity Overview

Figure 3.9 shows on a high level the options available to connect Crystal Reports to an SAP ERP system.

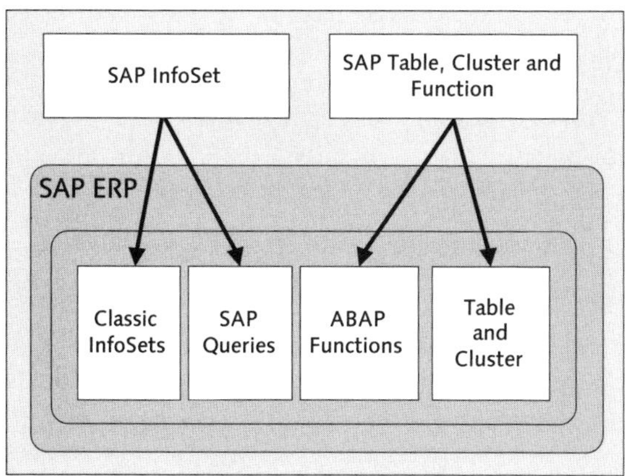

Figure 3.9 Crystal Reports Connectivity for SAP ERP

Classic InfoSet and SAP Queries

The combined connectivity for classic InfoSets and SAP queries allows you to connect to InfoSets and SAP queries (sometimes referred to as ABAP queries) directly from Crystal Reports. When you create a Crystal Reports object on top of an InfoSet or an SAP query, the newly created report will inherit all of the available metadata from the underlying SAP source. For an InfoSet and an SAP query this includes items such as long text for keyfields and the selections defined.

Selections created in the InfoSet or SAP query result in parameter fields in Crystal Reports that can be used to filter the actual result set.

The connectivity between InfoSets and SAP queries also honors the security on various levels:

- Each user viewing or designing a report based on an InfoSet or SAP query needs to authenticate against the SAP system, the general access to the source is secured, but also the configured data-level security in the SAP system will be used.
- Crystal Reports differentiates between global and local InfoSets and SAP queries and honors the assignment to User Groups (Transaction SQ02) as well.

Table and ABAP Function

With the connectivity to tables and ABAP functions in your SAP ERP system, you can access ABAP functions, transparent tables, cluster tables, pool tables, and views with Crystal Reports. This connectivity provides you with huge flexibility for your SAP ERP reporting because you can now use Crystal Reports to directly access this information and leverage those sources.

- The connectivity references the ABAP Dictionary to retrieve all of the metadata for the tables, which includes items such as the language-dependent description of tables and fields.
- When accessing ABAP functions in Crystal Reports you can preprocess the data in ABAP before passing it to Crystal Reports. In addition, this connectivity allows you to use a large set of your existing ABAP reports in your SAP ERP system directly as a source for Crystal Reports so that you can use Crystal Reports to create presentation-style reports based on your existing investment on the ABAP side.

ABAP functions that will be used in Crystal Reports need to fulfill the following requirements:

- The ABAP function needs to have defined return types for each of the outputs.
- The ABAP function cannot use complete tables as input parameters.
- You cannot call entire programs. You can only use individual functions.

As an example we'll use the ABAP function BAPI_SFLIGHT_GETLIST, shown in Listing 3.1.

```
FUNCTION BAPI_SFLIGHT_GETLIST
IMPORTING
   VALUE(FROMCOUNTRYKEY) LIKE  BAPISFDETA-COUNTRYFR
   VALUE(FROMCITY) LIKE  BAPISFDETA-CITYFROM
   VALUE(TOCOUNTRYKEY) LIKE  BAPISFDETA-COUNTRYTO
   VALUE(TOCITY) LIKE  BAPISFDETA-CITYTO
   VALUE(AIRLINECARRIER) LIKE  BAPISFDETA-CARRID DEFAULT SPACE
   VALUE(AFTERNOON) LIKE  BAPI_AUX-AFTERNOON DEFAULT SPACE
   VALUE(MAXREAD) LIKE  BAPI_AUX-MAXREAD DEFAULT 0
   EXPORTING
   VALUE(RETURN) LIKE  BAPIRET2 STRUCTURE  BAPIRET2
TABLES
   FLIGHTLIST STRUCTURE  BAPISFLIST
```

Listing 3.1 ABAP Function BAPI_SFLIGHT_GETLIST

Given the above example, you'll receive a list of fields in Crystal Reports (see Figure 3.10).

- All input parameters will result in fields with a prefix "I_" in the technical name.
- The output fields are available in Crystal Reports, and the technical name depends on the type of output. In our case the output is a table with the name FLIGHTLIST, so the fields are named with the prefix "T_" (for table) and the name of table (for example, T_FLIGHTLIST.CARRID).
- In Crystal Reports you can either use the input parameters of an ABAP function in the record selection formula, or you can link fields from another table to these fields and use the values from the table as input for the ABAP function.

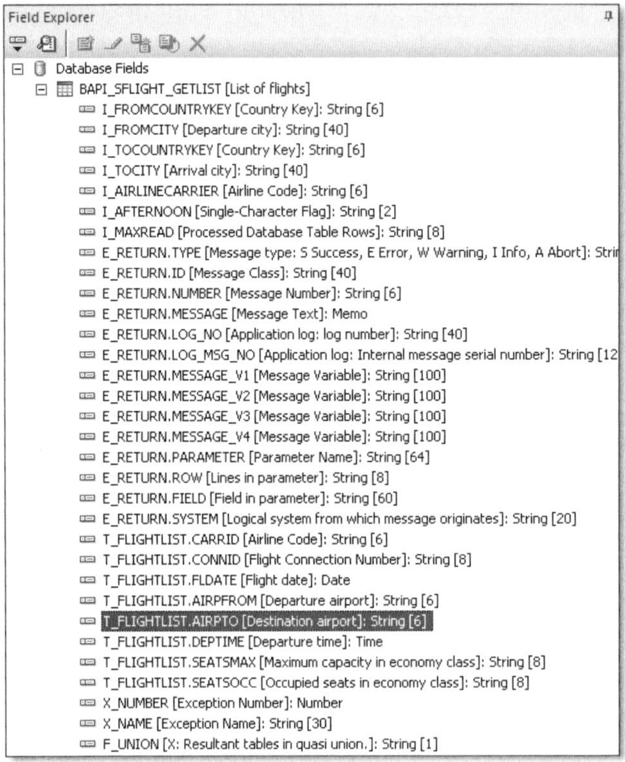

Figure 3.10 Crystal Reports Field Explorer

Data Cluster

Data clusters are specific databases in the ABAP dictionary. The structure is divided into a standard section containing several fields and one large field for the actual data cluster. Usually data clusters contain complex structures containing multiple pieces of information. The ABAP Dictionary might contain the table in which the data cluster is stored, but unfortunately the ABAP Dictionary does not contain the definition of the data cluster.

Therefore, SAP BusinessObjects Integration for SAP Solutions includes a Cluster Definition tool (Transaction ZCDD), which allows you to create a dictionary for the data cluster and map the individual components to tables. The dictionary can then be used with the table, ABAP function, and data cluster connectivity in Crystal Reports.

Data Cluster Example

Because this book focuses on the installation and configuration of the SAP BusinessObjects software in combination with your SAP landscape, explaining how you can configure your data cluster for the usage of Crystal Reports would go beyond the scope of this book. The user guide for SAP BusinessObjects Integration for SAP Solutions contains a very good example of how you can map an existing data cluster to a structure that can be used in Crystal Reports. You can download the user guide from *https://service.sap.com/bosap-instguides*.

3.2.2 Data-Level Security Editor

Because Crystal Reports can access the tables directly, SAP BusinessObjects Integration for SAP Solutions also includes a tool that allows you to define the user security for tables and the data stored in those tables. The Security Definition Editor (Transaction /CRYSTAL/RLS) is part of the ABAP transports that you received as part of SAP BusinessObjects Integration for SAP Solutions. Using this tool, not only can you define which user will have access to which table, but you can configure row-level security.

In this section you'll learn how to configure global access (or global restriction) on all tables and how to configure data-level security on top of the tables in your SAP ERP system.

1. To configure global access or global restriction, you can start the Security Definition Editor with Transaction /CRYSTAL/RLS (see Figure 3.11).

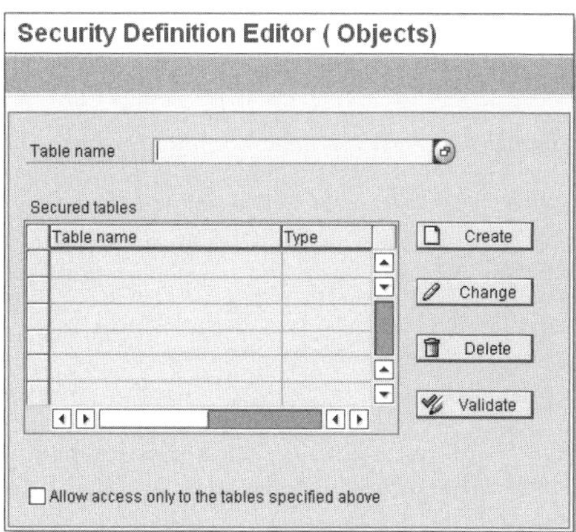

Figure 3.11 Security Definition Editor

2. If you want to restrict your users to a specific set of tables, you can select the ALLOW ACCESS ONLY TO THE TABLES SPECIFIED ABOVE checkbox. By default, the checkbox is not selected, and your users have access to all tables.
3. If you select the option to restrict your users to a specific set of tables, you first need to create a new authorization object via Transaction SU21. In our example we'll name the authorization object ZTABCHECK. The authorization object needs to contain one field; we'll call the field TABLE (see Figure 3.12).

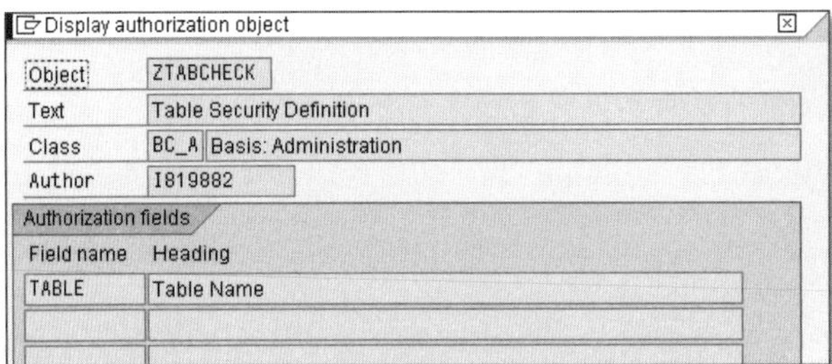

Figure 3.12 Authorization Object

4. After you have created the authorization object, you go back to the Security Definition Editor (Transaction /CRYSAL/RLS). Enter the name of the table you want to allow your users to access and click CREATE. We'll use the table SFLIGHT (see Figure 3.13). You can also use wildcards such as "*" to define the settings for multiple tables at once.

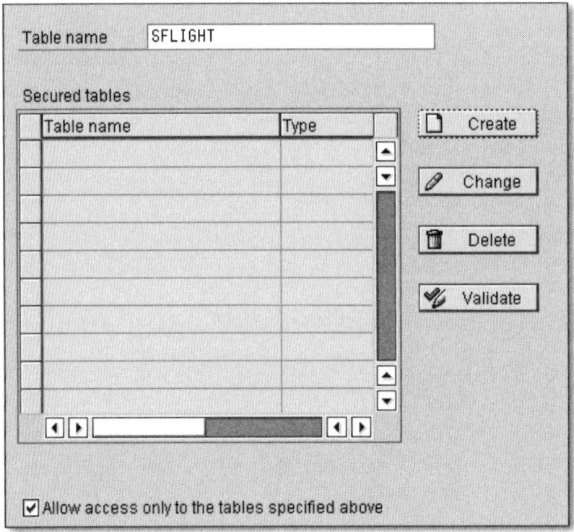

Figure 3.13 Security Definition Editor

5. In the next screen you click CREATE to set up a new authorization entry. You can select REFERENCE TO AN AUTHORIZATION OBJECT when asked for the entry type.
6. Enter your previously created authorization object (in our example ZTABCHECK) and click CREATE (see Figure 3.14).

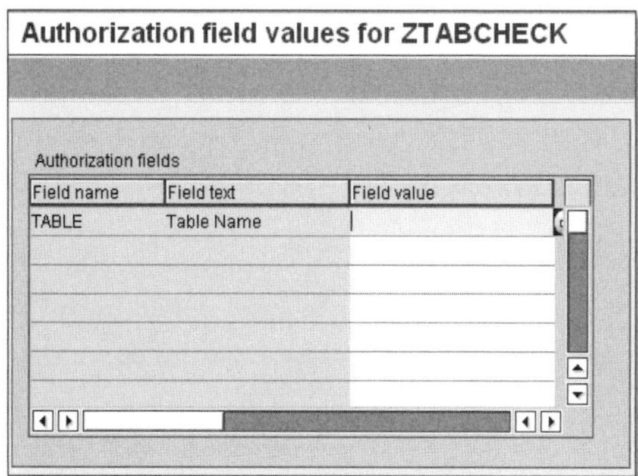

Figure 3.14 Authorization Field Values

7. Enter the table name (in our example SFLIGHT) as the FIELD VALUE and save your changes.
8. For the final step you need to add the authorization object (in our example ZTABCHECK) to the role of your users and specify the table to which you want to grant access.

If you want to set up row-level security, the steps are very similar to those above.

1. Create a new authorization object with a single field in Transaction SU21. The field represents the table field that we'll use to define the row-level security. We'll use the field CARR_ID (carrier ID) to define the row-level security for the table SFLIGHT.
2. Start the Security Definition Editor (Transaction /CRYSTAL/RLS). Enter the name of the table where you want to define the row-level security; we'll use SFLIGHT) and click CREATE.
3. In the next screen you click CREATE to set up a new authorization entry. You can select REFERENCE TO AN AUTHORIZATION OBJECT when asked for the entry type.
4. Enter your previously created authorization object and click CREATE.

5. Enter the field name that you want to use to define the row-level security. In our example we'll use the field CARR_ID.
6. For the final step you need to add the authorization object to the role of your users and specify as part of the role the actual value that you want the users to be able to use as row-level security for the field.

3.2.3 Creating Your First Crystal Report with SAP ERP

We will now use the knowledge from the previous sections and create our first report with Crystal Reports on top of an SAP ERP system.

1. Start Crystal Reports and follow the menu path File • New • Standard Report.
2. Double-click Create new connection and Crystal Reports will show a list of available data sources configured on your machine. By scrolling down the list you can identify the SAP options as well (see Figure 3.15).

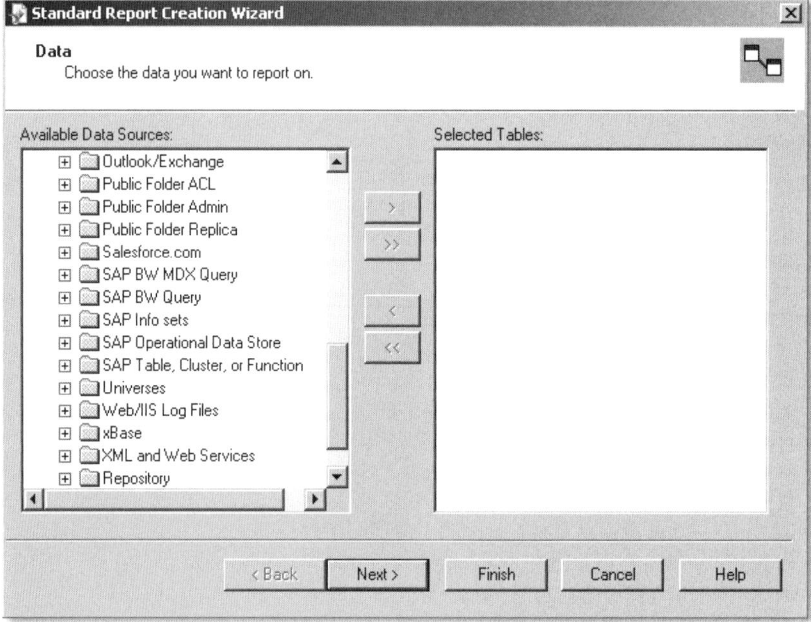

Figure 3.15 List of Available Data Sources

3. Double-click to select SAP Table, Cluster, or Function.

4. You will be asked to select the SAP system and to provide the necessary user credentials.
5. After a successful logon you'll be presented with the three options: Data Dictionary, ABAP Function modules, and Data Cluster.
6. Select DATA DICTIONARY, right-click to open the context menu, and select OPTIONS.
7. To reduce the list of tables retrieved by Crystal Reports you can configure a filter in the field TABLE NAME LIKE (see Figure 3.16). In our example we'll use the filter "s%" . After changing the filter value, you need to refresh the connection by either pressing the F5 button on your keyboard or right-clicking on your connection and selecting the option REFRESH.

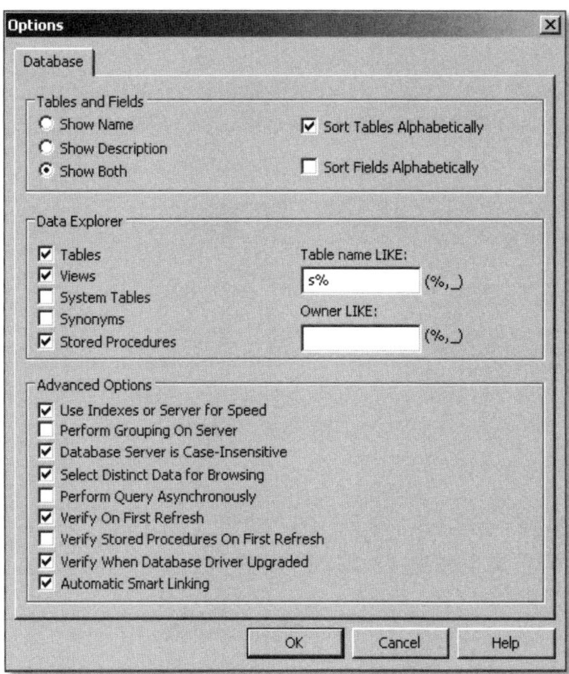

Figure 3.16 Options

8. Double-click DATA DICTIONARY, and Crystal Reports will show the tables from your SAP system. You can then add the tables SCARR, SPFLI, and SFLIGHT to the list of tables that will be used in Crystal Reports (see Figure 3.17).

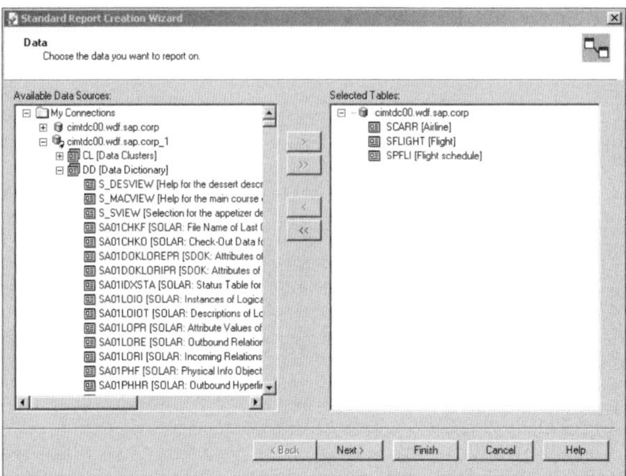

Figure 3.17 Selected Tables

9. In the next screen you can define the linking between the tables (see Figure 3.18). You have the option to define the linking yourself or to receive suggestions based on names or keys.

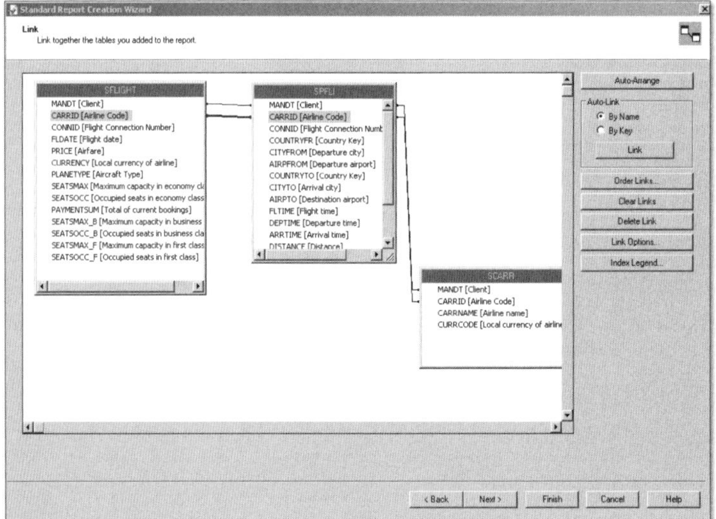

Figure 3.18 Table Linking

10. Click FINISH and you can now use all of the fields from all of the tables in Crystal Reports, and you can build your first Crystal Reports objects on top of SAP ERP data much like you created your first report on top of the BW query.

In the following chapter you will learn how to use Web Intelligence on top of your SAP NetWeaver Business Warehouse system and how to offer your end users an ad-hoc and self-service reporting solution.

4 SAP BusinessObjects Web Intelligence and SAP NetWeaver Business Warehouse

In the following sections we'll go into detail about how to use OLAP Universes and SAP BusinessObjects Web Intelligence on top of SAP NetWeaver Business Warehouse. We'll start by outlining the connectivity options available to you, go to the metadata mapping between SAP NetWeaver Business Warehouse and OLAP Universes, and finally create our first OLAP Universe and an SAP Business-Objects Web Intelligence report on top of this universe.

4.1 Data Connectivity Overview

Figure 4.1 shows an overview of the data connectivity for SAP BusinessObjects Web Intelligence via OLAP Universes.

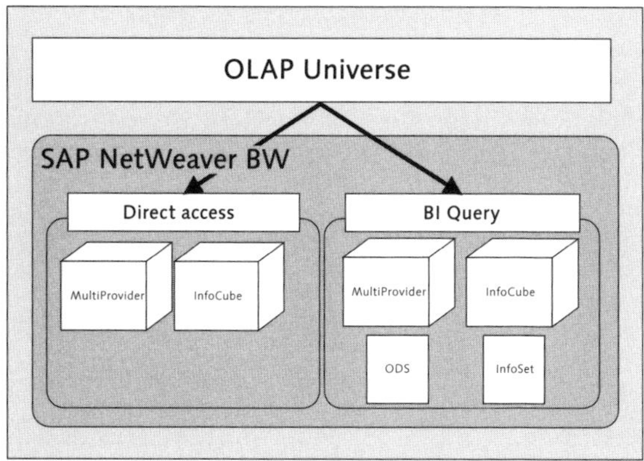

Figure 4.1 Data Connectivity for SAP BusinessObjects Web Intelligence and SAP NetWeaver Business Warehouse

SAP BusinessObjects Web Intelligence depends on the existence of a universe, and as you can see in Figure 4.1, in release XI 3.1 the universe is only able to connect to the SAP NetWeaver Business Warehouse system, which means there is no solution to connect SAP BusinessObjects Web Intelligence directly to the SAP ERP system.

The connectivity for the OLAP Universe is purely based on the OLAP BAPI interface from SAP NetWeaver Business Warehouse, so the connectivity of the OLAP Universe does not require any ABAP transports to be imported into the SAP system. However, to use the Single Sign-On functionality of SAP BusinessObjects Integration for SAP Solutions, those ABAP transports need to be imported at least.

SAP BusinessObjects Web Intelligence and SAP ERP

If you want to connect SAP BusinessObjects Web Intelligence to your SAP ERP data, a possible solution is SAP BusinessObjects Rapid Marts. SAP BusinessObjects offers *Rapid Marts* for customers who don't necessarily use SAP NetWeaver Business Warehouse as a data warehouse solution but want to create a data mart on top of their SAP ERP system. Rapid Marts are prebuilt extractors for Data Integrator with a predefined database schema for a data mart on top of your SAP ERP system. On top of the prebuilt database schema, the Rapid Mart includes universes and SAP BusinessObjects Web Intelligence reports that you can use out of the box.

4.2 Supported and Unsupported SAP NetWeaver Business Warehouse Elements

Table 4.1 shows the supported and unsupported features for OLAP Universes and for SAP BusinessObjects Web Intelligence reports based on those OLAP Universes. The table represents the level of support for release XI 3.1.

SAP Variables – Variable Types	OLAP Universes
InfoProvider	
Direct access to InfoCube and MultiProvider	Yes
Access to BW queries	Yes

Table 4.1 Supported and Unsupported BW Query Features for OLAP Universes

SAP Variables – Variable Types	OLAP Universes
InfoProvider	
Characteristic Values	
Key	Yes
Short description	Yes
Medium and long description	Yes
BW Query Features	
Support for hierarchies	Yes
Support for free characteristics	Yes
Support for calculated and restricted keyfigures	Yes
Support for currencies and units	Yes
Support for multiple structures	Yes
Support for formulas and selections	Yes
Support for filters	Yes
Support for display and navigational attributes	Yes
Support for conditions and exceptions	No
Data Types	
Support for type CHAR (characteristics)	Yes
Support for type NUMC (characteristics)	Yes
Support for type DATS (characteristics)	Yes
Support for type TIMS (characteristics)	No
Support for type Date (keyfigures)	Yes
Support for type Time (keyfigures)	No
SAP Variable – Processing Type	
User Input	Yes
Authorization	Yes

Table 4.1 Supported and Unsupported BW Query Features for OLAP Universes (cont.)

SAP Variables – Variable Types	OLAP Universes
InfoProvider	
Replacement Path	Yes
SAP Exit/Custom Exit	Yes
Precalculated Value Set	Yes
General Features for Variables	
Support for optional and mandatory variables	Yes
Support for keydate dependencies	Yes
Support for default values	Yes
Support for personalized values	No
SAP Variables – Variable Type	
Single value	Yes
Multiple single value	Yes
Range value	Yes
Complex selection	Yes, as range filter
Formula variable	Yes
Hierarchy variable	Yes
Hierarchy node variable	Yes
Text variable	No
Keydate variable	Yes
Currency variable	Yes
Hierarchy version variable	No

Table 4.1 Supported and Unsupported BW Query Features for OLAP Universes (cont.)

In Table 4.2 you can see how the Universe Designer uses the elements from the BW query and what types of objects in the OLAP universe map to which BW query elements.

BW Query Element	OLAP Universe Element
Cube Dimension	Each dimension of the InfoCube results in a top-level class and provides the structure for the universe.
Characteristic	Each characteristic results in a subclass folder with a level 00 and a level 01 dimension object, where the level 00 object represents the "All members" view for the characteristic.
Hierarchy	**BW query as source**: A characteristic with an activated hierarchy results in a subclass folder with the number of dimension objects representing the number of hierarchy levels available at the point of creating the universe. **BW InfoCube as source**: If the universe is created directly on top of an InfoCube, each available hierarchy for each characteristic is represented by a subclass folder, and the number of dimension objects depends on the number of levels for each hierarchy available at the point of creating the universe.
Keyfigure	Each keyfigure can have up to three elements: numeric value, unit, and formatted value, so each keyfigure is created in a subclass folder below the class folder *Keyfigures*, with up to one measure object (numeric value) and two dimension objects (unit and formatted values). The formatted value is based on the user preferences configured in the SAP system.
Calculated and restricted keyfigures	Each calculated and restricted keyfigure is treated like a keyfigure. The user does not have access to the underlying definition in the OLAP Universe.
Filter	Filters are applied to the underlying query but are not visible in the Universe Designer.
Navigational attribute	Navigational attributes are treated just like a characteristic.
Display attribute	Display attributes become detail objects and are subordinates of the linked characteristic.
SAP variables	Each variable with the property *Ready for Input* results in a predefined filter in the OLAP Universe.

Table 4.2 SAP NetWeaver BW Metadata Mapping for OLAP Universes

4.3 Creating Your First SAP BusinessObjects Web Intelligence Report

In this section we'll create our first OLAP Universe on top of a BW query. We'll use the same query we used for our first Crystal Reports example. You can find the details of the query in Section 3.1.3, Creating Your First Crystal Reports Report with SAP NetWeaver Business Warehouse. Keep in mind that, like for Crystal Reports, BW queries have to be configured to allow external access via the property in the BW Query Designer.

1. You can start the Universe Designer by following the menu path START • PROGRAMS • BUSINESSOBJECTS XI RELEASE 3 • BUSINESSOBJECTS ENTERPRISE • DESIGNER.
2. Before you can build a new OLAP Universe, you need to authenticate yourself against your SAP BusinessObjects Enterprise system (see Figure 4.2).

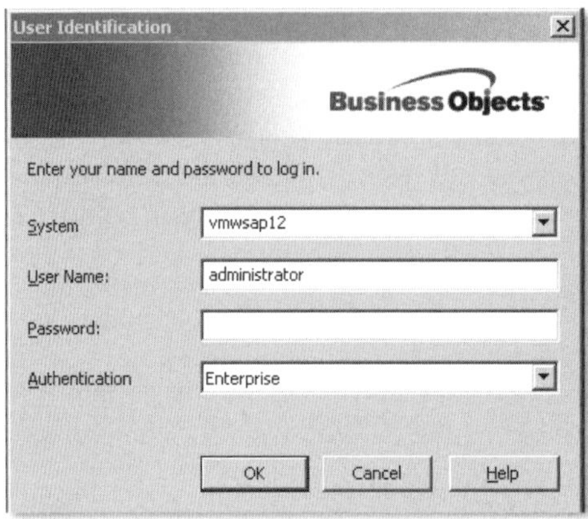

Figure 4.2 Universe Designer Authentication

3. Select SAP as the authentication and enter your SAP credentials. Because the Universe Designer does not offer an SAP-specific UI, you need to enter your user name in the following syntax:

   ```
   [SAP System ID]~[SAP System client]/[SAP user name]
   ```

   Example:

   ```
   CIM~003/DEMO
   ```

4. Select the menu path FILE • NEW to create a new OLAP Universe. The Universe Parameters screen of your new universe will come up (see Figure 4.3).

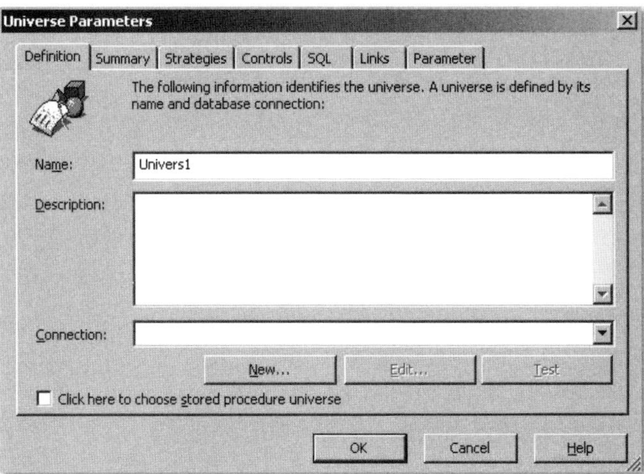

Figure 4.3 Universe Parameters

5. Click New to create a new connection to your SAP system.
6. In the list of connections scroll down to SAP and select SAP Business Warehouse as the connection type.
7. Enter a name for the connection at the top of the screen and move to the next screen (see Figure 4.4).

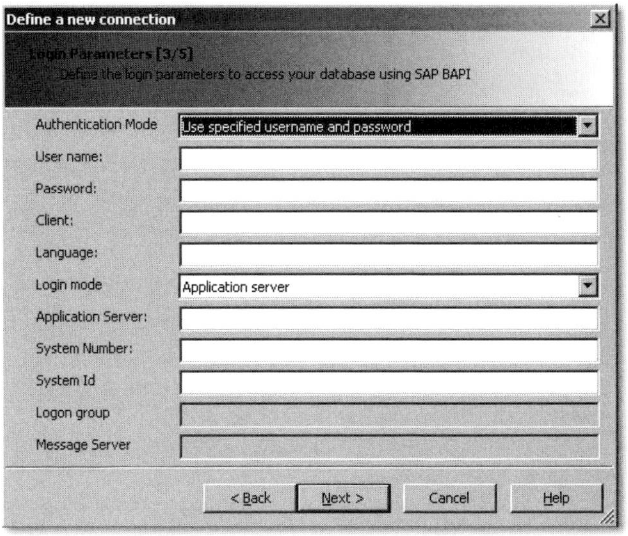

Figure 4.4 Login Parameters for Universe Connection

8. In this screen you need to provide the details of your SAP system and your SAP credentials, and you need to select the authentication mode for your universe connection. In our example we want to use Single Sign-On later on, so we'll select the option USE SINGLE SIGN-ON WHEN REFRESHING REPORTS AT VIEWTIME.
9. You can enter the details for your SAP system and set the authentication mode to USE SINGLE SIGN-ON WHEN REFRESHING REPORTS AT VIEWTIME. If you did use your SAP credentials to log on to the Universe Designer, you can also use Single Sign-On in the Universe Designer.
10. Click NEXT to go to the next screen (see Figure 4.5).

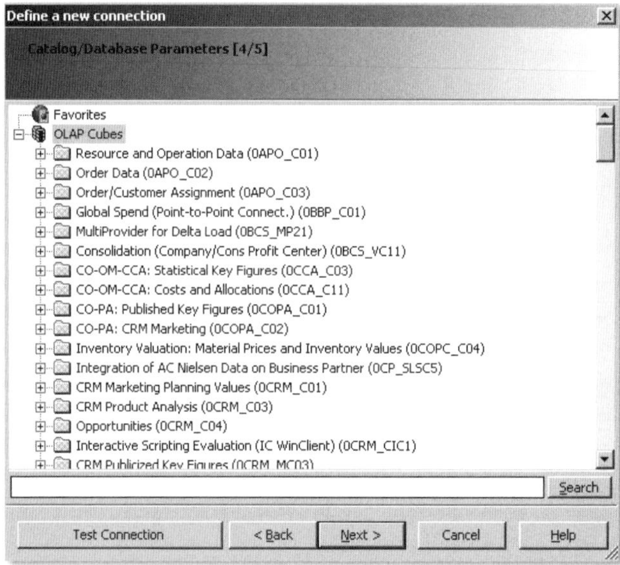

Figure 4.5 Available OLAP Cubes and Queries from SAP NetWeaver Business Warehouse

11. In this screen you can see all of the BW InfoCubes with BW queries that have been configured to be available via the OLAP BAPI interface. At the end of the list you'll find an entry called $INFOCUBE, which gives you direct access to all of the InfoCubes.
12. Navigate down to your InfoCube and open the list of BW queries by clicking the "+" symbol in front of the cube.
13. Select the BW query and navigate to the next screen by clicking the NEXT button (see Figure 4.6).

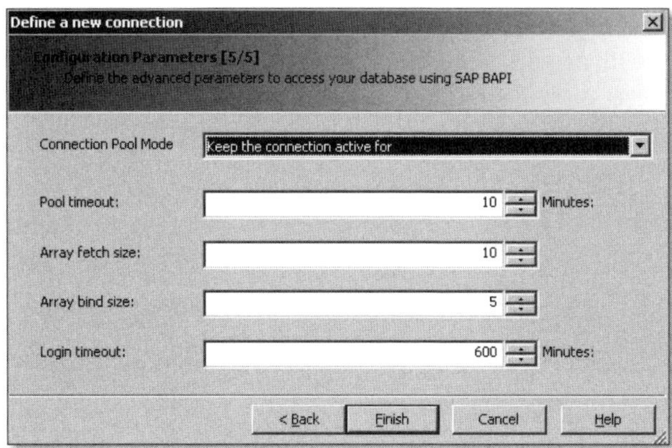

Figure 4.6 Connection Parameters

14. In this dialog you can configure the connection parameters; the connection pool mode is especially important. Here you define for how long the connection will be kept active. The default value is 10 minutes. You also have the option to select the option Disconnect after each transaction, which you want to avoid because it will result in a log on and log off process for every single function call to your SAP system from this universe connection. Select Keep the connection active for and leave the default value for Pool timeout.
15. Click Finish and navigate to the Controls tab from the Universe Parameter screen (see Figure 4.7). Uncheck all of the controls on this screen unless you are sure you want to set those limits for this connection.

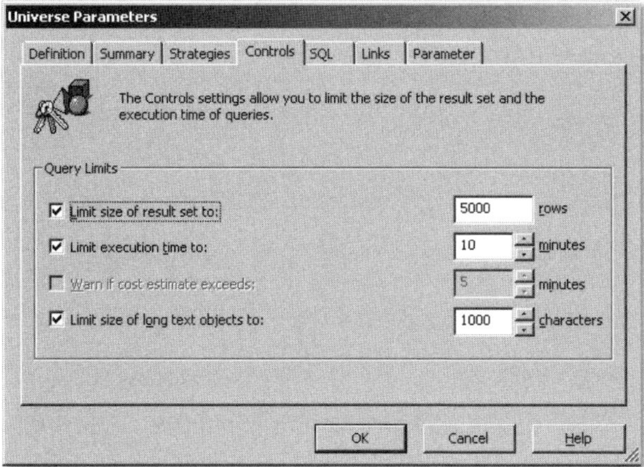

Figure 4.7 Universe Parameters – Controls

16. Click OK, and the Universe Designer will use the existing metadata in your SAP NetWeaver BW system and create a new universe (see Figure 4.8). Figure 4.8 shows the resulting universe based on the BW query that we selected for this example.

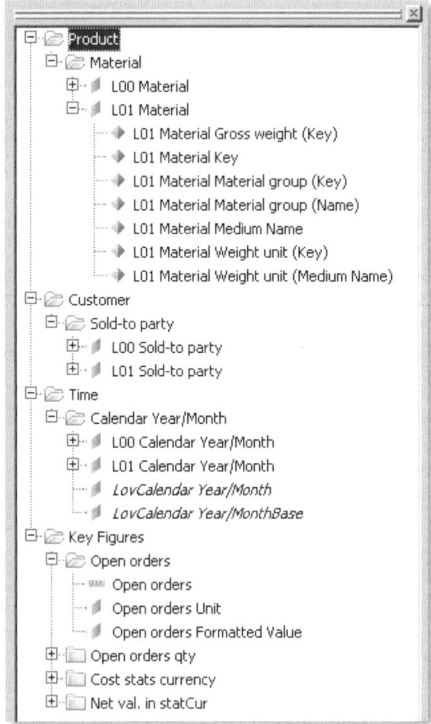

Figure 4.8 OLAP Universe Based on Sample BW Query

17. Select the menu path File • Save to save the universe and then select the menu path File • Export to save the universe to your SAP BusinessObjects Enterprise system so that you can use it with SAP BusinessObjects Web Intelligence.
18. After exporting the universe, you can log on to InfoView using the SAP authentication and your SAP credentials.
19. In InfoView select the menu path New • Web Intelligence Report.
20. You can then select the universe that you previously exported to the SAP BusinessObjects Enterprise system to create a new SAP BusinessObjects Web Intelligence report.

21. You will then be shown the SAP BusinessObjects Web Intelligence query panel (see Figure 4.9).

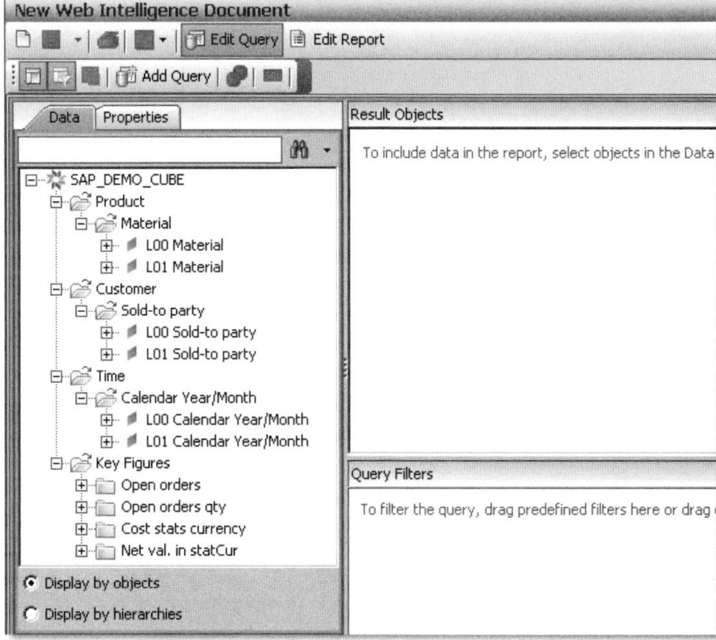

Figure 4.9 SAP BusinessObjects Web Intelligence Query Panel

Here you can select the objects for the result set, and you can create your own filter objects.

22. Drag and drop the following objects to the Result Objects panel:
    - L01 Calendar Year/Month
    - L01 Sold-to party
    - L01 Material
    - Open orders
    - Open order qty
23. Click Refresh Query (top-right corner).
24. Based on the variable that exists in our BW query, you'll be asked to provide values for the start and end of the range for the Calendar Year/Month characteristic.

Optional Variables

If the underlying variable in the BW query is configured to be an optional variable, SAP BusinessObjects Web Intelligence shows the word *optional* behind the prompting text, and you can run the query without entering any values. If you don't enter any values for the variable, SAP BusinessObjects Web Intelligence will remove the variable from the actual data retrieval to ensure that all records are considered.

If the optional variable has a configured default value in the underlying BW query, the SAP BusinessObjects Web Intelligence report will be executed for the default value even in cases where you removed the default value explicitly.

25. After providing the values, you can click Run Query. You've just created your first SAP BusinessObjects Web Intelligence report on top of SAP NetWeaver Business Warehouse (see Figure 4.10).

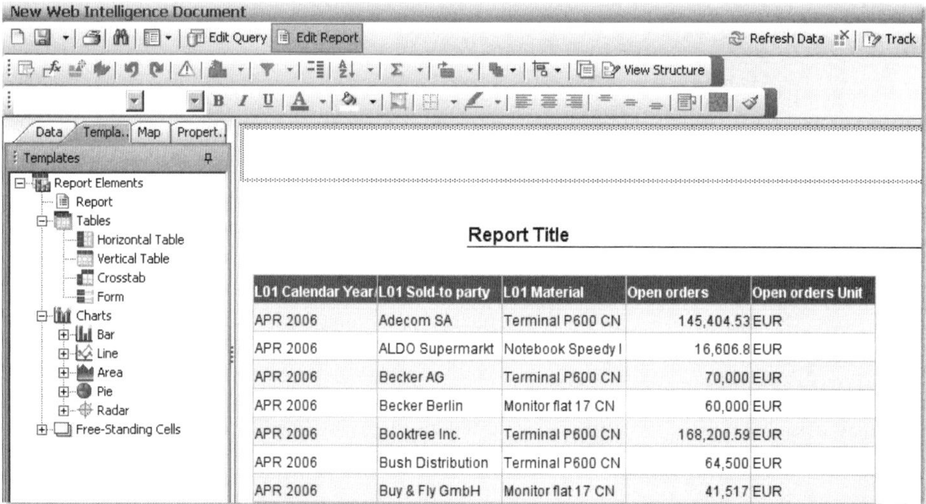

Figure 4.10 Web Intelligence Report

26. Click the icon to save your SAP BusinessObjects Web Intelligence report to your SAP BusinessObjects Enterprise system.

Saving to Roles

When you're looking at a deployment of Crystal Reports and SAP BusinessObjects Web Intelligence reports, you might want to consider storing the SAP BusinessObjects Web Intelligence reports in the role folders that are created based on the publishing process in your SAP BusinessObjects Enterprise system.

In that way you can also use the imported SAP roles in your SAP BusinessObjects Enterprise system to assign rights to those reports including the SAP BusinessObjects Web Intelligence-related content. Keep in mind that the role folders only appears after at least one Crystal Reports object has been published to the role folder.

4.4 OLAP Universe Change Management

Universes on top of your SAP NetWeaver Business Warehouse are created automatically based on the metadata available in your SAP system. Starting with the XI 3.x release, the Universe Designer also provides the functionality to update the universe based on changes in the underlying source system.

1. You can call the Update Wizard by following the menu path View • Refresh Structure in the Universe Designer.
2. In the second screen of the Update Wizard you'll be asked which of your changes you want to keep (see Figure 4.11).

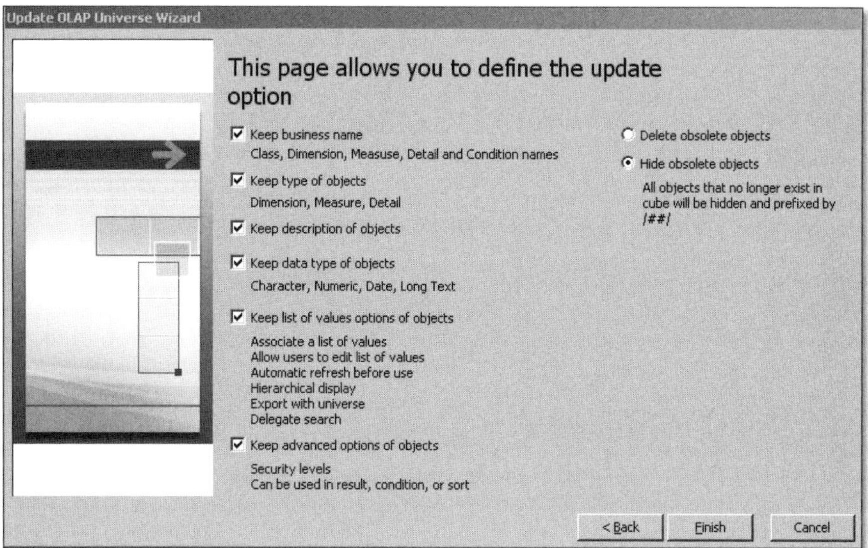

Figure 4.11 OLAP Universe Update Wizard

3. After setting the options, the Update Wizard connects to the underlying SAP system and provides a list of updates that have been submitted to your uni-

verse. The options to select depend on the changes you made and the changes you want to keep in the universe. By default, the Update Wizard comes with all of the options selected, to keep all custom changes in the universe.

Connection Timeout and Updates

Depending on the setting for the connection timeout for your universe, the Update Wizard might not be able to provide any updates, or the updates might be incomplete. For example, if your connection timeout is set to 10 minutes and you adding and removing characteristics to your BW query and go directly to the Update Wizard in the Universe Designer, some of the changes might not get picked up from the Update Wizard because of caching.

Therefore, it is highly recommend that, if you want to update your universe, you ensure that you start with a fresh connection to the SAP NetWeaver BW system by ensuring that there are no open connections. The best way to do so is to close the Universe Designer and start it again and then call the Update Wizard.

In this chapter you will receive an overview of how to leverage Query as a Web Service on top of your OLAP Universe in order to create a Web service that leverages the data of your SAP NetWeaver Business Warehouse system.

5 Query as a Web Service and OLAP Universes

Query as a Web Service (QaaWS) is an application that allows you to expose a query on top of a universe as a Web service. This Web service can then be consumed by other applications, for example, Xcelsius. QaaWS consists of two main components: the administrative client application that allows you to create Web services on top of universes and a backend component that stores the definition of the Web service and hosts the Web services. QaaWS is included in your SAP BusinessObjects Enterprise XI release 3.1 package, and if you followed the steps in Section 2.1.1, Installation of SAP BusinessObjects Enterprise, for the server side and for the client side, you should have the components installed on your system.

The focus of this section is to use the client tool for creating Web services so that we can use Web services based on OLAP Universes and consume those later on in Xcelsius.

5.1 Data Connectivity Overview

Before we start creating a new Web service, let's take a look at Figure 5.1, which provides an overview of the connectivity that's available to you with QaaWS on top of your SAP landscape. QaaWS sits on top of universes, so the only connectivity you can use in combination with QaaWS is with the OLAP Universe. QaaWS can also use any other universe based on relational or other OLAP sources, but the focus here is the connectivity with your SAP systems.

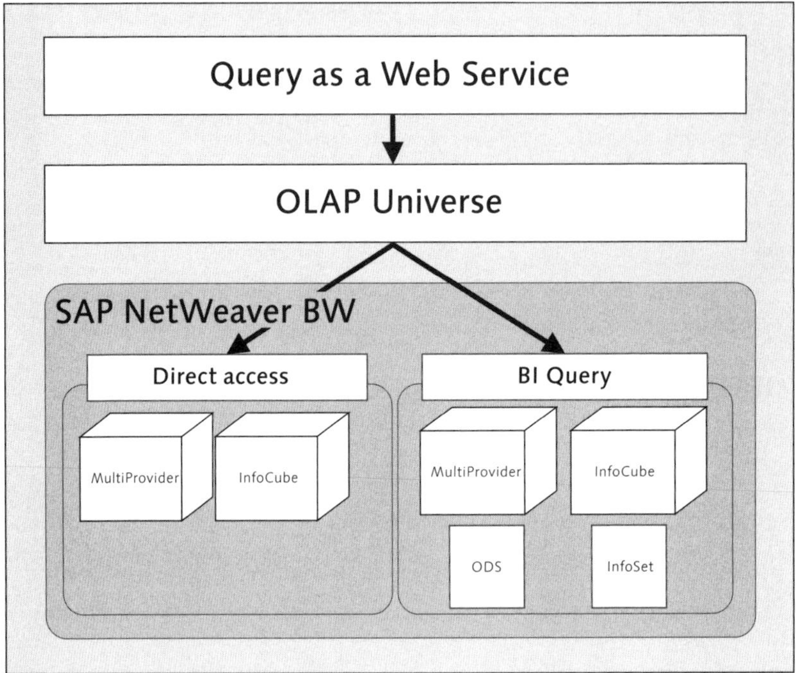

Figure 5.1 Connectivity for QaaWS

5.2 Creating Your First Query as a Web Service

Before you can start using the QaaWS tool, you need to ensure that your user is either part of the *Administrator* user group or part of the *QaaWS Group Designer* user group in your SAP BusinessObjects Enterprise system. You can ensure this by going to the USERS AND GROUPS area in the Central Management Console and add either your SAP role or your SAP user to one of the existing user groups.

Inside the Central Management Console you'll also find an area QaaWS that allows you to define your own user groups and security in regard to the QaaWS tool.

1. To start the QaaWS tool, follow the menu path PROGRAMS • BUSINESSOBJECTS XI 3.1 • BUSINESSOBJECTS ENTERPRISE • QUERY AS A WEB SERVICE.
2. Because you haven't used the tool previously, you'll be asked to add a new host to the list of available systems (see Figure 5.2).

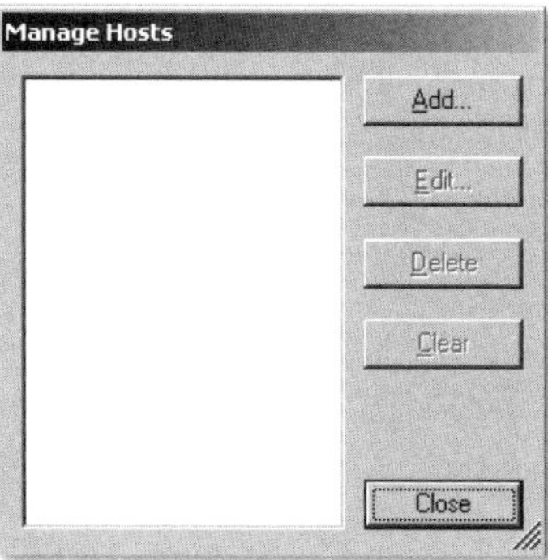

Figure 5.2 Managing Hosts for QaaWS

3. Click the ADD button and define a new host. The pop-up window shown in Figure 5.3 will appear and provide you the functionality to enter the details for the new host.

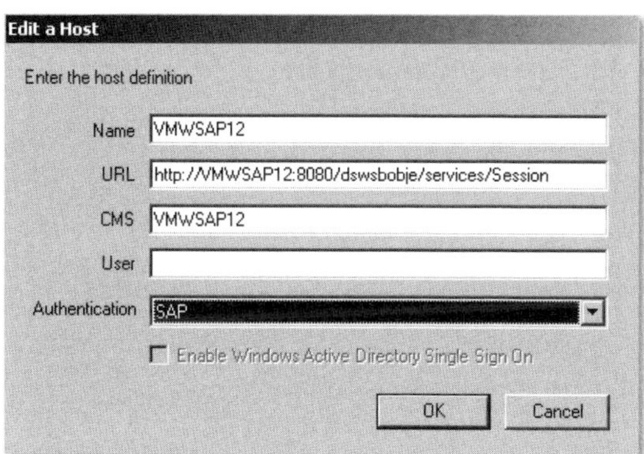

Figure 5.3 Creating a New Host

4. Enter a name (VMWSAP12 in our example) for your new system. When typing, you'll see that the value for the URL field will be entered for you based on the name. Therefore, you should use the name of your application server hosting the Web service as the name.

   Enter the name of your Central Management Server, and as soon as the system has verified your Web service deployment, you can select SAP as the authentication mode. There is no need to enter a user right away because you are creating a host entry. You'll be asked to authenticate against your system later on.

After you confirmed all of your entries and clicked OK, the tool will bring you to the logon screen (see Figure 5.4).

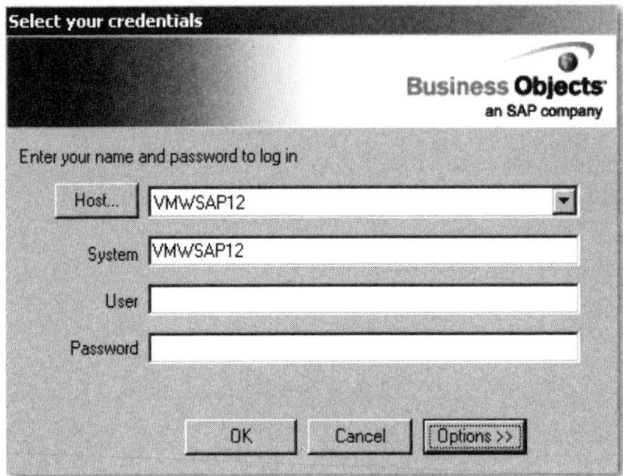

Figure 5.4 Log On to the QaaWS Tool

5. As you can see, the QaaWS tool does not provide an SAP-specific logon dialog. You need to enter your user name in the following syntax:

   ```
   [SAP System ID]~[SAP System client]/[SAP user name]
   ```

   Example:

   ```
   CIM~003/DEMO
   ```

6. The OPTIONS button allows you to select the authentication method.
7. After a successful logon you'll be presented with the list of available Web services on your SAP BusinessObjects Enterprise system, which most likely is empty at this stage.

Query as a Web Service with Universes and Single Sign-On

If you configured the universe connection to leverage Single Sign-On with your SAP system, you need to log on with your SAP credentials using the SAP authentication to the QaaWS tool because otherwise you won't be able to finish the creation of a Web service, because the final step includes a preview of the data that will be retrieved.

8. Follow the menu path QUERY • NEW • QUERY to create your first Web service on top of an OLAP Universe.
9. In the next screen (see Figure 5.5) you can enter the name of your Web service (in our example SAP_DEMO_WEBSERVICE).

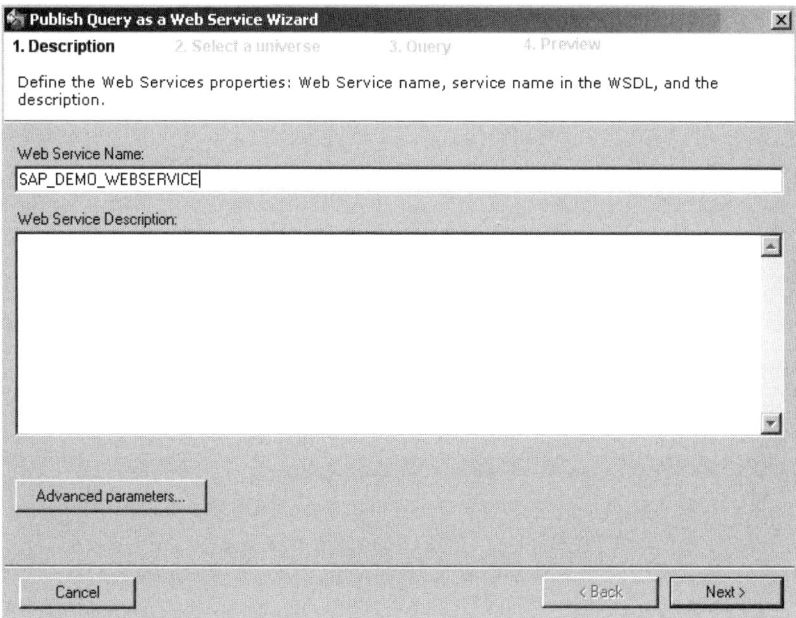

Figure 5.5 New QaaWS

10. Click the ADVANCED PARAMETERS button to configure the authentication mode for the Web service.

11. In the ADVANCED PARAMETERS screen (see Figure 5.6) ensure that the authentication mode is set to "secSAPR3", which is the value for the SAP authentication. In this way you can use the Web service inside an Xcelsius dashboard on top of an OLAP Universe but still achieve Single Sign-On using the SAP authentication.

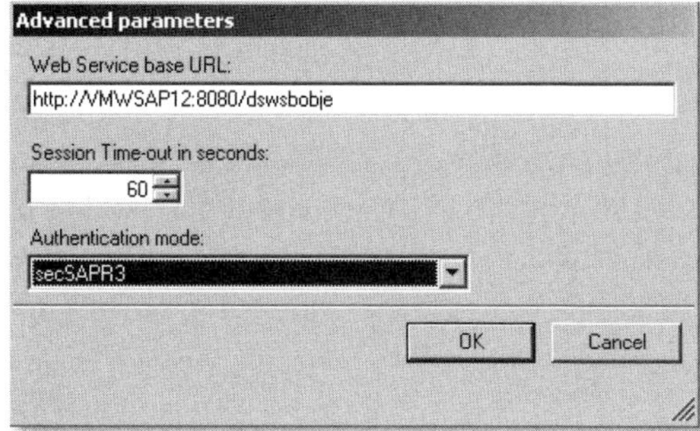

Figure 5.6 Advanced Parameters

Session Time-out

The session time-out can be configured per Web service connection. The connection to the server is cached to improve the overall performance of QaaWS.

12. Confirm the changes and move to the next screen. The system will present you with a list of universes, and you should be able to select the OLAP Universe that we created in Section 4.3, Creating Your First SAP BusinessObjects Web Intelligence Report.
13. In the next screen (see Figure 5.7) you are presented with the query panel, which is similar to the query panel from SAP BusinessObjects Web Intelligence that you used in the previous chapter.

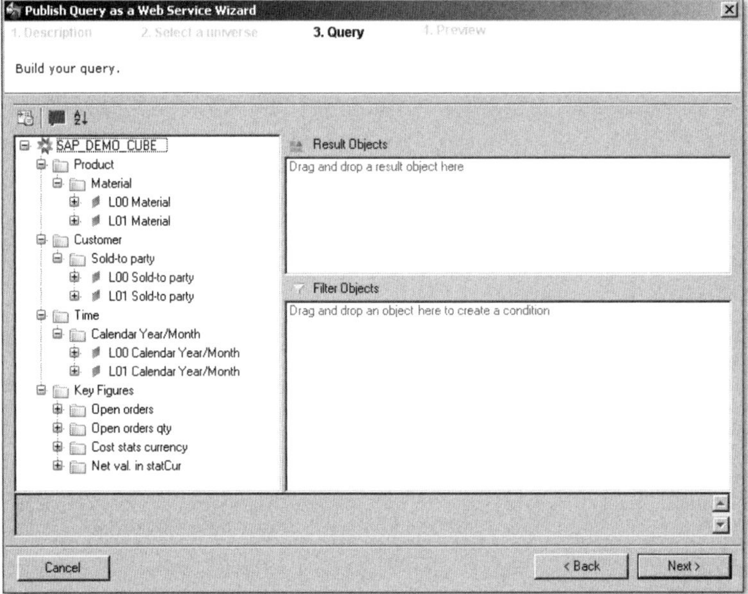

Figure 5.7 Query Panel in QaaWS

14. You can now add the elements from the OLAP Universe to the Result Objects area. If you want to add an additional filter, you can also add objects to the Filter Objects area. In our example we add the following objects to the Result Objects area:
    - L01 Calendar Year/Month
    - L01 Sold-to party

- L01 Material
- Open Orders

QaaWS for Prompting and List of Values

When you plan to use QaaWS to provide a Web service for list of values being used in Xcelsius dashboards, please ensure that your Web service provides the actual key value (detail object in the universe) and the value description (either a dimension object or a detail object). It is important to use the actual key value as input to any SAP variables in the underlying BW queries.

15. By clicking the OPTIONS icon in the top left corner, you can set constraints for your defined query. The possible limits are:
    - **Max. fetched time**
      Allows you to set a maximum time value for data retrieval
    - **Max. rows fetched**
      Allows you to set a maximum number of rows for your result set
16. If your universe has prompts (SAP variables), you'll receive a prompting screen in the next step (see Figure 5.8). In our example we'll receive a prompting screen for the CALENDAR YEAR/MONTH variable from the underlying BW query.

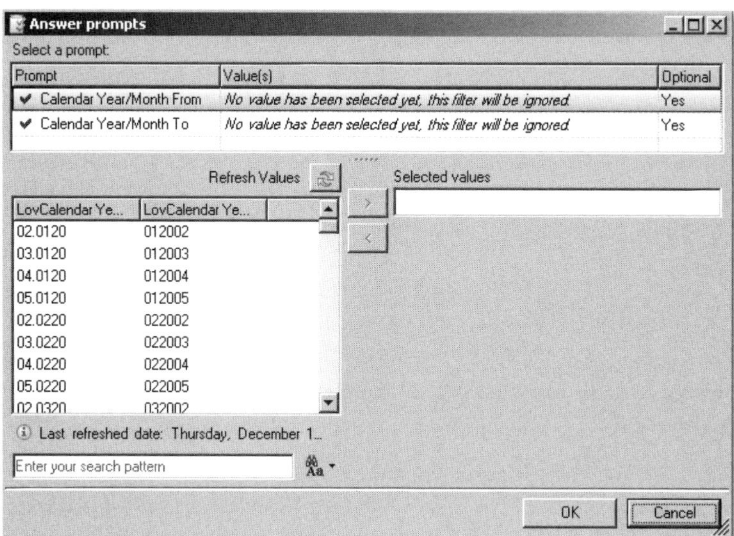

Figure 5.8 Prompting Screen

The reason for the prompting screen is that the system is now trying to provide an example result set for your Web service. After you entered the values for the variables, the system will present the example result set (see Figure 5.9).

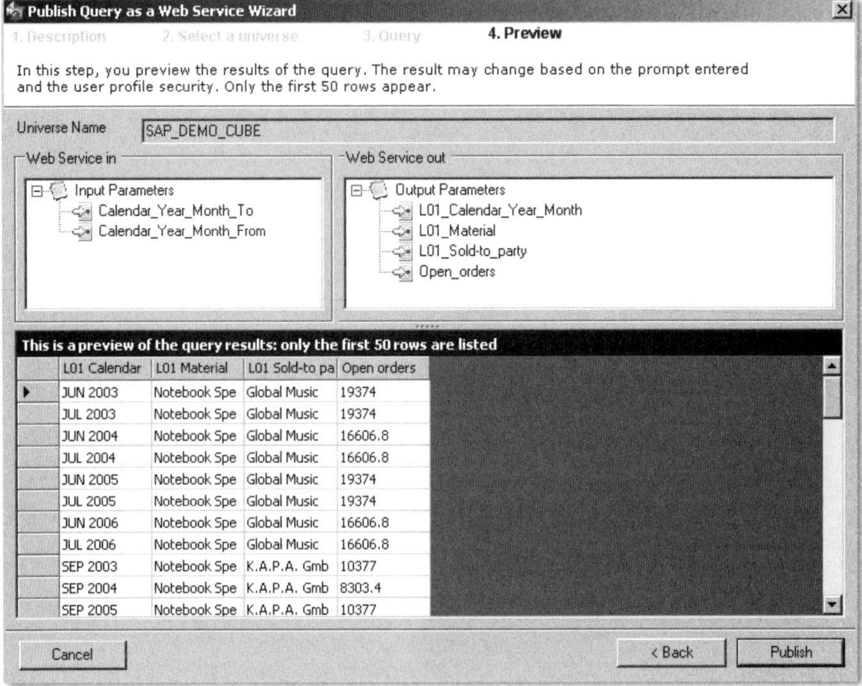

Figure 5.9 Preview for QaaWS

Not only will the system present the sample rows, but you can also see the input and output parameters of your Web service.

17. Click PUBLISH to save your Web service definition to your SAP BusinessObjects Enterprise system (see Figure 5.10).

    The tool goes back to the starting point, and you receive the URL for your new Web service. You can click the TO CLIPBOARD button to copy the URL to the clipboard and use it in another tool such as Xcelsius.

You've just created your first QaaWS, and by navigating to the URL, you can see the complete details including the WSDL definition.

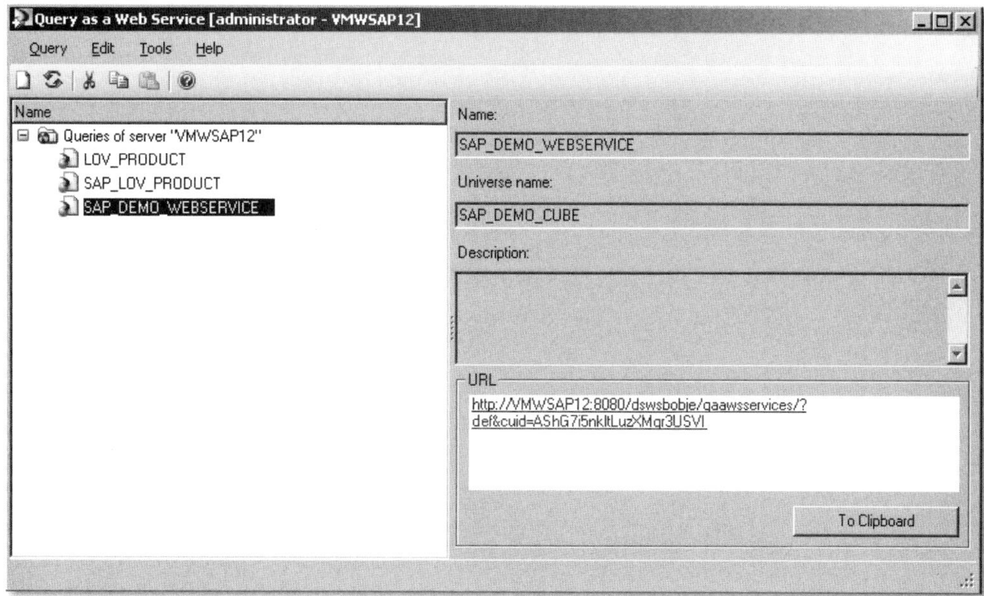

Figure 5.10 QaaWS Final Step

When using QaaWS, keep in mind that it creates a Web service for the data retrieval and that if you want to retrieve a larger set of data — for example, for your Xcelsius dashboard — SAP BusinessObjects Live Office might be the better choice. From a technical point of view, SAP BusinessObjects Live Office uses the Web service architecture as well, but it provides more functionality to use already scheduled reports, and in that way it provides more flexibility to handle larger data volumes.

In the following sections you will learn how to leverage objects from your BusinessObjects platform via Live Office and use the data inside Microsoft Office and inside Xcelsius.

6 SAP BusinessObjects Live Office

SAP BusinessObjects Live Office allows you use the content of Crystal Reports and SAP BusinessObjects Web Intelligence inside the Microsoft Office environment. You could, for example, take a chart from your Crystal Reports content and place it as part of a presentation you created with Microsoft PowerPoint. The advantage of SAP BusinessObjects Live Office is that the actual connection to the underlying data source is not lost, and you can refresh the data inside the Microsoft Office environment.

6.1 Data Connectivity Overview

In this section we'll focus on how you can use Crystal Reports and Web Intelligence inside of Microsoft Office. In Chapter 7, Xcelsius and SAP NetWeaver, we'll discuss how you can use SAP BusinessObjects Live Office to act as the middle layer to use the data from Crystal Reports and SAP BusinessObjects Web Intelligence inside Xcelsius.

Figure 6.1 shows the possible data sources you can use in SAP BusinessObjects Live Office and, as you will see later, in Xcelsius. Because SAP BusinessObjects Live Office can use Crystal Reports and SAP BusinessObjects Web Intelligence, you can use your SAP ERP system (via Crystal Reports) and your SAP NetWeaver Business Warehouse system (via Crystal Reports and SAP BusinessObjects Web Intelligence) as data sources. SAP BusinessObjects Live Office can use Crystal Reports, SAP BusinessObjects Web Intelligence, and universes as sources and can provide the reports and the underlying data source inside the Microsoft Office environment. In addition, you can use SAP BusinessObjects Live Office as a tool to provide those data sources to Xcelsius for data visualization:

- Via Crystal Reports objects you can use SAP ERP and SAP NetWeaver Business Warehouse inside SAP BusinessObjects Live Office.
- Via SAP BusinessObjects Web Intelligence reports and universes you can use SAP NetWeaver Business Warehouse as the data source inside SAP BusinessObjects Live Office.
- In addition to the possible SAP data source, you can also use all other available data sources from Crystal Reports, SAP BusinessObjects Web Intelligence, and universes inside SAP BusinessObjects Live Office.

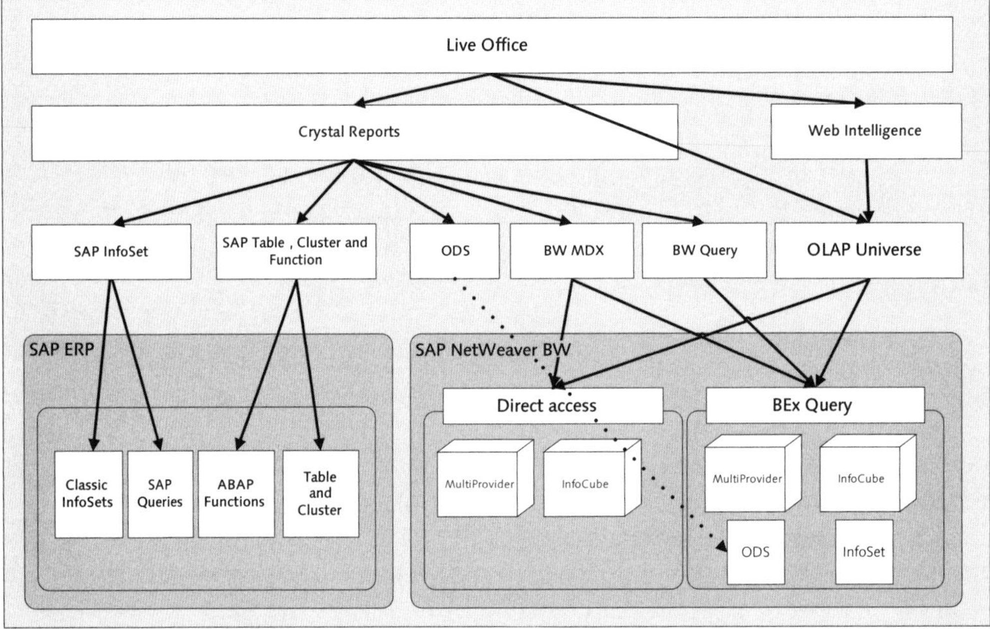

Figure 6.1 Data Connectivity for SAP BusinessObjects Live Office

SAP BusinessObjects Live Office vs. Query as a Web Service

As you will see, you can use SAP BusinessObjects Live Office and Query as a Web Service to provide data for Xcelsius. The advantage of using SAP BusinessObjects Live Office is the ability to use scheduled report instances or a publication (see Chapter 8, Publications with SAP Security) in combination with SAP BusinessObjects Live Office. Using those features gives you the option to provide on-demand data access and allows you to use scheduled reports for cases with very large data volumes.

6.2 SAP BusinessObjects Live Office Combined with Crystal Reports

In this section we'll take a look how you can use Crystal Reports content in SAP BusinessObjects Live Office. Assuming you installed SAP BusinessObjects Live Office during the client installation as described in Section 2.2.1, Installation of SAP BusinessObjects BI Client Tools, you can start Microsoft Excel now, and you should see an additional menu item, LIVE OFFICE.

1. Select the menu LIVE OFFICE and select the menu item OPTIONS. Here you can navigate to the ENTERPRISE tab (see Figure 6.2).

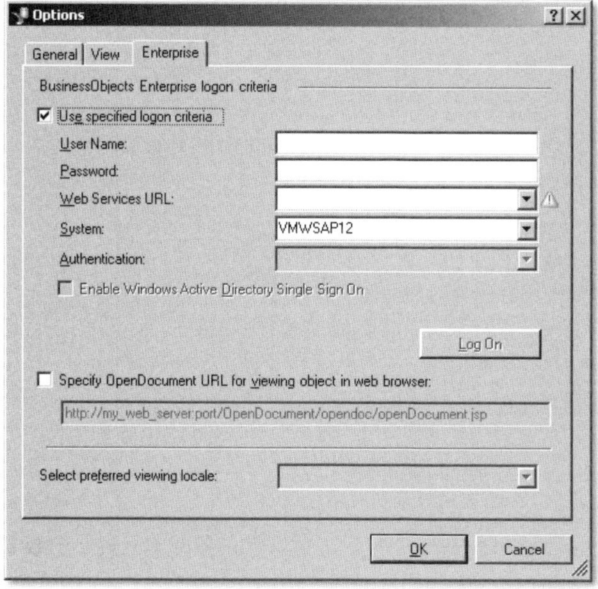

Figure 6.2 SAP BusinessObjects Live Office Options

2. Enter your system details. The Web service URL follows the standard syntax:

   http://[APPSERVER]:[PORT]/dswsbobje/services/session

   Example:

   `http://vmwsap12:8080/dswsbobj/services/session`

   Ensure that you set SAP as the authentication mode. You can leave the user and password empty because SAP BusinessObjects Live Office will ask you for the user credentials later on when you trying to use a Crystal Reports object.

SAP BusinessObjects Live Office Authentication

If you decide to leave the user and password empty in the OPTIONS dialog, you'll receive an error message when you try to insert content from your SAP BusinessObjects Enterprise system. You can just click OK in the error message and then provide the user credentials you want to use. The reason for the error message is the attempt by SAP BusinessObjects Live Office to leverage the user and password in the options to authenticate, which fails if they're empty.

3. Navigate to the VIEW tab, and in the COLUMN HEADING area select BOTH to show both the field description and the technical field name. In that way SAP BusinessObjects Live Office will show you the technical field names and the field description, which will make it easier for you to identify the correct fields.
4. Follow the menu path LIVE OFFICE • INSERT • CRYSTAL REPORTS CONTENT. SAP BusinessObjects Live Office will come up with a logon screen. As you can see, SAP BusinessObjects Live Office also does not provide an SAP-specific logon screen, so you need to use the same syntax for your user as you did for the Universe Designer and the QaaWS tool.
5. After you authenticated against the system, SAP BusinessObjects Live Office will present you with the repository of your SAP BusinessObjects system. You can use the shortcut MY ROLES to navigate directly to the roles that contain content for your SAP credentials (see Figure 6.3).

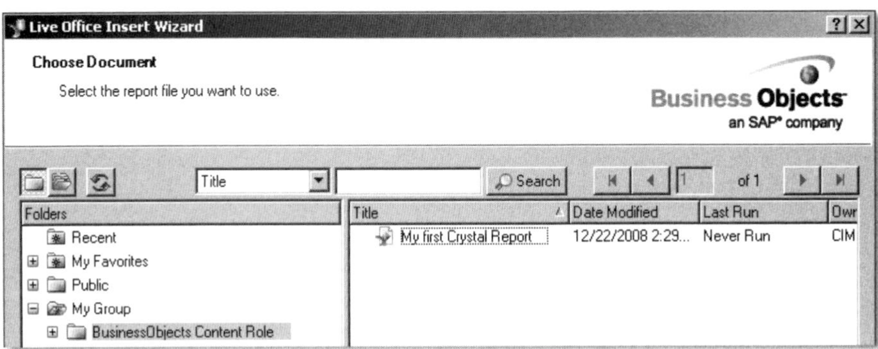

Figure 6.3 SAP BusinessObjects Live Office – Selecting a Document

6. You should be able to select the Crystal Report object from Section 3.1.3, Creating Your First Crystal Reports Report with SAP NetWeaver Business Warehouse, that we created on top of SAP NetWeaver Business Warehouse and published to our SAP BusinessObjects Enterprise system (called "My First Crystal

Report" in our example). Because you logged on with your SAP credentials, you'll be able to view the report content with Single Sign-On.

7. In the next screen you'll be asked to provide the values for the parameters. You can select values for the parameters or select SET TO NULL to retrieve the complete result set.
8. In the next screen SAP BusinessObjects Live Office presents the report, including the layout (see Figure 6.4).

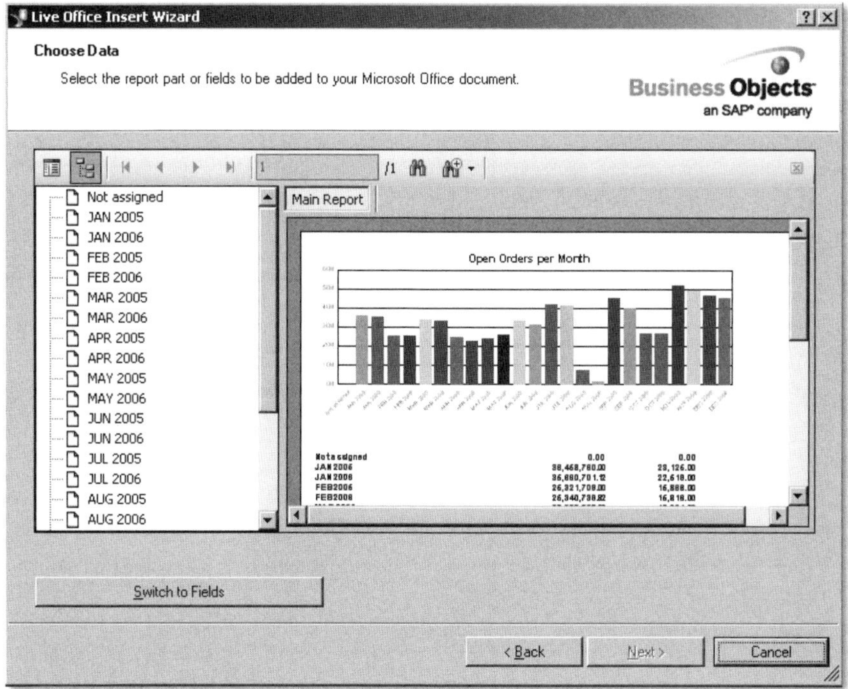

Figure 6.4 SAP BusinessObjects Live Office – Crystal Reports Document

The advantage of this option is that you can actually select parts of your report. In our example you can select the chart from the report, place it inside Microsoft Excel, and refresh it against the data source. For now we're interested in the actual fields of the reports, so we'll click the SWITCH TO FIELDS button.

9. As you can see, SAP BusinessObjects Live Office now offers the fields (see Figure 6.5) from the Detail section and the summaries we created previously in the report. You can select the three fields from the summary for the calendar month and move to the next screen.

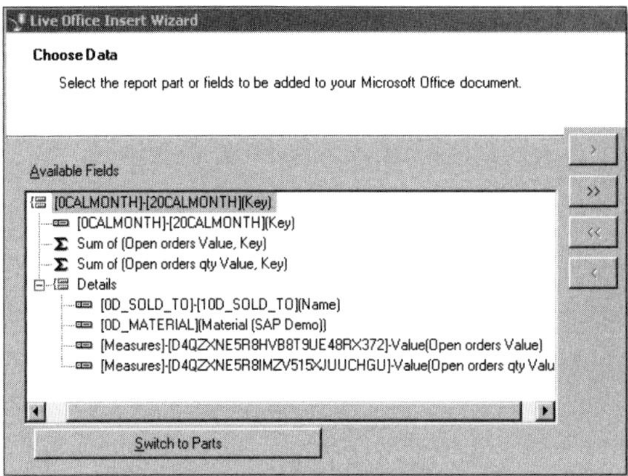

Figure 6.5 SAP BusinessObjects Live Office – Crystal Reports Fields

10. In the next screen you can create additional filters that are specific to your SAP BusinessObjects Live Office document. In our example we created a variable in the underlying BW query so we can move to the next screen.
11. In the final step you can assign a name for the spreadsheet inside SAP BusinessObjects Live Office, and as soon as you click FINISH, SAP BusinessObjects Live Office will retrieve the data and show it inside Microsoft Excel (see Figure 6.6).

	Month	Open Orders	Open Order Quantity
2	#	0	0
3	01.2005	36458760	23125
4	01.2006	35660701.12	22519
5	02.2005	25321709	15866
6	02.2006	25340739.82	15816
7	03.2005	33988827	18034
8	03.2006	33960511.7	17662
9	04.2005	24925426	15529
10	04.2006	23002790.99	14378
11	05.2005	24541905	15770
12	05.2006	26247528.93	17613
13	06.2005	33525345	19268
14	06.2006	31312664.18	17867
15	07.2005	42042069	24193
16	07.2006	41479460.13	23654
17	08.2005	8073297	3023
18	08.2006	1596865.63	650
19	09.2005	45598535	24490
20	09.2006	40496756.44	20860
21	10.2005	27033044	20299
22	10.2006	27157157.14	19882
23	11.2005	51901444	27276
24	11.2006	49529592.13	26061
25	12.2005	47175394	24249
26	12.2006	45319434.65	23359

Figure 6.6 Crystal Reports Data in SAP BusinessObjects Live Office

12. Navigate again to LIVE OFFICE • PROPERTIES FOR ALL OBJECTS to define the refresh options for the report object.
13. Open the REFRESH tab. Here you can define how a refresh in SAP BusinessObjects Live Office should be leveraged against the underlying data source. You can click the EDIT button and select which data you want to show in SAP BusinessObjects Live Office (see Figure 6.7).

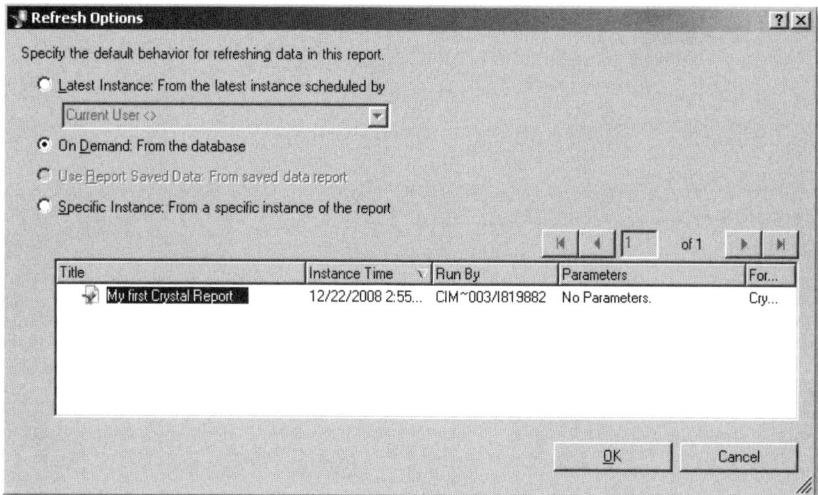

Figure 6.7 Refresh Option in SAP BusinessObjects Live Office

14. You have the option to select a specific instance, the latest instance, or on demand. These options allow you to select the data in your SAP BusinessObjects Live Office document that is refreshed each time you open the document in the spreadsheet (ON DEMAND) or if you want to use a prescheduled report that has been prepared for you (SPECIFIC INSTANCE or LATEST INSTANCE). This gives you a lot of flexibility to use SAP BusinessObjects Live Office, even against already existing scheduled reports.
15. Navigate back to the PROPERTIES area and select the PROMPTS tab (see Figure 6.8).

Parameter Values

If you don't have the PROMPTS tab, follow the menu path LIVE OFFICE • REFRESH ALL OBJECTS to ensure that you're not using a Crystal Reports report with cached data. After the refresh the PROMPTS tab should show up.

Another option to avoid this problem is to unselect the menu item SAVE DATA WITH REPORT in the menu FILE in the Crystal Reports designer, which ensures that only the report layout without any data is published to your SAP BusinessObjects Enterprise system.

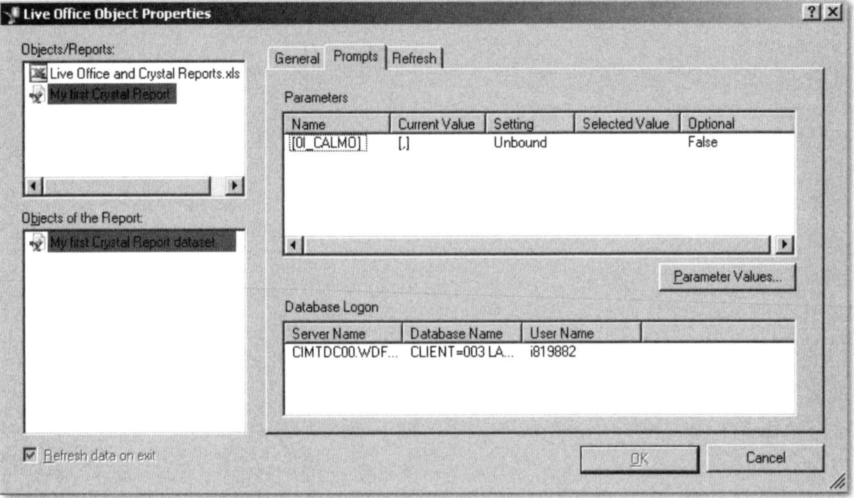

Figure 6.8 Object Properties in SAP BusinessObjects Live Office

16. Our example report that we are using inside SAP BusinessObjects Live Office contains parameters based on the underlying BW query containing variables. SAP BusinessObjects Live Office gives you the ability to link those parameters to cell values in Microsoft Excel, which you then can use to change the parameter values.

    Click the PARAMETER VALUES button. Now you can define for each parameter which cells will be used as input values when the report is refreshed (see Figure 6.9).

17. You can now select CHOOSE EXCEL DATA RANGE for each parameter and bind a spreadsheet cell to the parameter as input value. The other two options allow you to prompt the user for a value (ALWAYS ASK FOR VALUE checkbox) or to specify a value from a list of values (CHOOSE VALUES LIST checkbox). The reason we are binding our parameters to cells is that we can later use a selector created in Xcelsius to send in the value to this cell, and in that way update our underlying report object.

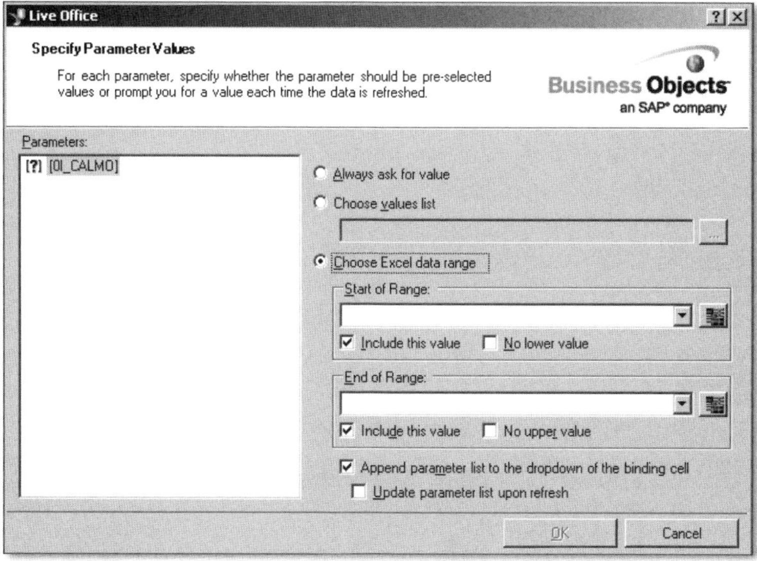

Figure 6.9 Parameter Options in SAP BusinessObjects Live Office

18. Confirm your changes and then follow the menu path LIVE OFFICE • PUBLISH TO BUSINESSOBJECTS ENTERPRISE • SAVE TO BUSINESSOBJECTS ENTERPRISE to save your SAP BusinessObjects Live Office document to SAP BusinessObjects Enterprise.

6.3 SAP BusinessObjects Live Office Combined with SAP BusinessObjects Web Intelligence and Universes

Very similar to the workflow for Crystal Reports, you can also use the SAP BusinessObjects Web Intelligence report that you created in Section 4.3, Creating Your First SAP BusinessObjects Web Intelligence Report, as a source in SAP BusinessObjects Live Office.

Because you already configured the options in the previous section, you can go directly to the menu LIVE OFFICE • INSERT • WEB INTELLIGENCE CONTENT.

1. You'll be presented with the repository from your SAP BusinessObjects Enterprise system, and you can select the SAP BusinessObjects Web Intelligence report that you created previously. We will use the SAP BusinessObjects Web Intelligence report that we created in Section 4.3.

2. Click NEXT to go to the next screen. Here you'll be presented with the output of your SAP BusinessObjects Web Intelligence report (see Figure 6.10). As you can see, there's no option to switch to the query panel similar to the option to switch to the fields in Crystal Reports. The reason for that is that in Live Office there's a separate menu item, INSERT • NEW QUERY, that allows you to create a new query based on universes.

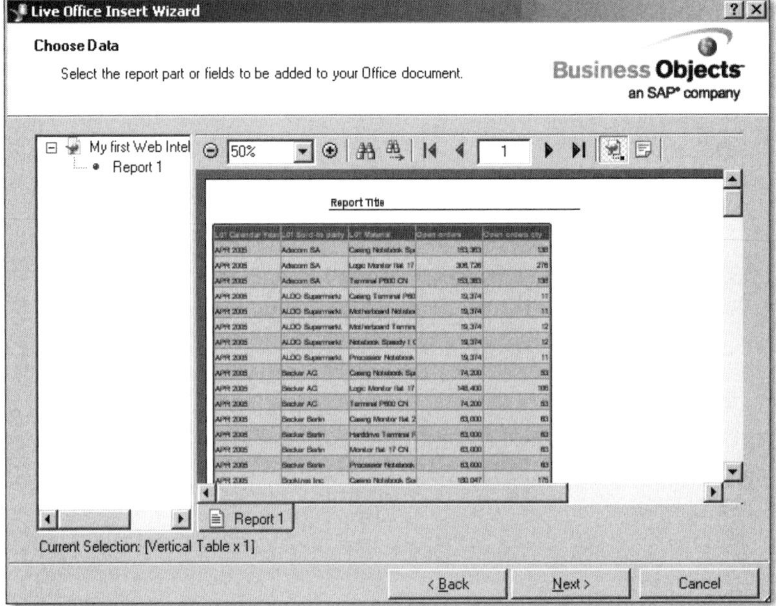

Figure 6.10 SAP BusinessObjects Web Intelligence Report for Live Office

3. Select the table of your SAP BusinessObjects Web Intelligence report and move to the next screen (see Figure 6.11).

   Here you can enter a name for the spreadsheet you're creating, and after clicking FINISH, you receive the data from your SAP BusinessObjects Web Intelligence report inside Microsoft Excel.

4. Our example SAP BusinessObjects Web Intelligence report contains parameters. Those parameter values can be linked to cells in your SAP BusinessObjects Live Office document the same way you did this task for the Crystal Reports object in the previous section.

   Follow the menu path LIVE OFFICE • PROPERTIES FOR ALL OBJECTS and select the PROMPTS tab.

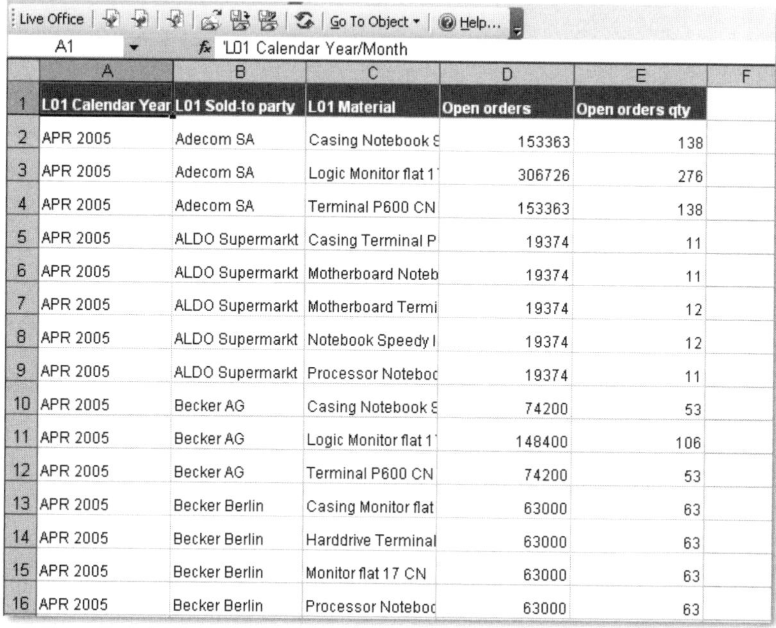

	A	B	C	D	E	F
1	L01 Calendar Year	L01 Sold-to party	L01 Material	Open orders	Open orders qty	
2	APR 2005	Adecom SA	Casing Notebook S	153363	138	
3	APR 2005	Adecom SA	Logic Monitor flat 1	306726	276	
4	APR 2005	Adecom SA	Terminal P600 CN	153363	138	
5	APR 2005	ALDO Supermarkt	Casing Terminal P	19374	11	
6	APR 2005	ALDO Supermarkt	Motherboard Noteb	19374	11	
7	APR 2005	ALDO Supermarkt	Motherboard Termi	19374	12	
8	APR 2005	ALDO Supermarkt	Notebook Speedy I	19374	12	
9	APR 2005	ALDO Supermarkt	Processor Noteboc	19374	11	
10	APR 2005	Becker AG	Casing Notebook S	74200	53	
11	APR 2005	Becker AG	Logic Monitor flat 1	148400	106	
12	APR 2005	Becker AG	Terminal P600 CN	74200	53	
13	APR 2005	Becker Berlin	Casing Monitor flat	63000	63	
14	APR 2005	Becker Berlin	Harddrive Terminal	63000	63	
15	APR 2005	Becker Berlin	Monitor flat 17 CN	63000	63	
16	APR 2005	Becker Berlin	Processor Noteboc	63000	63	

Figure 6.11 SAP BusinessObjects Live Office with SAP BusinessObjects Web Intelligence

Parameter Values

If you're missing the PROMPTS tab, follow the menu path LIVE OFFICE • REFRESH ALL OBJECTS to ensure that you're not using an SAP BusinessObjects Web Intelligence report with cached data. After the refresh, the PROMPTS tab should show up.

5. Click the PARAMETER VALUES button. Now you can define for each parameter which cells will be used as input values when the report is refreshed.
6. You can now select CHOOSE EXCEL DATA RANGE for each parameter and bind a spreadsheet cell to the parameter as input value.
7. Confirm you changes and then follow the menu path LIVE OFFICE • PUBLISH TO BUSINESSOBJECTS ENTERPRISE • SAVE TO BUSINESSOBJECTS ENTERPRISE to save your SAP BusinessObjects Live Office document to SAP BusinessObjects Enterprise.

In this chapter we will focus on how you can leverage Xcelsius to create stunning data visualizations on top of your SAP ERP and SAP NetWeaver Business Warehouse data.

7 Xcelsius and SAP NetWeaver

In this chapter we'll take a look at how you can leverage the data sources from your SAP systems inside Xcelsius. We'll look at how you can use SAP BusinessObjects Live Office and Query as a Web Service (QaaWS) to provide the data for your visualization.

7.1 Data Connectivity Overview

Xcelsius allows you to create great data visualization and use very intuitive user navigation elements. Figure 7.1 shows the data connectivity options that are available to you in your SAP landscape.

Xcelsius can use a broad range of connectivity including Web services, XML data, Adobe LiveCycle data services, QaaWS, and SAP BusinessObjects Live Office. For your SAP system you can see in Figure 7.1 that you use SAP BusinessObjects Live Office and Crystal Reports to provide the data from your SAP ERP system to Xcelsius and that you can use Crystal Reports and SAP BusinessObjects Web Intelligence in combination with SAP BusinessObjects Live Office or QaaWS and OLAP Universes to provide the data from your SAP NetWeaver Business Warehouse system to Xcelsius.

In the following sections we'll create a simple dashboard showing the data from the previously created Crystal Reports and SAP BusinessObjects Web Intelligence objects, and we'll use QaaWS to provide the list of values for a parameter. At the end of this chapter you'll have an Xcelsius dashboard that shows data from your SAP NetWeaver Business Warehouse system, and each time you change the value of the parameters (derived via QaaWS,) the data will be refreshed using the connectivity via SAP BusinessObjects Live Office to the SAP NetWeaver Business Warehouse system.

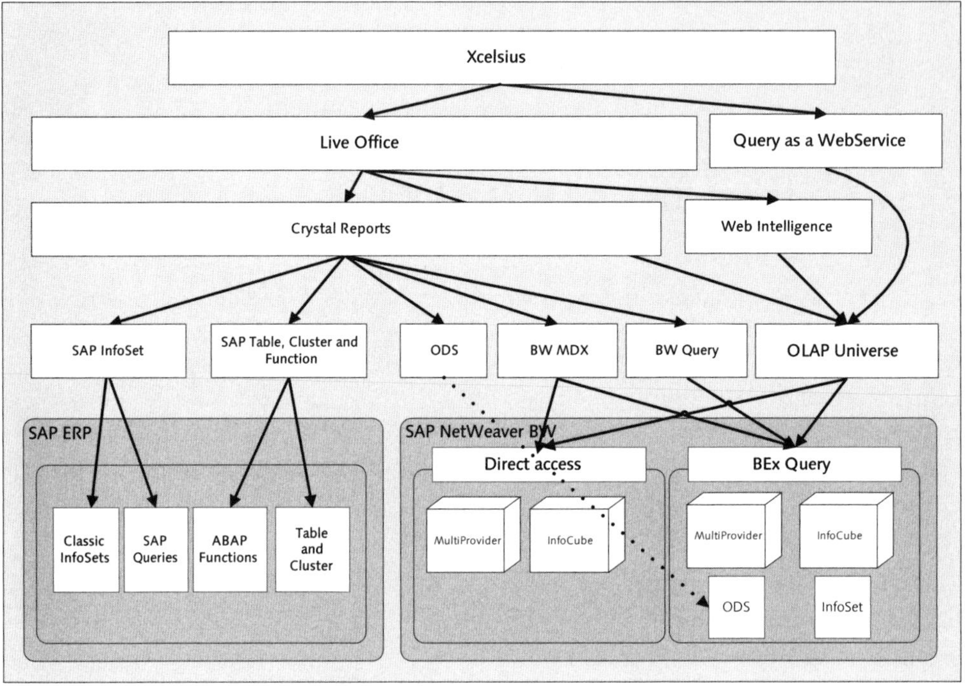

Figure 7.1 Xcelsius and SAP Connectivity

7.2 Xcelsius Combined with SAP BusinessObjects Live Office

In this section you'll learn how to use the previously created SAP BusinessObjects Live Office documents as a source for your Xcelsius object. In the following section we'll then use a QaaWS Web service to provide the list of values that will act as an input to the SAP BusinessObjects Live Office document.

1. Start the Xcelsius Designer and follow the menu path Data • Import from Enterprise. Log on on to your SAP BusinessObjects Enterprise system using your SAP credentials and SAP authentication mode.
2. Navigate to the SAP BusinessObjects Live Office document you created in Section 6.2, SAP BusinessObjects Live Office Combined with Crystal Reports. SAP

BusinessObjects Live Office will present you with the data inside Xcelsius (see Figure 7.2).

Key	Open Orders Value	Open Order Quantity
01.2005	36458760	23125
01.2006	35660701.12	22519
02.2005	25321709	15866
02.2006	25340739.82	15816
03.2005	33988827	18034
03.2006	33960511.7	17662

Figure 7.2 SAP BusinessObjects Live Office Document Inside Xcelsius

SAP BusinessObjects Live Office and Xcelsius

When using SAP BusinessObjects Live Office inside Xcelsius, ensure that you enable the Live Office compatibility mode. You can follow the menu path FILE • PREFERENCES • EXCEL OPTIONS to enable the compatibility mode. If you prefer to use SAP Business-Objects Live Office directly inside Xcelsius, the above is the correct approach. If you prefer to work with SAP BusinessObjects Live Office in Microsoft Excel, you should unselect the compatibility mode and prepare your SAP BusinessObjects Live Office documents for Xcelsius directly in Microsoft Excel.

3. Follow the menu path DATA • CONNECTIONS and click the ADD button to add a Live Office connection (see Figure 7.3).

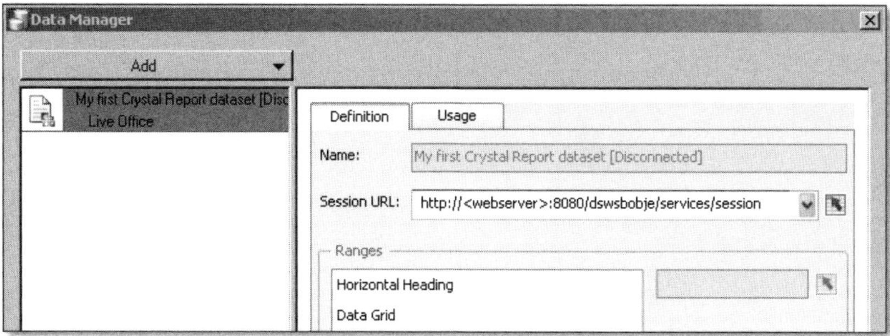

Figure 7.3 Data Manager in Xcelsius

4. On the DEFINITION tab you can find the SESSION URL FIELD, where you have to replace the placeholder `<webserver>` with the machine name of your application server, in our example VMWSAP12.

5. Click the USAGE tab (see Figure 7.4). Click on the icon next to the TRIGGER CELL field and select the two cells that you configured in Section 6.2, SAP BusinessObjects Live Office Combined with Crystal Reports, to become the cells for the parameter values. By using these cells as trigger cells, you configure your Live Office connection to refresh the data every time those values change.

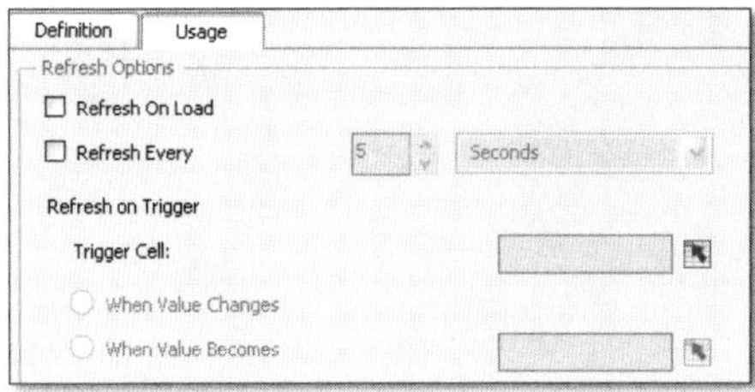

Figure 7.4 Usage for Live Office Connection

6. Select the WHEN VALUE CHANGES radio button. Then confirm your changes and close the Data Manager.
7. Add a column chart to your canvas, right-click the chart, and select the menu item PROPERTIES. A screen will come up that you can see in Figure 7.5.

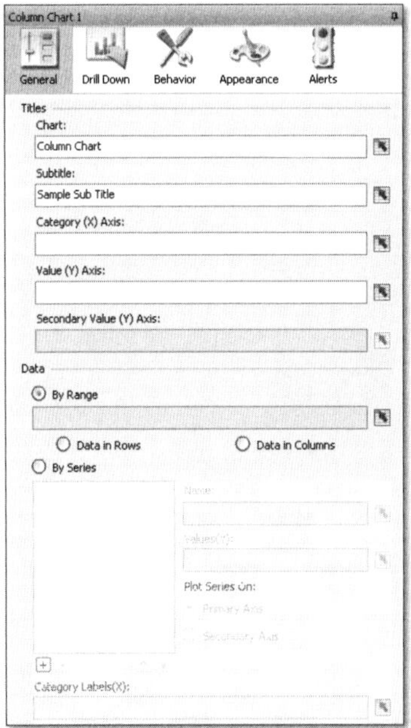

Figure 7.5 Column Chart Properties

8. Select the By Series radio button and click the "+" symbol to add your first data series, called Open Orders Value. Enter "Open Orders Value" as the name.
9. Click the icon next to the Values(Y) field and select cells B2 to B50 in the SAP BusinessObjects Live Office document shown inside Xcelsius.
10. Add another series by clicking the "+" symbol and enter "Open Orders Quantity" as the name.
11. Click the icon next to the Values(Y) field and select cells C2 to C50 in the SAP BusinessObjects Live Office document shown inside Xcelsius.
12. Select Plot Series on Secondary Axis.
13. Click the icon next to the Category Labels (X) field and select cells A2 to A50.
14. Enter a title for your chart.
15. Navigate to the Behavior area of the properties and click the Common tab (see Figure 7.6). Under Ignore cells at End-of-Range only select the In Series and In Values checkboxes. These two options result in the chart ignoring empty rows from the result set if the result set is smaller than the marked area in the spreadsheet.

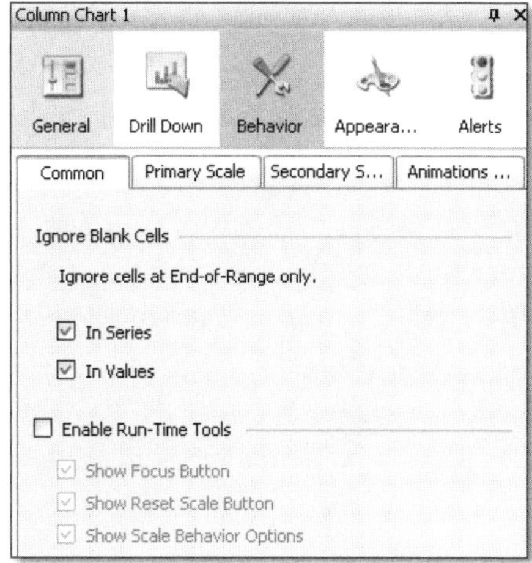

Figure 7.6 Behavior Options

16. Click the Preview button on the toolbar (an alternative is the menu path File • Preview). Xcelsius shows the chart (see Figure 7.7), but the data is retrieved

from the SAP BusinessObjects Live Office document and will not be refreshed right now because we configured the parameter cells as trigger cells and for now those cells stay unchanged.

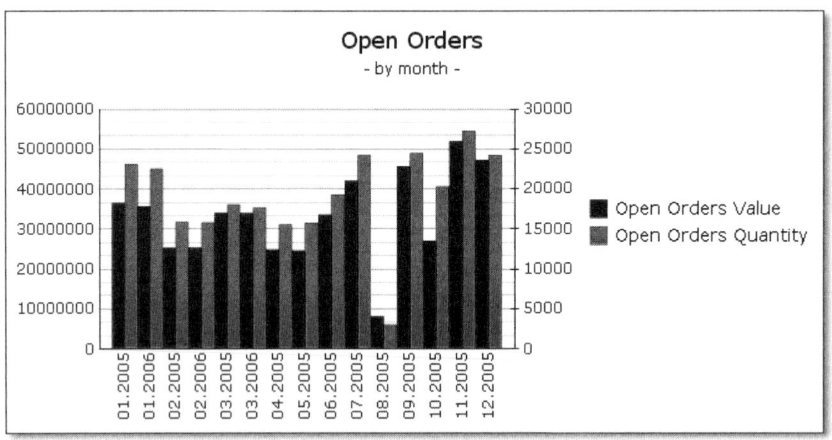

Figure 7.7 Xcelsius Dashboard Based on SAP BusinessObjects Live Office

7.3 Xcelsius combined with Query as a Web Service

In this section we'll use the QaaWS tool to generate a web service on top of an OLAP Universe to provide the list of values for a parameter that will act as an input for the Xcelsius dashboard. Those parameters will then trigger the update of your SAP BusinessObjects Live Office document and refresh the chart.

1. We'll use the BW query that we used in Section 3.1.3, Creating Your First Crystal Reports Report with SAP NetWeaver Business Warehouse, as our starting point. Open the query in the BW query designer and save it under a new name.
2. Because we want to use the BW query as a provider for our list of values, we can remove all of the elements from the query except the Calendar Year/Month characteristic. In this way you create a query with a single characteristic that can provide the list of values.

Using BW Queries for Lists of Values

The reason for creating an additional query in the previous step is that the initial query contains an SAP variable for the Calendar Year/Month characteristic, so you cannot create a Web service providing a list of values for the Calendar Year/Month without being prompted for it. It's always good practice to have BW queries without any SAP variables as providers for the list of values.

3. After you created the second BW query, you can use Section 4.3, Creating Your First SAP BusinessObjects Web Intelligence Report, to create a new OLAP Universe on the new BW query. You don't need to create an SAP BusinessObjects Web Intelligence report at this stage because you're going to use the QaaWS tool to build a Web service.
4. After you created the OLAP Universe, you can use Section 5.2, Creating Your First Query as a Web Service, to create a new Web service with the QaaWS tool. Ensure that you include the following objects in the query panel for the Web service (see Figure 7.8):
    - L01 Calendar Year/Month Key (detail object)
    - L01 Calendar Year/Month (dimension object)

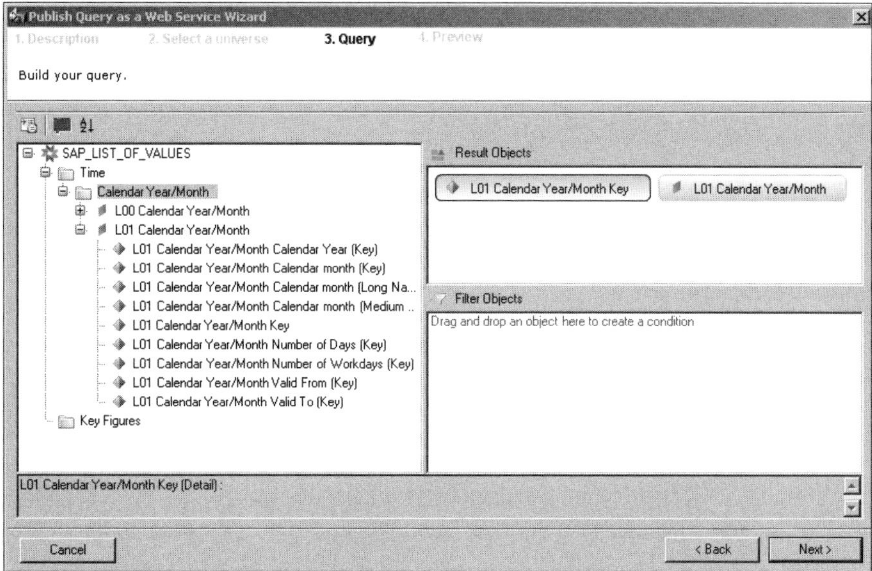

Figure 7.8 QaaWS Query Panel

5. Now you have created a Web service on top of an OLAP Universe that you can use inside Xcelsius to provide the values for a prompt.
6. Start the Xcelsius Designer via the menu path START • PROGRAMS • XCELSIUS • XCELSIUS 2008.
7. Open the Xcelsius object from the previous section and as a first step ensure that you add another spreadsheet to your included Microsoft Excel sheet so that we'll have a separate spreadsheet for the QaaWS Web service configurations.
8. Follow the menu path DATA • CONNECTIONS.
9. Click the ADD button and select QUERY AS A WEB SERVICE (see Figure 7.9).

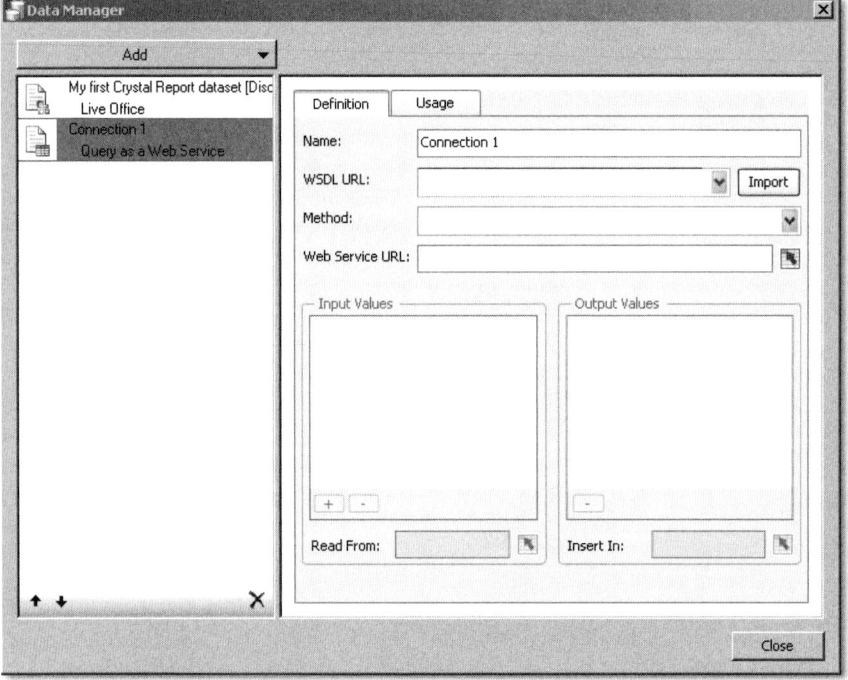

Figure 7.9 Xcelsius Data Manager

10. Paste the URL from your previously created Web service into the WSDL URL field and click the IMPORT button. The details of your Web service are shown in the INPUT VALUES and OUTPUT VALUES areas (see Figure 7.10).

11. To be able to use the data from the Web service, you need to map the output values to the Microsoft Excel spreadsheet. Select ROW from the OUTPUT VALUES area and click the icon next to the INSERT IN field.

Using Microsoft Excel in Xcelsius

Xcelsius uses the Microsoft Excel sheet during the design of the dashboard. The spreadsheet is not used for data retrieval or as data storage; it is used purely for the design of the dashboard.

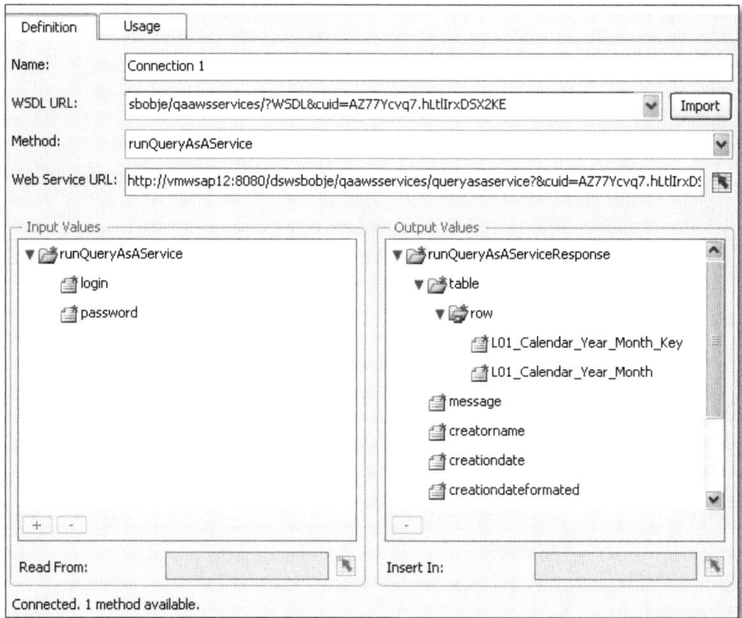

Figure 7.10 QaaWS Definition in Xcelsius Data Manager

12. Xcelsius now asks you to specify the range in the spreadsheet. Keep in mind that your Web service returns two columns, so you need to mark a range of at least two columns. In our example we'll select the first 100 rows from columns A and B in the newly added sheet (see Figure 7.11).

Use of Colors

It is good practice to mark the cells in the areas you use in the spreadsheet with a color so that you do not reuse those cells for another connectivity.

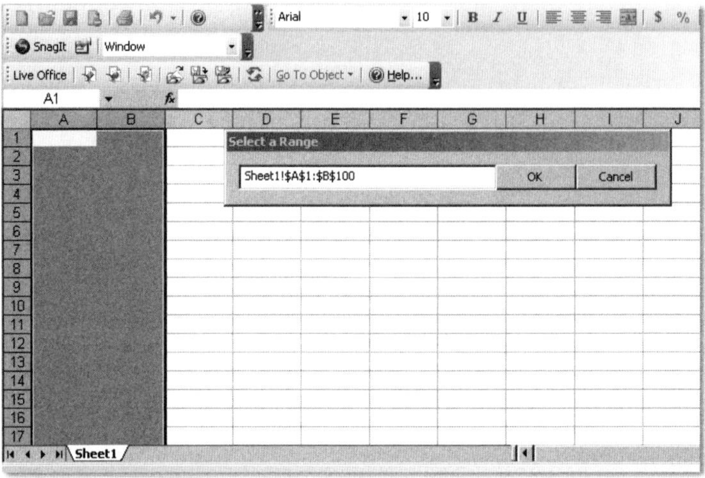

Figure 7.11 Selecting a Range in Xcelsius

13. After you confirmed the range, return to the Data Manager in Xcelsius. Because you configured the OLAP Universe and the QaaWS Web service to use the SAP authentication and Single Sign-On, there's no need to provide your credentials for the input values.
14. Navigate to the USAGE tab (see Figure 7.12). Here you can configure how often the data should be refreshed for your Web service. In our example the Web service represents a list of values, so the REFRESH ON LOAD option is all you need because the values will not change frequently. Select REFRESH ON LOAD and close the Data Manager.

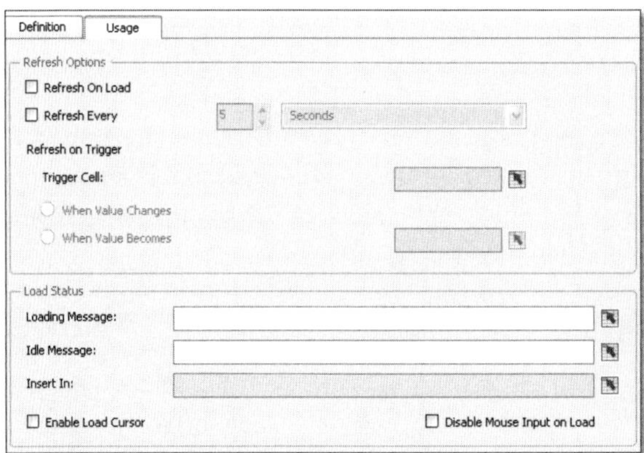

Figure 7.12 Usage Tab for QaaWS Connection

15. Now follow the menu path VIEW • COMPONENTS to ensure that you can see all available components.
16. Drag and drop two combo boxes onto your canvas. The reason for using two combo boxes is that your underlying SAP NetWeaver Business Warehouse query requires a range, so you need to provide a start and end value for the range.
17. Right-click the first combo box and select PROPERTIES to open the screen shown in Figure 7.13.

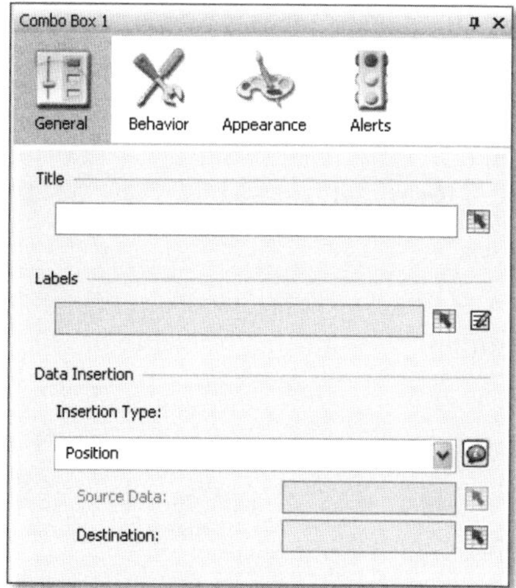

Figure 7.13 Combo Box Properties

18. Set "Value" in the INSERTION TYPE field and click the icon next to the SOURCE DATA field. Select the range for the key values that are returned from the Web service. In our example this is the range from cell A1 to cell A100.
19. Now click the icon next to the LABELS field and select the range that represents the value description from your Web service. In our example this is the range from cell B1 to cell B100.
20. The DESTINATION field represents the cell in the spreadsheet where the combo box will store the value. For the first combo box select the cell you used in your SAP BusinessObjects Live Office document to bind the *FROM* value of the parameter as destination cell for the parameter input.
21. Navigate to the BEHAVIOR area and the COMMON tab for your combo box and select IGNORE BLANK CELLS IN VALUES (see Figure 7.14).

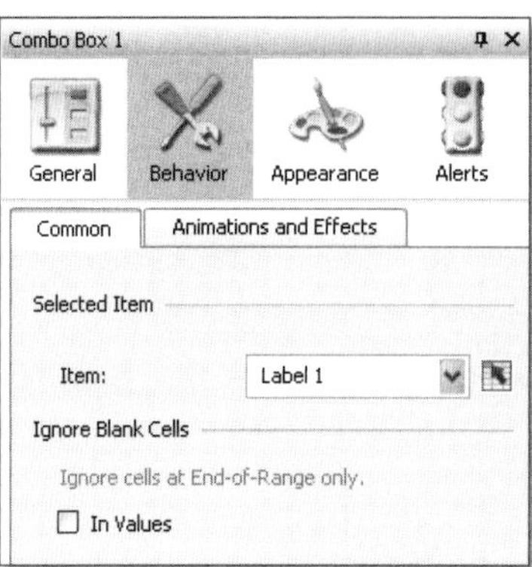

Figure 7.14 Behavior Options for Combo Box

22. Repeat the previous steps for your second combo box, select "Value" in the INSERTION TYPE field, and define the identical cell ranges for the source data and labels.
23. Set the destination for the second combo box to the cell that you used in your SAP BusinessObjects Live Office document to bind the *TO* value of the parameter as input cell to.

    With these steps you have created a simple Xcelsius dashboard that retrieves data from a Crystal Reports object on top of SAP NetWeaver Business Warehouse via SAP BusinessObjects Live Office, and you are using a Web service on top of an OLAP Universe to provide values for two combo boxes that will allow you to set the time range for your chart.
24. Click the PREVIEW button on the toolbar (an alternative is the menu path FILE • PREVIEW).

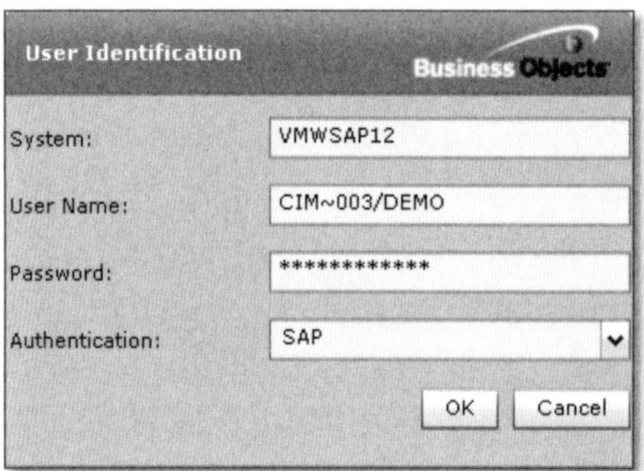

Figure 7.15 User Identification in Xcelsius Designer

Because you haven't authenticated against your SAP BusinessObjects Enterprise system, you need to provide the name of your system and your credentials (see Figure 7.15), and you need to set the authentication. In our example the system is VMWSAP12, the user name is CIM~003/DEMO, and the authentication is SAP.

After a successful logon you'll be presented with a preview of your Xcelsius dashboard (see Figure 7.16).

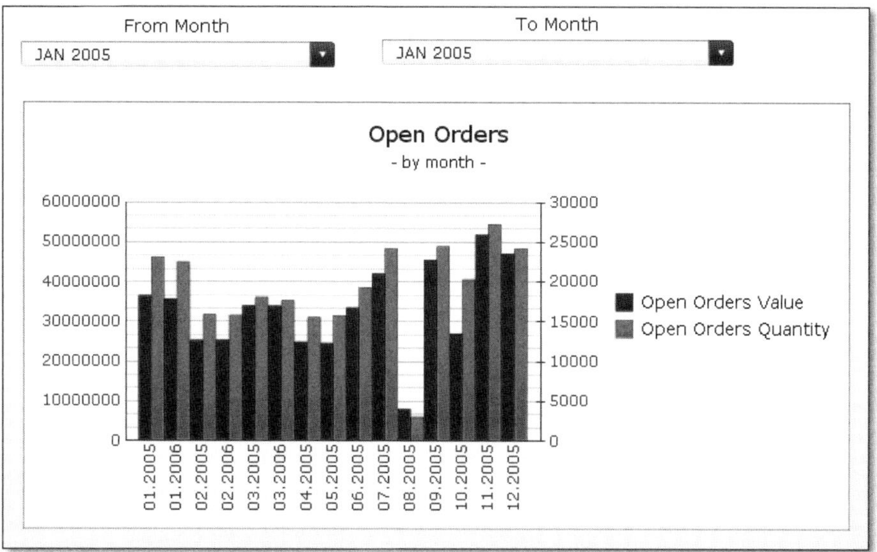

Figure 7.16 Xcelsius Dashboard

Each time you change the values in the combo boxes, the values of your chart will be updated.

25. Follow the menu path File • Export • BusinessObjects Platform and export your Xcelsius dashboard to your SAP BusinessObjects Enterprise system.

Save to and Export to

The Xcelsius Designer offers the menu path File • SAVE TO ENTERPRISE and the menu path File • Export • SAP BusinessObjects Platform. When you use the Save option, you save the actual design (XLF file) to your SAP BusinessObjects system, and when you use the Export option you generate a Flash file (SWF file) that is stored on your SAP BusinessObjects system and can be viewed by your end users.

Saving to Roles

If you're looking at a deployment of multiple tools such as Crystal Reports, SAP BusinessObjects Web Intelligence, and Xcelsius, you might want to consider storing the Xcelsius content in the role folders that are created based on the publishing process with Crystal Reports in your SAP BusinessObjects Enterprise system. In that way you can also use the imported SAP roles in your SAP BusinessObjects Enterprise system to assign rights to those reports including the Xcelsius-related content.

Publications provide you with the capabilitiy to distribute a report to a large set of users. In this chapter you will learn how to setup your system in order to run publications with Crystal Reports and Web Intelligence and still keeping the security intact.

8 Publications with SAP Security

In this chapter we'll take a look at how you can use publications on your SAP BusinessObjects Enterprise system in combination with server-side trust configured on your SAP NetWeaver system to set up a scheduling process that will distribute your report objects to a large number of users.

8.1 What Is Server-Side Trust?

In your SAP BusinessObjects Enterprise landscape you can use server-side trust to set up a publication job for a multipass bursting process, so that you can schedule a Crystal Reports or SAP BusinessObjects Web Intelligence object for a large set of SAP roles and users by keeping the SAP data-level security intact.

Server-side trust allows the SAP BusinessObjects system to impersonate other users during the scheduling process without requiring the password for each user account. Impersonation allows the SAP BusinessObjects system to act on behalf of different users or a different security context.

For example, your SAP NetWeaver Business Warehouse system grants your SAP BusinessObjects system the trust to authenticate with different users in a password-free authentication mode. Your SAP BusinessObjects system can then use the granted trust and the impersonation capability, and can schedule a Crystal Reports or SAP BusinessObjects Web Intelligence object on behalf of a set of users.

In combination with the publication capabilities of your SAP BusinessObjects Enterprise system, this means you can set up a publication process, and use the granted trust between your two systems, and create a multipass publication process and still ensure the data-level security that you configured in your SAP system. After the configuration steps, your SAP system grants your SAP BusinessObjects system the trust to execute a report against the SAP system by using impersonation and authenticate with a set of user toward the SAP server without the need for a password.

In order for the SAP BusinessObjects system to perform the above-described process the actual processing services such as the Crystal Reports job service and the SAP BusinessObjects Web Intelligence processing service need to be configured to authenticate with a Secure Network Communication (SNC) account that is also configured to allow impersonation.

In this section you will learn about the required components to configure the server side trust and the necessary steps that are involved to configure the trust on the SAP BusinessObjects system and your SAP system.

SAP Cryptographic Library

SAP delivers the SAP Cryptographic Library as part of your SAP system, and you can use the SAP Cryptographic Library to configure SNC between server components.

After you downloaded and unpacked the SAP Cryptographic software, you'll receive three main components:

- The SAP Cryptographic Library (`sapcrypto.dll` for Windows; `libsapcrypto.<ext>` for Unix)
- A license file `ticket`
- The configuration tool `sapgenpse.exe`

SAP Cryptographic Library

You can only use the delivered SAP Cryptographic Library for SNC between server components. If you want to use SNC for frontend components (for example, SAP GUI for Windows), then you must purchase an SNC-certified partner product.

You can download the SAP cryptographic library from the SAP Service Marketplace (*http://service.sap.com/SWDC*) in the SAP Cryptographic Software area.

For detailed information you can also look at SAP Notes 711093, 597059, and 397175 at *http://service.sap.com/notes*.

Personal Security Environment

The personal security environment (PSE) file contains the certificate of the component that created the PSE file and a list of components and parties that are identified as trusted components. The PSE file is password-protected to avoid exploits where certificates are added or valid certificates are removed but operating system credentials can be tied to the PSE file for password-free access.

Steps to Configure Server-Side Trust

Figure 8.1 shows the steps required to deploy and configure server-side trust between your SAP system and your SAP BusinessObjects system. What you need to do is:

1. Deploy and configure the SAP Cryptographic Library on your SAP system
2. Deploy and configure the SAP Cryptographic Library on your SAP BusinessObjects Enterprise system
3. Generate a PSE file and a certificate from your SAP BusinessObjects Enterprise system
4. Import the certificate file from your SAP BusinessObjects Enterprise system to the trust manager of your SAP system
5. Export a certificate file from your SAP system
6. Import the certificate file from your SAP system to the PSE file from your SAP BusinessObjects Enterprise system
7. Grant the credentials being used to run the SAP BusinessObjects Enterprise services access to the PSE file from the SAP BusinessObjects system

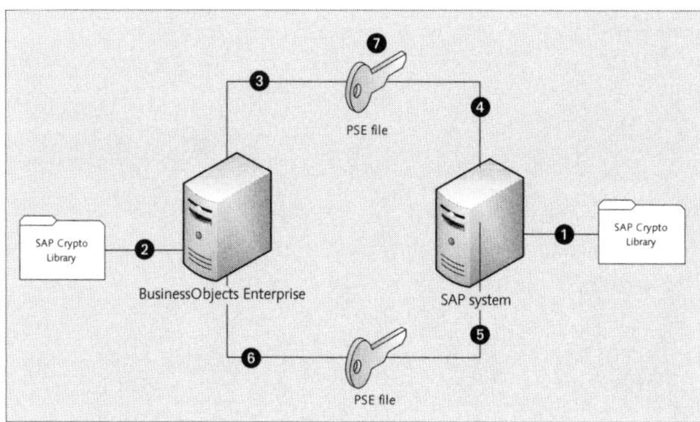

Figure 8.1 Server-Side Trust

8.2 Configuring Your SAP Server

In the following sections we'll prepare your SAP system for server-side trust. This involves four main steps:

1. Deploying the SAP Cryptographic Library
2. Configuring profile parameters for your SAP system
3. Configuring the trust manager for your SAP system
4. Configuring additional profile parameters

We'll go through these steps in detail in Sections 8.2.1, SAP Cryptographic Library, to 8.2.4, Profile Parameters.

8.2.1 SAP Cryptographic Library

1. Download and unpack the SAP Cryptographic Library for your SAP system according to the platform of your SAP system.
2. On your SAP server copy the SAP Cryptographic Library to the folder *\usr\sap\<SID>\SYS\exe\run*, where the placeholder `<SID>` represents your System ID — in our example, CIM.
3. On your SAP server copy the file `ticket` that is part of the SAP Cryptographic Library to the folder *\usr\sap\<SID>\<instance>\sec*, where the placeholder `<SID>` needs to be replaced with your system ID (in our example CIM), and the placeholder `<instance>` needs to be replaced with the instance number (in our example 00).
4. You need to create an environment variable SECUDIR pointing to the path for the file `ticket` from the previous step. This environment variable needs to be accessible by the user account that is used to run the dispatcher process for your SAP system.

Folder Structure

The folder structure mentioned above should already exist based on the installation of your SAP System. You might have changed the base folder or some of the naming; therefore, I'll always refer to the basic installation folders here.

8.2.2 Profile Parameters

1. Log on to your SAP system.
2. Start Transaction RZ10 to go to the server profile parameters (see Figure 8.2).

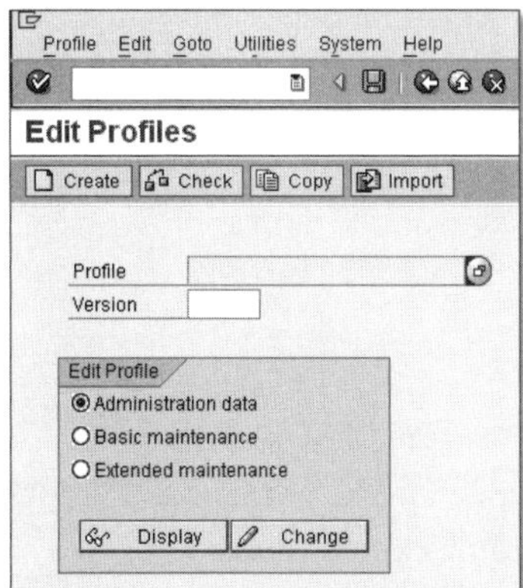

Figure 8.2 Profile Parameters

3. Select the instance profile and select EXTENDED MAINTENANCE.
4. Click the CHANGE button.
5. Add the profile parameters and values according to Table 8.1 to the profile settings and value of your SAP system.

Profile Parameter	Value
ssf/name	SAPSECULIB
ssf/ssfapi_lib	Enter the full path including the file name to the SAP Cryptographic Library on your SAP server.
sec/libsapsecu	Enter the full path including the file name to the SAP Cryptographic Library on your SAP server.
snc/gssapi_lib	Enter the full path including the file name to the SAP Cryptographic Library on your SAP server.
snc/identity/as	Enter the Distinguished Name (DN) for your SAP system.

Table 8.1 SAP Server Profile Parameters and Values

6. The Distinguished Name (DN) of your SAP system should follow the *Lightweight Directory Access Protocol* (LDAP) naming convention according to Table 8.2.

Tag	Meaning	Description
CN	Common name	Name of the certificate proprietor
OU	Organizational unit	Name of the organizational unit
O	Organization	Name of the organization
C	Country	Country in which the proprietor resides

Table 8.2 Distinguished Name Values

For our example the Distinguished Name could look like

```
p:CN=CIM;OU=PM;O=SAP;C=CA
```

where CIM is the system ID of our example SAP server, PM stands for product management, SAP is the name of the organization, and CA stands for Canada. After making these changes you need to restart your SAP system.

SAP Cryptographic Library and Distinguished Name

When referring to the Distinguished Name of your SAP system, ensure that you always include the "p:" in front of the name.

8.2.3 Trust Manager

1. After you restarted your SAP server, log on to your SAP system.
2. Start Transaction STRUST to start the trust manager for your SAP system. You should now have two additional entries on the left side: one entry for SNC SAPCRYPTOLIB and entries for SSL (*Secure Sockets Layer*).
3. Right-click on the entry "SNC SAPCryptolib" and select CREATE (see Figure 8.3).

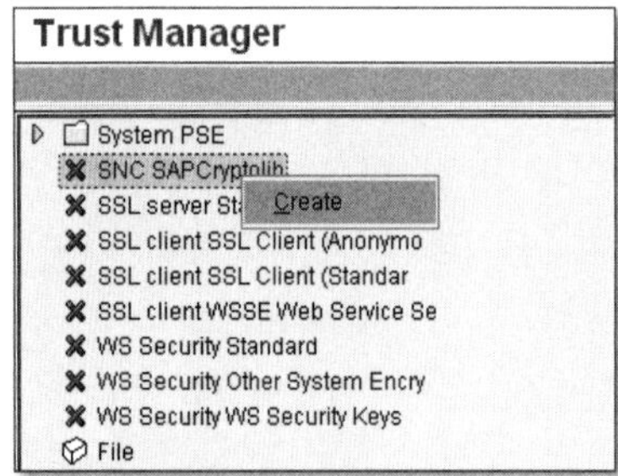

Figure 8.3 Trust Manager

4. The Distinguished Name (SNC ID) of your SAP system should show up now (see Figure 8.4). Click OK.

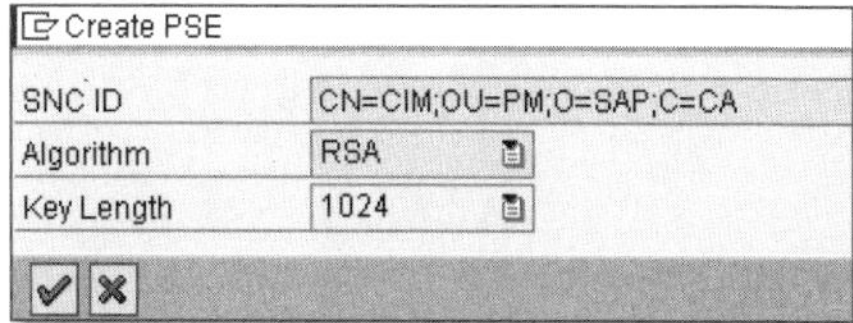

Figure 8.4 Create PSE

5. Click on the PASSWORD button (see Figure 8.5). Now you need to assign a password to the PSE file. Each time you try to view or edit the content of the PSE file, you'll be prompted for the password. Click SAVE.

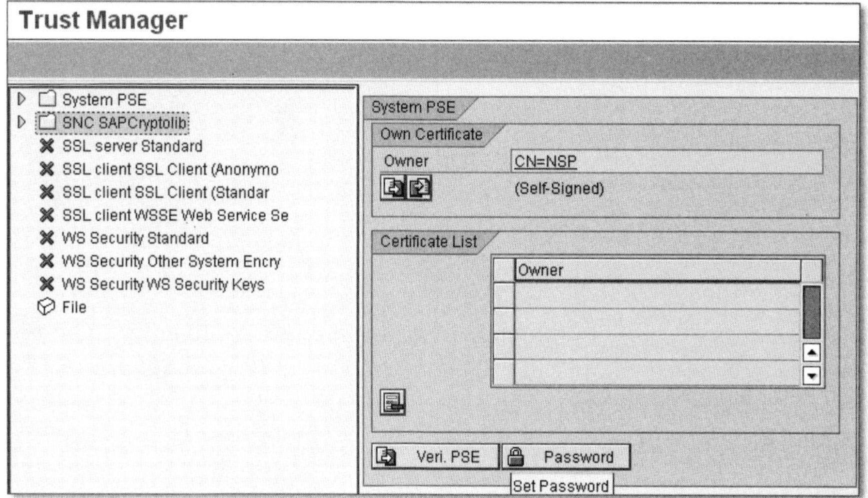

Figure 8.5 Password

Important Note

If you skip the two previous steps (assigning a password and saving the changes), your SAP server won't start after you enabled SNC.

8.2.4 Profile Parameters

1. Log on to your SAP system.
2. Start Transaction RZ10 to go to the server profile parameters.
3. Select the instance profile and select EXTENDED MAINTENANCE. Click the CHANGE button.
4. Add the profile parameters and values according to Table 8.3.

Profile Parameter	Value
snc/accept_insecure_rfc	1
snc/accept_insecure_r3int_rfc	1
snc/accept_insecure_gui	1
snc/accept_insecure_cpic	1
snc/permit_insecure_start	1
snc/data_protection/min	1
snc/data_protection/max	3
snc/enable	1

Table 8.3 SAP Server Profile Parameters and Values

5. The snc/accept_insecure_* parameters and values are set to ensure that previous, unsecure communication methods are still permitted. The snc/data_protection parameter is set to the minimum value (1) for authentication and to the maximum value (3) for privacy.
6. Restart your SAP system.

8.3 Configuring Your SAP BusinessObjects System

In the following sections we'll prepare your SAP BusinessObjects system for server-side trust. This involves several steps:

1. Deploying the SAP Cryptographic Library onto your SAP BusinessObjects system
2. Generating a PSE file and certificate file for your SAP BusinessObjects system

3. Importing the certificate file with the trust manager of your SAP system
4. Exporting the SAP server certificate file
5. Adding a entry to the SNC access control list
6. Importing the SAP server certificate file to the SAP BusinessObjects PSE file
7. Granting access to the SAP BusinessObjects PSE file
8. Configuring the SAP BusinessObjects services
9. Configuring the SNC options in the Central Management Console

8.3.1 SAP Cryptographic Library

As the first step you need to configure the SAP Cryptographic Library on your SAP BusinessObjects Enterprise system.

1. Download and unpack the SAP Cryptographic Library for your SAP BusinessObjects Enterprise system according to the platform of your SAP BusinessObjects Enterprise system (for example, Microsoft Windows, Sun Solaris, IBM AIX).
2. Log on with an administrative account to the operating system of your SAP BusinessObjects Enterprise system.
3. Create the folder *<Drive>:\Program files\SAP\CRYPTO*. This is just an example. You can select the location and create your own folder.
4. Add the folder that you created to the environment variable PATH on your SAP BusinessObjects system.
5. Copy the SAP Cryptographic Library (*sapcrypto.dll*) to the folder you just created.
6. Copy the PSE tool (*sapgenpse.exe*) to the same folder.
7. Add a system-wide variable SNC_LIB with the value pointing to the complete path including the file name of the SAP Cryptographic Library, in our example *<Drive>:\Program files\SAP\CRYPTO\sapcrypto.dll.*
8. Add a subfolder called *SEC* to the previously created folder, in our example *<Drive>:\Program files\SAP\CRYPTO\SEC.*
9. Add a system-wide variable SECUDIR with the value pointing to the subfolder.
10. Copy the file `ticket` from the SAP Cryptographic Library to the subfolder.

8.3.2 Generating PSE Files

Now that you've configured the SAP Cryptographic Library, you can generate a PSE file and export it as a certificate so that the trust manager from your SAP system can import it.

1. Log on with an administrative account to the operating system of your SAP BusinessObjects Enterprise system.
2. Open a command prompt.
3. Navigate to the folder into which you copied the PSE maintenance tool (*sapgenpse.exe*), in our example *<Drive>:\Program Files\SAP\CRYPTO*.
4. Use the following command to generate a PSE file for your SAP BusinessObjects system:

   ```
   sapgenpse.exe gen_pse -v -p BOE.pse
   ```

   In this command *BOE.pse* represents the file name for the PSE file.
5. The system will ask you to configure a PIN code to secure the PSE file. Provide a PIN code and enter the PIN a second time (see Figure 8.6).

```
C:\Program Files\SAP\CRYPTO>sapgenpse.exe gen_pse -v -p BOE.pse
 Got absolute PSE path "C:\Program Files\SAP\CRYPTO\SEC\BOE.pse".
Please enter PIN:
```

Figure 8.6 Generating a PSE File

6. In the next step you'll be asked to provide a Distinguished Name (DN) for your SAP BusinessObjects Enterprise system. The Distinguished Name should follow the LDAP naming convention (see Table 8.2 for details). At this command you do not have to enter the name with the "p:" prefix.

   For our example, this would be

   ```
   CN=BOESERVER,OU=PM,O=SAP,C=CA
   ```
7. Press ↵ to confirm your Distinguished Name for the SAP BusinessObjects system.
8. As the final step for generating the PSE file, you should see a window similar to Figure 8.7, and you should have a PSE file located in the folder *<Drive>:\Program files\SAP\CRYPTO\SEC*.

```
C:\Program Files\SAP\CRYPTO>sapgenpse.exe gen_pse -v -p BOE.pse
 Got absolute PSE path "C:\Program Files\SAP\CRYPTO\SEC\BOE.pse".
Please enter PIN:
Please reenter PIN:
get_pse: Distinguished name of PSE owner: CN=BOESERVER,OU=PM,O=SAP,C=CA
 Supplied distinguished name: "CN=BOESERVER,OU=PM,O=SAP,C=CA"
 Creating PSE with format v2 (default)
 Generating key (RSA, 1024-bits) ... succeeded.
 certificate creation... ok
 PSE update... ok
 PKRoot... ok
Generating certificate request... ok.
PKCS#10 certificate request for "C:\Program Files\SAP\CRYPTO\SEC\BOE.pse":

-----BEGIN CERTIFICATE REQUEST-----
MIIBezCB5QIBADA8MQswCQYDVQQGEwJDQTEMMAoGA1UEChMDU0FQMQswCQYDVQQL
EwJQTTESMBAGA1UEAxMJQk9FU0VSVkVSMIGfMA0GCSqGSIb3DQEBAQUAA4GNADCB
iQKBgQD9m5zxVnciagA8TeZIJ294Nl0fcly4qSSa8OL0TD2FWWzVFlHYCppOIPbL
LlT8sAotejKU2NNTkyZAjPPGEJi3bqozwn6BEpcgkmc8EBol7Mxdu4QeoAHprk0U
ldEzd9UACsLtIWRd6H956gSFjLVPuaZDkXTyTnx4FNsNg6qinwIDAQABoAAwDQYJ
KoZIhvcNAQEFBQADgYEARZt8nsjm3wVt07TfxUal+rJv62TkQhPOYVjq18RrSn5a
5HFvbpdAn6vRLE/ahq/To8KNcTIk8m/FlKaM+4z+TuDuacWYYGdQgrcRP5M33E7X
Kq32rJlMiq9EqeCc2/xs+dkuzvstqewJpbc+MAemK5MHZhFNMUC8vOoUPOD425k=
-----END CERTIFICATE REQUEST-----
```

Figure 8.7 Final Step for PSE Generation

9. Next you need to export the PSE file into a certificate so that the trust manager from your SAP system can import it. You can use the following command to export the PSE file:

   ```
   sapgenpse.exe export_own_cert -v -p BOE.pse
     -o myBOEcertificate.cert
   ```

   In this command `BOE.pse` represents the PSE file you generated for your SAP BusinessObjects Enterprise system in the previous steps, and `myBOEcertificate.cert` is the file name for the certificate.

10. You'll be asked to enter the previously configured PIN.

11. You should now have the PSE file for your SAP BusinessObjects Enterprise system in the folder *<Drive>:\Program files\SAP\CRYPTO\SEC*, and you should have the certificate file in the folder *<Drive>:\Program files\SAP\CRYPTO*.

8.3.3 Trust Manager

Next you need to import the exported certificate from your SAP BusinessObjects system via the trust manager of your SAP system, and then you can export the SAP system PSE to a certificate file.

1. Log on to your SAP system and start Transaction STRUST.
2. Open the folder entry *SNC SAPCryptolib*.
3. Double-click your server entry and enter the password that you configured previously.

4. Click the IMPORT CERTIFICATE button (see Figure 8.8).

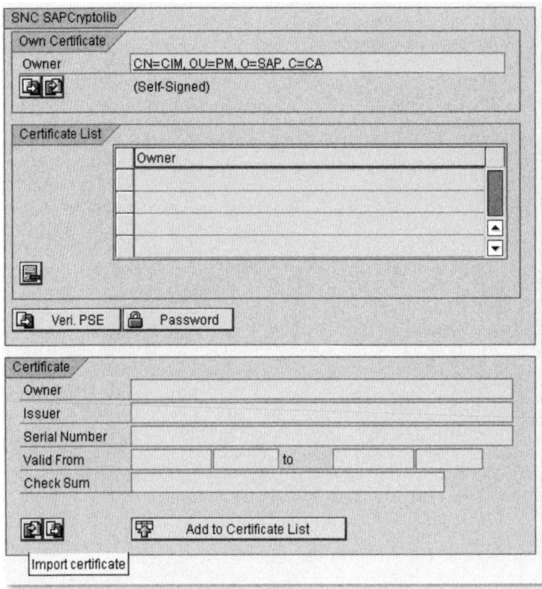

Figure 8.8 Import Certificate

5. Select the certificate file from your SAP BusinessObjects Enterprise system and then select BASE64 (see Figure 8.9). Click OK.

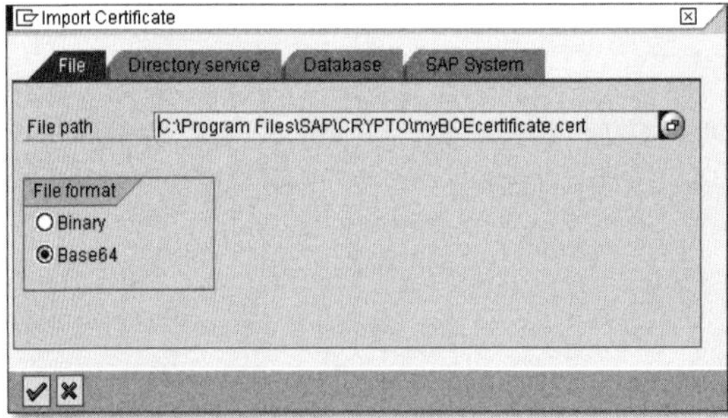

Figure 8.9 File Configuration for Import

6. Return to the screen shown in Figure 8.8. Click the ADD TO CERTIFICATE LIST button. The Distinguished Name of your SAP BusinessObjects system should now appear in the list on the top screen (see Figure 8.10).
7. Click SAVE and close Transaction STRUST.

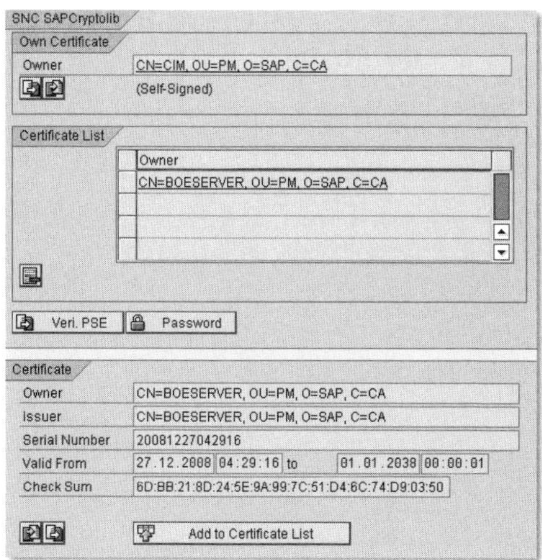

Figure 8.10 Updated Certificate List

You just imported the certificate from your SAP BusinessObjects Enterprise system to your SAP system. The next step is to export the certificate from your SAP system so you can import it to the PSE file of your SAP BusinessObjects Enterprise system.

1. Log on to your SAP system and start Transaction STRUST.
2. Open the folder entry *SNC SAPCryptolib*.
3. Double-click your server entry and enter the password that you configured previously.
4. Double-click the top entry of the SAP server, called "Own Certificate" (see Figure 8.11).

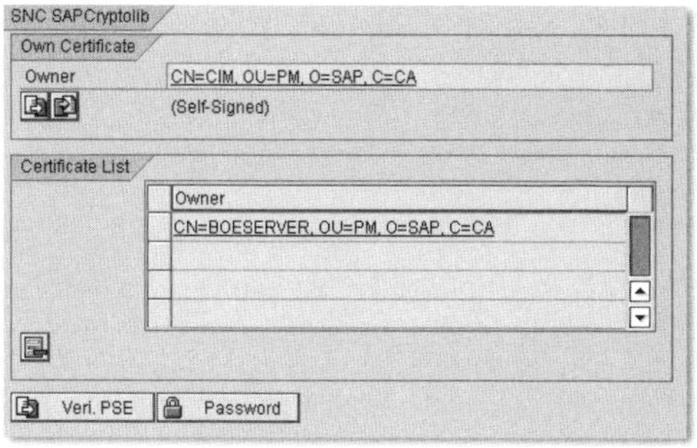

SNC SAPCryptolib
Own Certificate
Owner CN=CIM, OU=PM, O=SAP, C=CA
(Self-Signed)
Certificate List
Owner
CN=BOESERVER, OU=PM, O=SAP, C=CA
Veri. PSE
Password

Figure 8.11 Own Certificate

5. The Distinguished Name of your SAP system should now be listed in the bottom list of certificates (see Figure 8.12). Click the EXPORT CERTIFICATE icon, and you'll be presented with a screen similar to Figure 8.9.

Figure 8.12 Export Certificate

6. Select a path and filename with the extension *.cert*.
7. Select BASE64 and click OK.
8. Close Transaction STRUST.

8.3.4 SNC Access Control List

Before you import the certificate from your SAP server into the PSE file of your SAP BusinessObjects Enterprise system, you need to create a System ID as part of the SNC access control list (ACL).

1. Log on to your SAP system and start Transaction SNCO (see Figure 8.13).

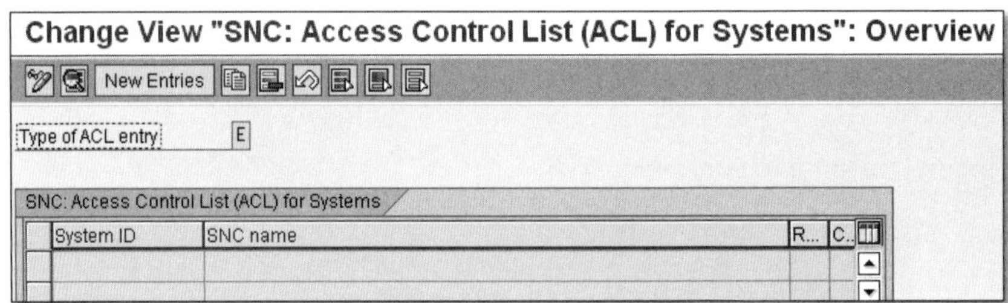

Figure 8.13 SNC Access Control List

2. Click the NEW ENTRIES button, and you'll see the configuration screen for a new entry (see Figure 8.14).
3. Enter the name of your SAP BusinessObjects system as the System ID, in our example VMWSAP12.

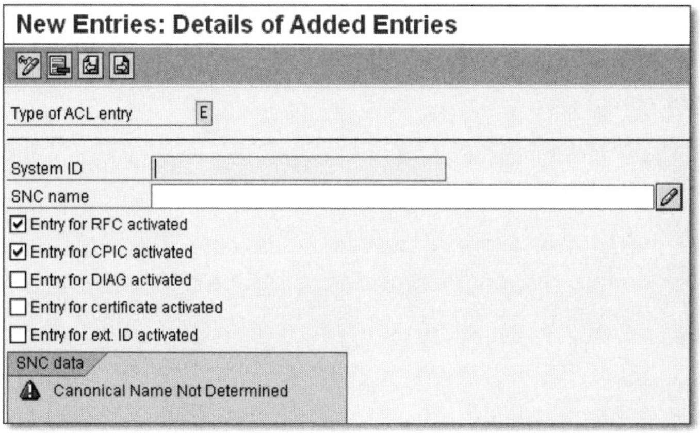

Figure 8.14 New Entry for SNC ACL

4. Enter the Distinguished Name that you configured previously for your SAP BusinessObjects server in the SNC name field. This time you need to enter the prefix "p:". In our example this would be

   `p:CN=BOESERVER,OU=PM,O=SAP,C=CA`

5. Select the ENTRY FOR RFC ACTIVATED and ENTRY FOR EXT ID ACTIVATED checkboxes (see Figure 8.15) and click SAVE.

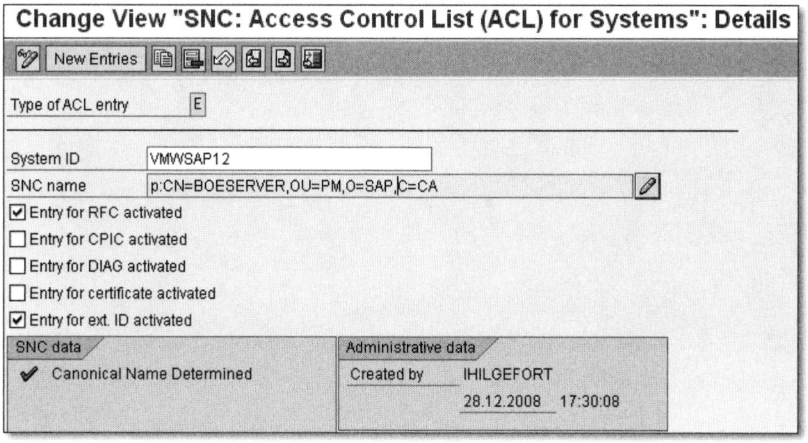

Figure 8.15 Filled Entry for SNC ACL

At this point you've configured your SAP BusinessObjects Enterprise system as a System ID that can use SNC and impersonation to log on with external IDs.

8.3.5 Importing SAP Server PSE Files

Next you need to import the SAP server certificate to the PSE file from your SAP BusinessObjects Enterprise system.

1. Log on with an administrative account to the operating system of your SAP BusinessObjects Enterprise system.
2. Copy the SAP server certificate to the folder where you copied the PSE maintenance tool, in our example *<Drive>:\Program Files\SAP\CRYPTO*.
3. Open a command box and navigate to the folder where you copied the PSE maintenance tool, in our example *<Drive>:\Program Files\SAP\CRYPTO*.
4. Use the following command to add the certificate to the PSE file of your SAP BusinessObjects Enterprise system:

   ```
   sapgenpse.exe maintain_pk -v -a SAPServer.cert -p BOE.pse
   ```

   In this command *SAPServer.cert* represents the file name of the SAP server certificate, and *BOE.pse* represents the file name of the PSE file from your SAP BusinessObjects Enterprise system.
5. You'll be asked to enter the PIN code that you configured previously.
6. You should then see the Distinguished Name of your SAP server as an added entry (see Figure 8.16).

```
C:\Program Files\SAP\CRYPTO>sapgenpse.exe maintain_pk -v -a SAPServer.cert -p BO
E.pse
 Opening PSE "C:\Program Files\SAP\CRYPTO\SEC\BOE.pse"...
 No SSO credentials found for this PSE.
Please enter PIN:
 PSE (v2) open ok.
 retrieving PKList
 Adding new certificate from file "SAPServer.cert"
----------
Subject : CN=CIM, OU=PM, O=SAP, C=CA
Issuer  : CN=CIM, OU=PM, O=SAP, C=CA
Serialno: 20:08:12:27:01:59:46
KeyInfo : RSA, 1024-bit
Validity  -  NotBefore:   Sat Dec 27 01:59:46 2008 (081227015946Z)

             NotAfter:    Fri Jan 01 00:00:01 2038 (380101000001Z)
------------------------------------------------------------------------

 PKList updated (1 entries total, 1 newly added)
```

Figure 8.16 Added Certificate

8.3.6 Granting Access to the PSE File

Before your SAP BusinessObjects service can use the PSE file that you created for your SAP BusinessObjects system, you need to grant access to a specific user account, which you then can use to run the services. In the following steps we'll use the administrator account from the system, but you can use any other account, and the steps are identical.

1. Log on with the account that you want to grant the access to the operating system of your SAP BusinessObjects system.
2. Open a command box and navigate to the folder for the PSE maintenance tool, in our example *<Drive>:\Program Files\SAP\CRYPTO*.
3. You can use the following command to grant access to the logged-on user:
   ```
   sapgenpse.exe seclogin -p BOE.pse
   ```
   In this command *BOE.pse* represents the file name for the PSE file of your SAP BusinessObjects system.
4. You'll be asked to enter your previously configured PIN code. If this is successful, the logged-on user is granted access to the PSE file. You can use the following command for verification:
   ```
   sapgenpse.exe maintain_pk -l
   ```
5. If the user was granted the access, you can view the content of the PSE file without being asked for the PIN code.

Adding other User Accounts

If you want to add a different user than the user that is currently logged on, you can use the command:

```
sapgenpse.exe seclogin -p BOE.pse -O <domain\username>
```

In this command *BOE.pse* represents the PSE file of your SAP BusinessObjects system, and the placeholder *<domain\username>* represents the domain user to which you can grant access.

8.3.7 SAP BusinessObjects Services

The next step is to configure your SAP BusinessObjects services to run under the account to which you granted access to the PSE file. The services that require access to the PSE file in this scenario are the processing services for Crystal Reports and SAP BusinessObjects Web Intelligence.

Starting with release XI 3.0 of SAP BusinessObjects Enterprise, the services are no longer configured in the Central Configuration Manager, but instead you now have an SIA, which acts as a parent process, and the assigned services use the credentials from the SIA.

You now have three options to configure this step:

- You can configure a single SIA for your SAP BusinessObjects Enterprise system and configure it to run under the credentials that have access to the PSE file. This is the easiest way but is the least secure because now all of the services of your SAP BusinessObjects system have access to the PSE file, which is not necessary.
- You can create a second SIA for your SAP BusinessObjects Enterprise system and add the processing service for Crystal Reports and SAP BusinessObjects Web Intelligence to this new SIA. You can then remove the original processing services for Crystal Reports and SAP BusinessObjects Web Intelligence. In this way all of your content is processed on services with access to the PSE file.
- In the third option you also create a second SIA for your SAP BusinessObjects Enterprise system, but you don't remove the original entries for the processing services. In this option you create server groups to differentiate between the two groups of processing services.

We'll configure our example system according to option three. Based on the steps outlined here for option three you should also be able to setup the other options because they are following the same concept.

1. Start the Central Configuration Manager of your SAP BusinessObjects Enterprise system (START • PROGRAMS • BUSINESSOBJECTS XI RELEASE 3.1 • BUSINESSOBJECTS ENTERPRISE • CENTRAL CONFIGURATION MANAGER).
2. Click the ADD SERVER INTELLIGENCE AGENT icon on the Central Configuration Manager toolbar (see Figure 8.17).

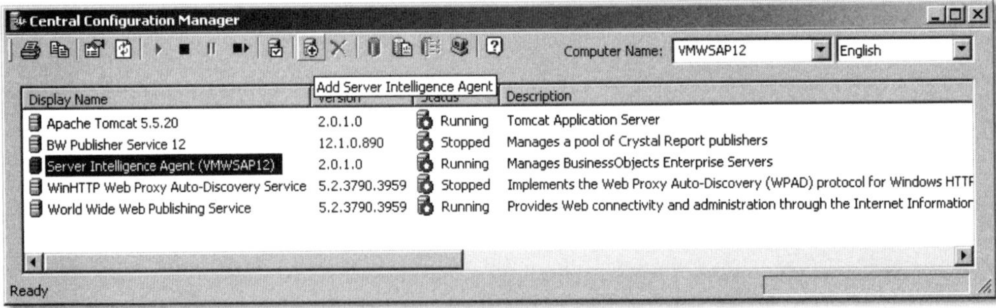

Figure 8.17 Central Configuration Manager

3. Enter the name of your SIA and enter the port number. In our example we'll use "SAPProcessingServices" for the name and "6420" for the port number (see Figure 8.18).

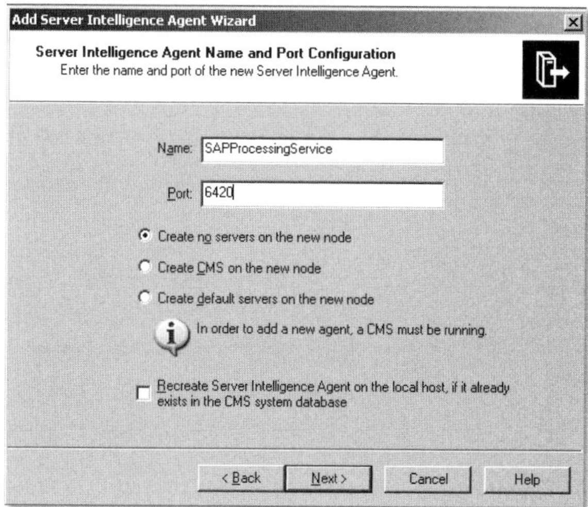

Figure 8.18 Adding the SIA

4. In the next screen you'll be asked to provide the credentials to authenticate against your SAP BusinessObjects Enterprise system.
5. After a successful authentication, you'll be presented with a summary. Click the FINISH button to add your new SIA (SAPProcessingService) to the system (see Figure 8.19).

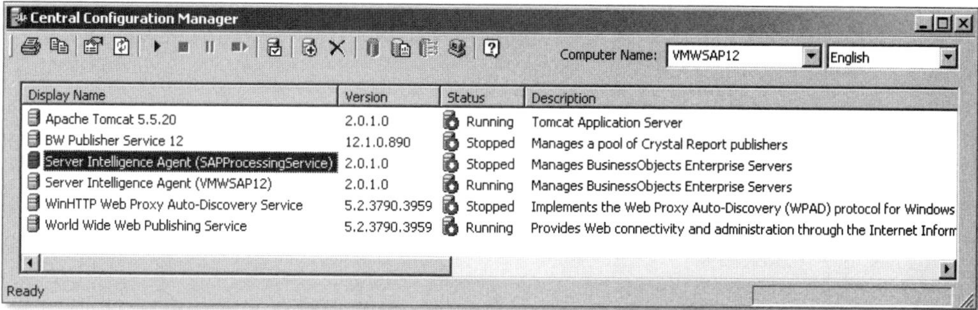

Figure 8.19 Central Configuration Manager

6. Select your new SIA and click the PROPERTIES icon (see Figure 8.20).

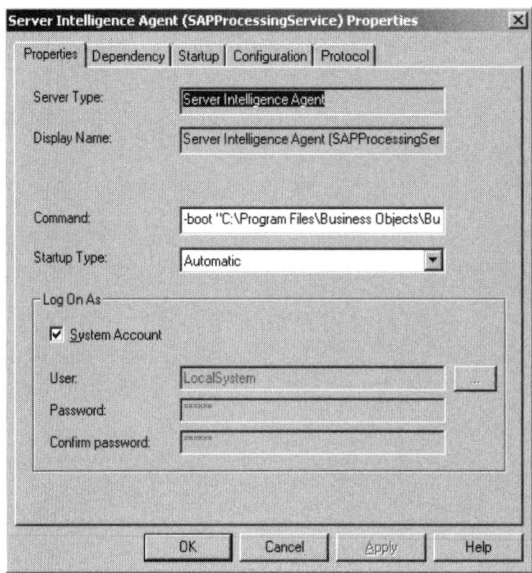

Figure 8.20 SIA Properties

7. Deselect the option LOG ON AS SYSTEM ACCOUNT checkbox and enter the credentials to which you granted access to the PSE file, in our example the administrator account.
8. Click OK and start the newly created SIA.
9. Now you need to add the processing services to the newly created SIA. To do so, log on to the Central Management Console of your SAP BusinessObjects system.
10. Navigate to the SERVERS area (see Figure 8.21).

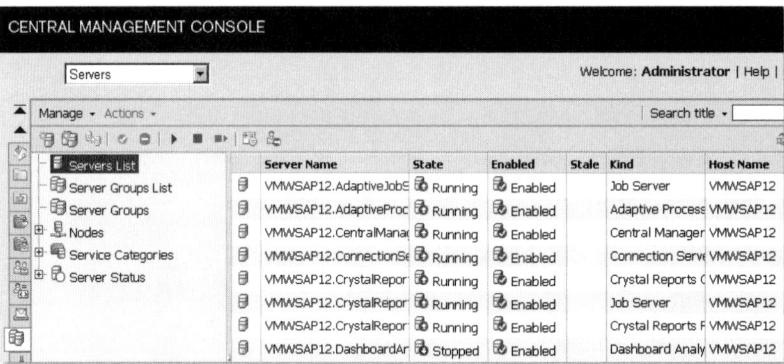

Figure 8.21 Servers

11. Follow the menu path MANAGE • NEW • NEW SERVER (see Figure 8.22).

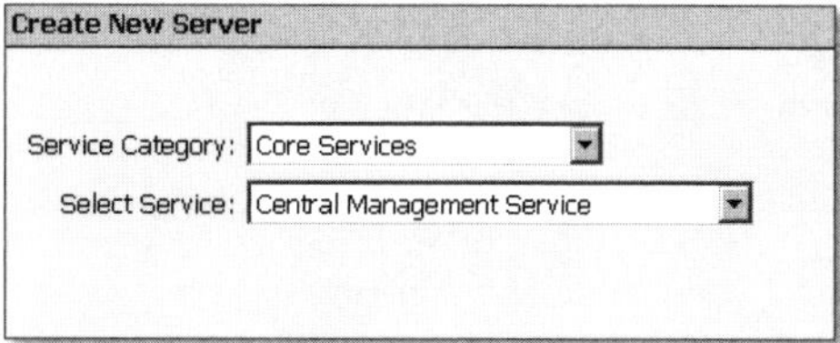

Figure 8.22 Create New Server

12. In the following pop-up, select "Crystal Reports" as SERVICE CATEGORY.
13. Select "Crystal Reports Scheduling Service" as SERVICE.
14. Click NEXT twice.
15. Select the newly created SIA as the NODE for the new Crystal Reports service (see Figure 8.23).

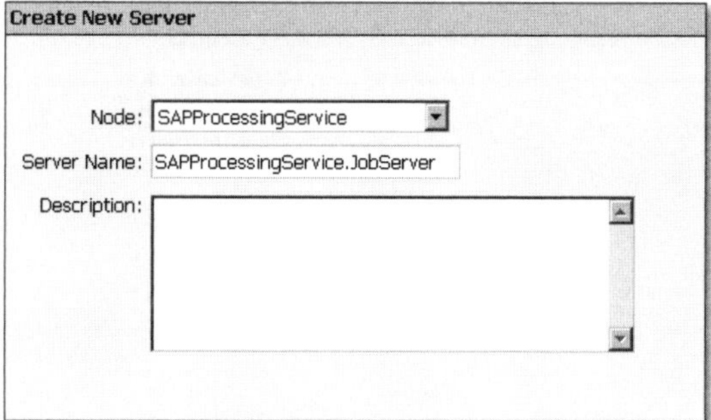

Figure 8.23 SIA Assignment

16. Click the CREATE button.
17. Repeat the steps for adding a new server for the additional services according to Table 8.4.

Service Category	Service Entry
Crystal Reports	Crystal Reports Scheduling Service
Crystal Reports	Crystal Reports Processing Service
Crystal Reports	Crystal Reports Cache Service

Table 8.4 Additional Services

Service Category	Service Entry
Crystal Reports	Crystal Reports Viewing and Modification Service
Web Intelligence	Web Intelligence Processing Service
Web Intelligence	Web Intelligence Scheduling and Publishing Service

Table 8.4 Additional Services (cont.)

18. After you added all of the additional services, select those services and follow the menu path Actions • Enable Servers. After you enabled all of the services, select all of the additional services again and follow the menu path Actions • Start Server.
19. Now navigate to the Server Groups area on the left-hand side (see Figure 8.24).

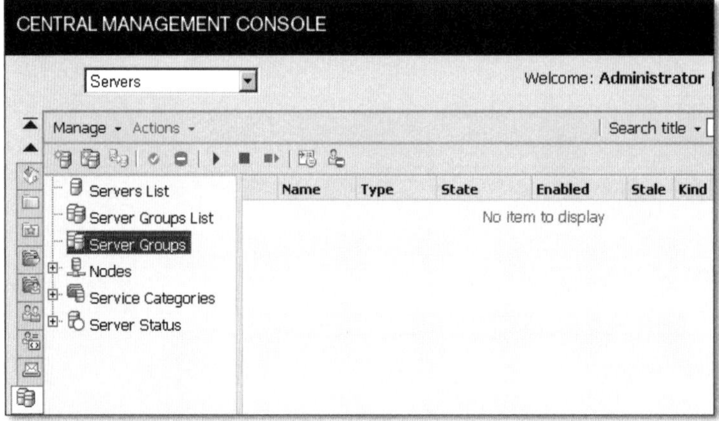

Figure 8.24 Server Groups

20. Follow the menu path Manage • New • Create Server Group (see Figure 8.25).

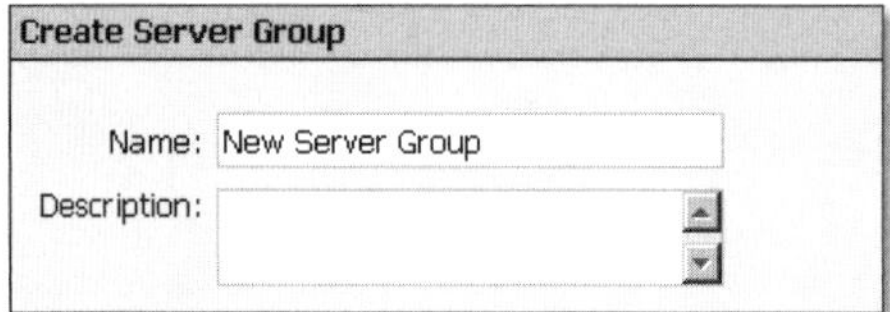

Figure 8.25 Create New Server Group

21. Enter a name for the new server group, in our example "SAPProcessing-Group". Then click OK.
22. Right-click the newly created server group SAPPROCESSINGGROUP and select the menu ADD MEMBERS.
23. Add the following services to your server group (see Figure 8.26):
    - ALL SIX PREVIOUSLY CREATED SERVICES ASSIGNED TO YOUR SECOND SIA
    - ADAPTIVE JOB SERVER
    - ADAPTIVE PROCESSING SERVER
    - DESTINATION JOB SERVER
    - PUBLICATION JOB SERVER

    By adding these services to your server group, you'll be able to use the server group during the scheduling process, and you can ensure that the report is scheduled on the services that have been configured properly.

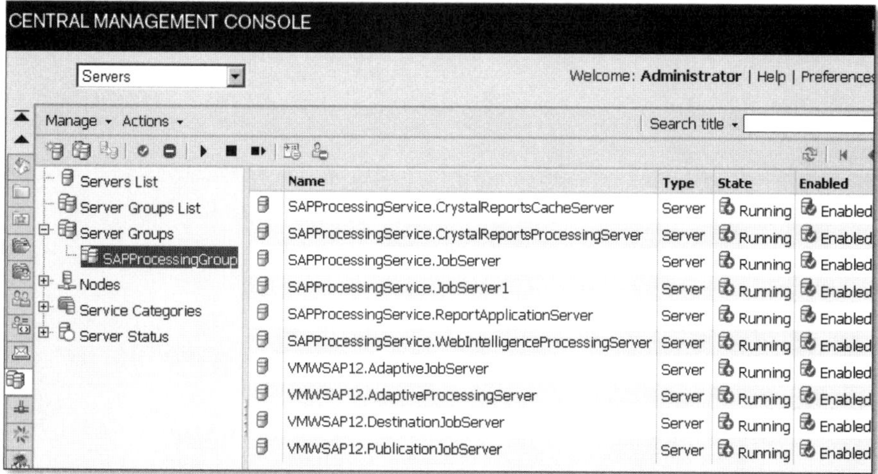

Figure 8.26 Newly Created Services

You've created an SIA controlling the user account for your processing services, and you've created a server group with all necessary services to be able to create a publication for Crystal Reports and SAP BusinessObjects Web Intelligence.

8.3.8 SNC Options in the Central Management Console

To finalize the SNC configuration, you need to provide the details of the SNC options as part of the SAP authentication in the Central Management Console.

1. Log on to the Central Management Console of your SAP BusinessObjects Enterprise system.
2. Navigate to the AUTHENTICATION area and select the SAP authentication.
3. Navigate to the SNC SETTINGS tab and ensure that your SAP system is selected as LOGICAL SYSTEM NAME (see Figure 8.27).

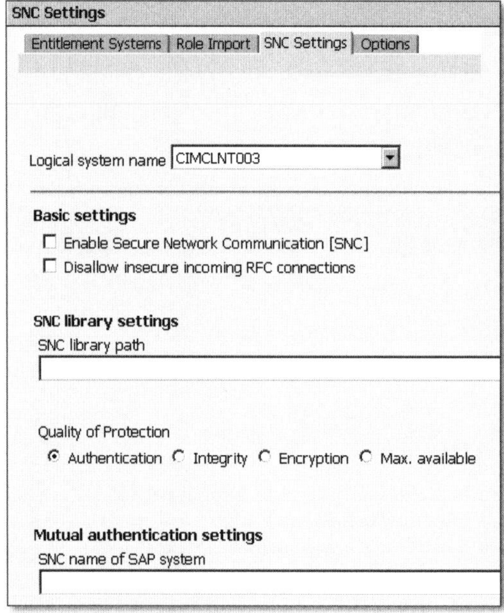

Figure 8.27 SNC Settings

4. Select the ENABLE SECURE NETWORK COMMUNICATION [SNC] checkbox under BASIC SETTINGS.
5. Enter the full path to the SNC library including the filename in the SNC LIBRARY PATH field under SNC LIBRARY SETTINGS.
6. Select AUTHENTICATION under QUALITY OF PROTECTION.
7. Enter the Distinguished Name of your SAP system in the SNC NAME OF SAP SYSTEM field under MUTUAL AUTHENTICATION SETTINGS. In this case you need to add the prefix "p:".

SNC Name of the SAP System

You can verify the SNC name of your SAP system in Transaction RZ10 by viewing the value for the profile parameter `snc/identiy/as`.

8. Enter the Distinguished Name of your SAP BusinessObjects system in the SNC NAME OF ENTERPRISE SYSTEM field under TRUST SETTINGS (Figure 8.28). In this case you need to add the prefix "p:".

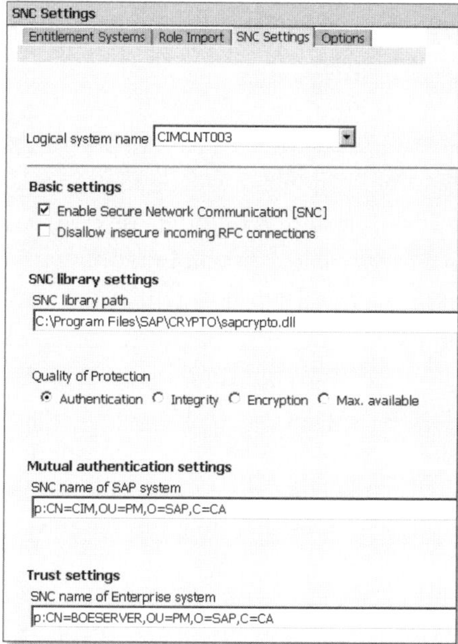

Figure 8.28 SNC Settings

You've achieved the following from the configuration steps you did:

- You deployed and configured the SAP Cryptographic Library on your SAP system.
- You deployed and configured the SAP Cryptographic Library on your SAP BusinessObjects Enterprise system.
- You exchanged certificates between your SAP and SAP BusinessObjects Enterprise systems to establish trust between them.
- You created a system ID in the SNC ACL to allow password-free impersonation for your SAP BusinessObjects Enterprise system.

- You added a new SIA to your SAP BusinessObjects system and added the processing tier for Crystal Reports and SAP BusinessObjects Web Intelligence.
- You configured the SNC options for your SAP system in the Central Management Console.

You are now ready to create a publication for a Crystal Reports or SAP BusinessObjects Web Intelligence object on your SAP BusinessObjects system.

8.4 Creating Publications with Crystal Reports and SAP BusinessObjects Web Intelligence

In this section you'll learn how to create a publication for a Crystal Reports or SAP BusinessObjects Web Intelligence object. A publication allows you to schedule an object for a large set of user groups or a set of users and define specific rules about the output format and delivery to each of the recipients. In combination with the now-configured server-side trust, you can use a publication to schedule a Crystal Reports or SAP BusinessObjects Web Intelligence object by keeping the data-level security from your SAP system without the need to replicate it, because the SAP BusinessObjects Enterprise system can now act on behalf of the SAP users in a password-free way and thus schedule the report for each SAP user (multipass bursting). Those more familiar with the SAP side than the SAP BusinessObjects side can compare a publication with the Information Broadcasting functionality offered as part of SAP NetWeaver Business Warehouse.

You can use the publication and the configured server-side trust without any data-level security defined in your SAP system, but in the next couple of steps we will make the following assumptions:

- You configured the characteristic material for the cube *0D_SD_C03* from our BW query (see Section 3.1.3, Creating Your First Crystal Reports Report with SAP NetWeaver Business Warehouse) to be authorization-relevant.
- You added an authorization variable to the BW query for the characteristic material.
- You created a new Crystal Report (or SAP BusinessObjects Web Intelligence) object based on this changed BW query. If you're using Crystal Reports, ensure that you publish the report to SAP BusinessObjects Enterprise.
- You configured two roles with the following data-level security (see Table 8.5).

- USER_A is assigned to the role BUSINESSOBJECTS_AUTH_ROLE_01.
- USER_B is assigned to the role BUSINESSOBJECTS_AUTH_ROLE_02.

Role Name	Assigned Values for Material
BUSINESSOBJECTS_AUTH_ROLE_01	CN00S1 – Notebook Speedy I CN CN00S2 – Notebook Speedy II CN
BUSINESSOBJECTS_AUTH_ROLE_02	CN0400 – Terminal P400 CN CN0600 – Terminal P600 CN
BUSINESSOBJECTS_CONTENT_ROLE	All values

Table 8.5 Authorization Roles with Values

These are only examples for a configuration of data-level security so that we can use those settings for our publications in the following steps.

1. Log on to the Central Management Console of your SAP BusinessObjects system.
2. Navigate to the AUTHENTICATION area and select SAP AUTHENTICATION.
3. Navigate to the OPTIONS tab and ensure that the AUTOMATICALLY IMPORT USERS and FORCE USER SYNCHRONIZATION checkboxes are selected (see Figure 8.29).

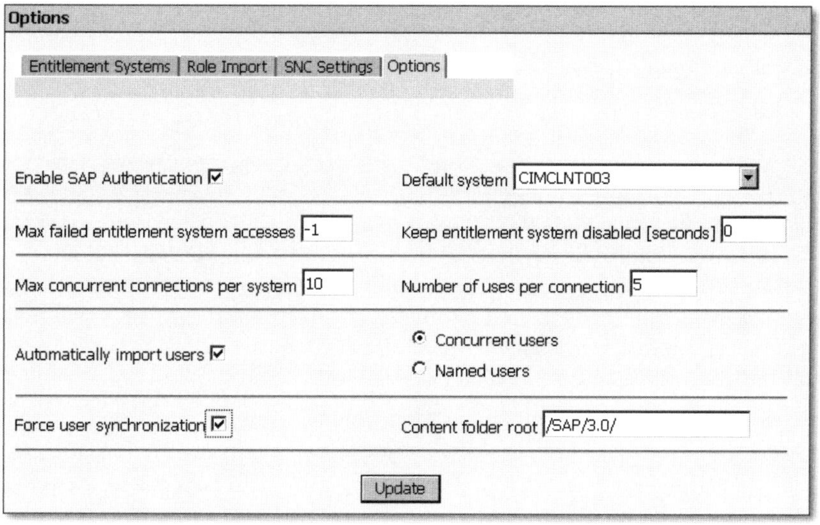

Figure 8.29 SAP Authentication Options

4. Navigate to the Role Import tab and ensure that your SAP system is the selected system for the Logical system name.
5. Import the roles listed in Table 8.5 into your SAP BusinessObjects Enterprise system (see Figure 8.30).

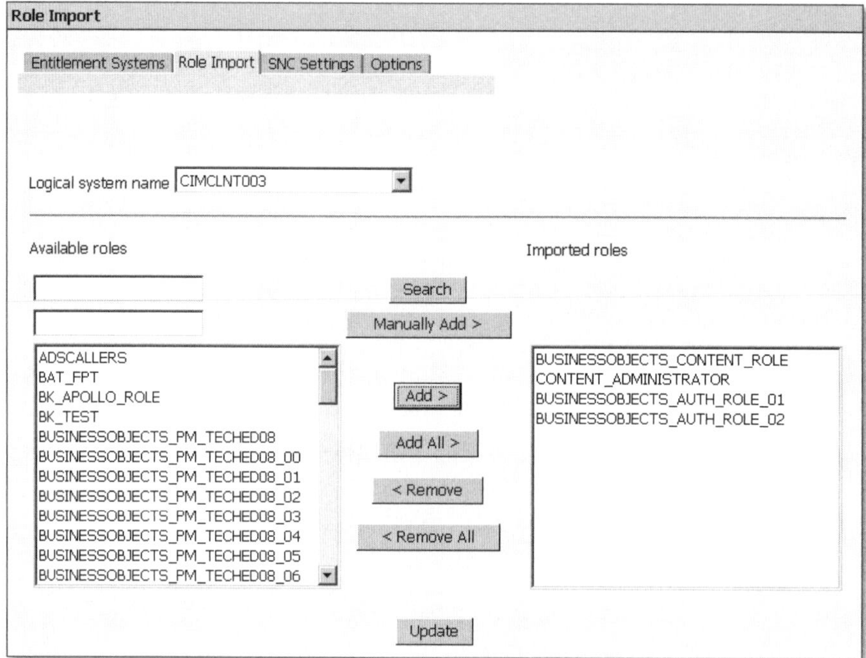

Figure 8.30 Role Import

Imported SAP Roles and Users and Publications

A publication can be configured to leverage user groups and individual users as recipients. If you're using the imported SAP roles, you need to ensure that the users for those roles have also been imported, so you should make sure the Automatically import users and Force user synchronization checkboxes are selected. If you're not sure, you can select the Force user synchronization checkbox and click the Update button on the Role Import tab of your SAP system.

If the users aren't imported, the publication won't process the user group, because the user group does not have any users assigned to it.

6. Now navigate to the Folders area.
7. Navigate to the folder of the report you created for this exercise.

8. Follow the menu path MANAGE • NEW • NEW PUBLICATION (see Figure 8.31).

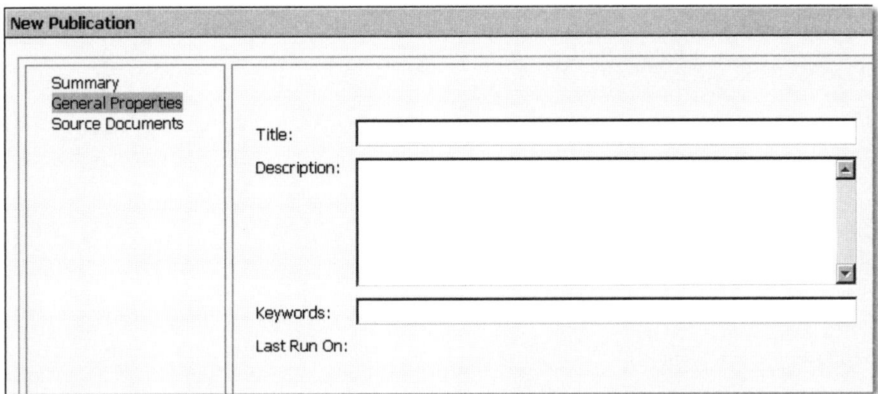

Figure 8.31 New Publication

9. Enter a title and description for your new publication.
10. Click SOURCE DOCUMENTS, and a screen will come up where you can select the documents that you'll use for your publication (see Figure 8.32).

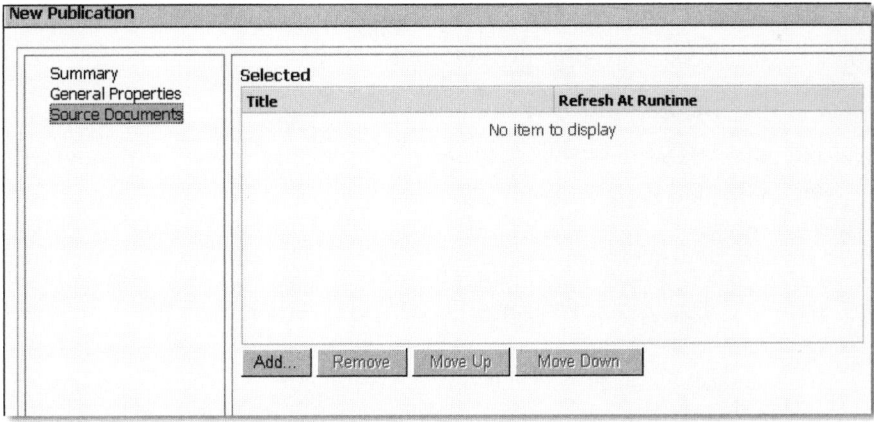

Figure 8.32 New Publication – Source Documents

11. Click ADD and select the Crystal Reports (or SAP BusinessObjects Web Intelligence) document that you created on the changed BW query. After you added the document, the screen will change to provide additional options, as you can see in Figure 8.33.

12. Click Enterprise Recipients (see Figure 8.33).

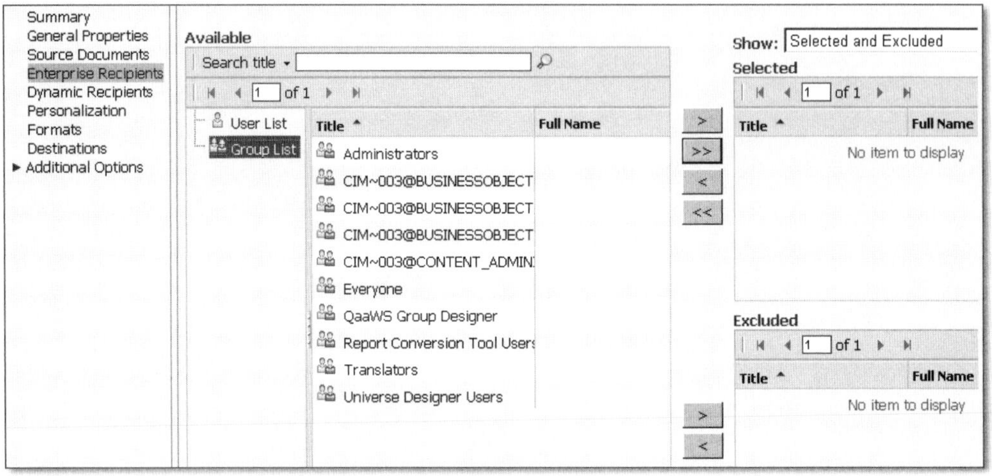

Figure 8.33 New Publication – Enterprise Recipients

13. Click Group List and add the following user groups as recipients to the Selected area:
    - CIM~003@BUSINESSOBJECTS_CONTENT_ROLE
    - CIM~003@BUSINESSOBJECTS_AUTH_ROLE_01
    - CIM~003@BUSINESSOBJECTS_AUTH_ROLE_02

    In your SAP BusinessObjects system the prefix of the roles will show with the logical system name of your SAP system.
14. Click Destinations in the menu on the left (see Figure 8.34). Here you can define where the output of the process is going to be delivered. The default option is Default Enterprise Location, which means the output will be delivered to the same location where the source document is being stored. In our example we'll also check the BusinessObjects Inbox checkbox so that each recipient will receive the output directly to the Inbox folder in your SAP BusinessObjects system.
15. Next open the list of Additional Options in the left-hand menu, and in the drop-down list, select Scheduling Server Group (see Figure 8.35). Select the server group that you created in Section 8.3.7, SAP BusinessObjects Services, under the Only use servers belonging to the selected group checkbox.

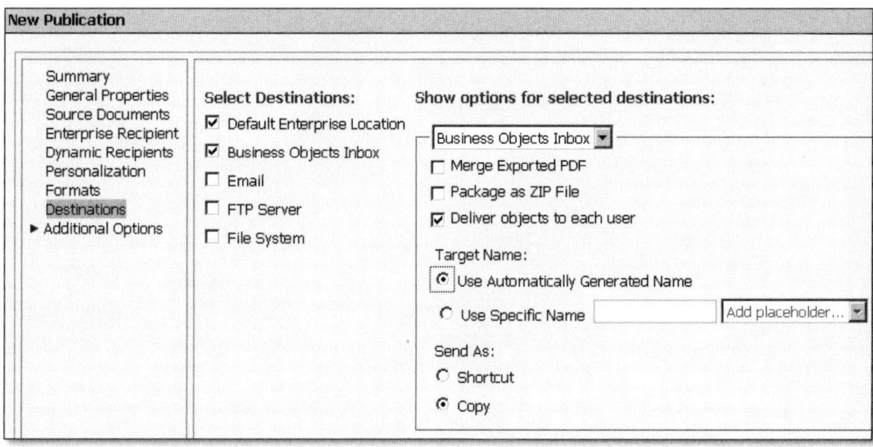

Figure 8.34 New Publication – Destinations

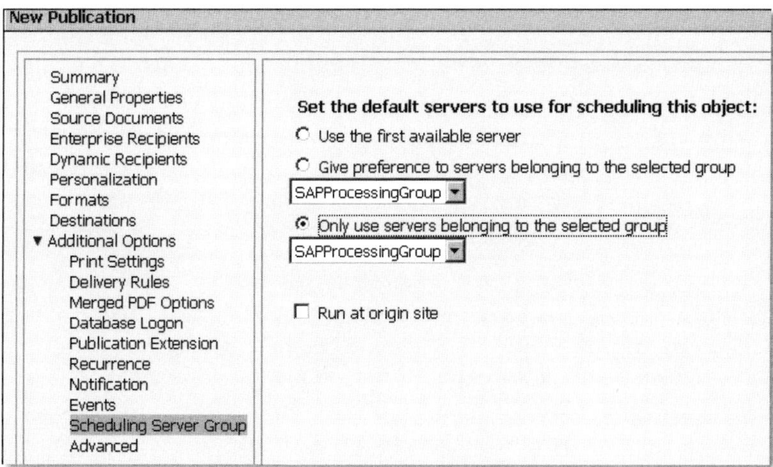

Figure 8.35 New Publication – Scheduling Server Group

16. Select ADVANCED in the drop-down list (see Figure 8.36).
17. Select ONE DATABASE FETCH PER RECIPIENT. In that way you create a multipass bursting process.
18. Click SAVE & CLOSE, and your publication will appear in the folder.
19. Next select the publication in the folder and follow the menu path ACTIONS • SCHEDULE.

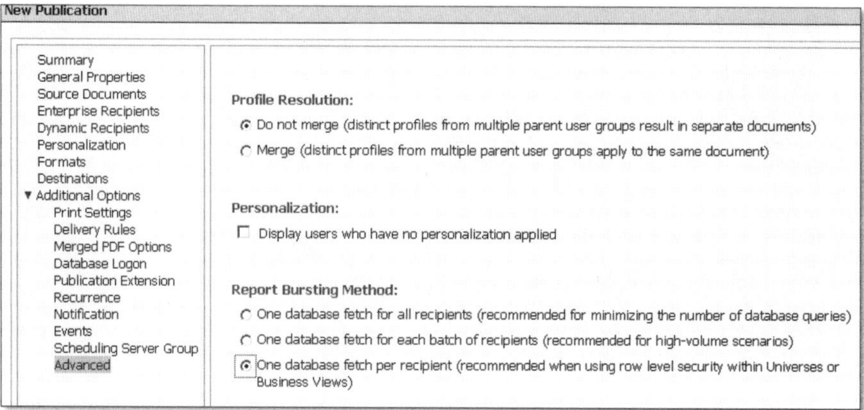

Figure 8.36 New Publication – Advanced

20. The scheduling screen appears with all of the settings you configured. You can go through them to verify them if you want.
21. Click SCHEDULE to start the process of your publication. When the publication is finished, you should see the message SUCCESS, and you should be able to log on with the SAP credentials to InfoView and see the output of the process in the INBOX of each recipient.

Scheduling SAP BusinessObjects Web Intelligence Documents

When you try to schedule an SAP BusinessObjects Web Intelligence document, you'll see that there is no option for you to enter the user credentials that will be used during the scheduling process. There are two options available to you to successfully schedule a SAP BusinessObjects Web Intelligence document:

- You can set up the connection for your SAP BusinessObjects Web Intelligence document to use a set of hard-coded credentials, which result in a scheduling process always using those credentials.
- The second option is to configure the connection to use Single Sign-On, to ensure that the required users are imported via the SAP authentication as proper SAP BusinessObjects users, and you can then use the server-side trust as described above also for a normal scheduling process. You do not have to create a publication, but the server-side trust configuration needs to be in place so a user can use his SAP credentials and schedule a SAP BusinessObjects Web Intelligence document.

In this chapter we will take a look at the different options to integrate your BusinessObjects Enterprise system with the SAP NetWeaver Portal in order to show the content to your users.

9 Integrating with the SAP NetWeaver Portal

In this chapter you'll receive an overview of how you can integrate SAP BusinessObjects Enterprise content into your SAP NetWeaver Portal. You'll learn how you can use iViews to show content to your users and how you can integrate with the Knowledge Management (KM) of your portal.

9.1 BI Content with SAP NetWeaver Portal iViews

The SAP BusinessObjects Integration for SAP Solutions offers two ways of integrating content from your SAP BusinessObjects Enterprise system into the SAP NetWeaver Portal. You can create iViews and show the content of those iViews in your portal, and you can use the Knowledge Management component of your portal implementation and use a repository manager to offer the functionality of your SAP BusinessObjects Enterprise system to your consumers.

In this section we'll focus on the option to use iViews as containers for the BI content and go step-by-step through the process of configuring your SAP NetWeaver Portal, your SAP NetWeaver Business Warehouse system, and your SAP BusinessObjects Enterprise system.

9.1.1 Technical Prerequisites

Before we look at the specific steps required to configure your system landscape so that you can share BI content via your portal, we'll take a look at the technical prerequisites.

To be able to use Single Sign-On between the SAP NetWeaver Portal, your SAP NetWeaver Business Warehouse system, and your SAP BusinessObjects Enterprise system, you require:

- That the SAP NetWeaver Portal and the SAP NetWeaver Business Warehouse system are configured as trusted systems (see Section 9.1.2, SAP NetWeaver Portal – Configuration Steps)
- That all involved systems (SAP NetWeaver Portal, SAP NetWeaver Business Warehouse, and SAP BusinessObjects Enterprise) are in the same domain
- That all involved URLs always use the full qualified domain names of the involved systems
- That the SAP authentication is configured on your SAP BusinessObjects Enterprise system (see Section 2.4.1, Configuration of SAP Authentication) and SAP roles and users have been imported
- That the SAP NetWeaver Business Warehouse system accepts Single Sign-On logon tickets (see Section 2.3.4, Single Sign-On)

The list above shows the prerequisites that need to be configured in addition to all of the steps outlined in the following sections.

9.1.2 SAP NetWeaver Portal – Configuration Steps

The following steps are configuration steps that are required to created content from your SAP BusinessObjects Enterprise system inside the SAP NetWeaver Portal with Single Sign-On.

Configuring Trust

You need to configure trust between your portal system and your SAP NetWeaver Business Warehouse or SAP ERP system so that Single Sign-On is possible between those two systems. In the outlined steps we'll refer to your SAP NetWeaver Business Warehouse system, but the steps are identical if you're using an SAP ERP system.

1. Log on to your SAP NetWeaver Portal system. You need to use a portal user that is part of the system administrator's role of your portal.
2. Follow the menu path System Administration • System configuration (see Figure 9.1) and select Keystore Administration.

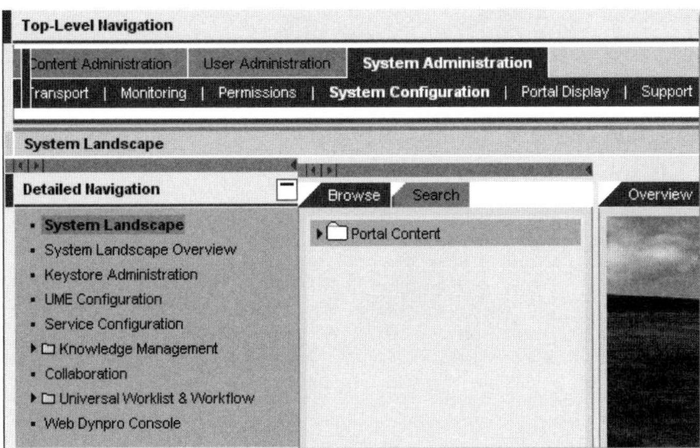

Figure 9.1 Enterprise Portal – System Configuration

3. Ensure that you select the CONTENT tab in the next screen (Figure 9.2).

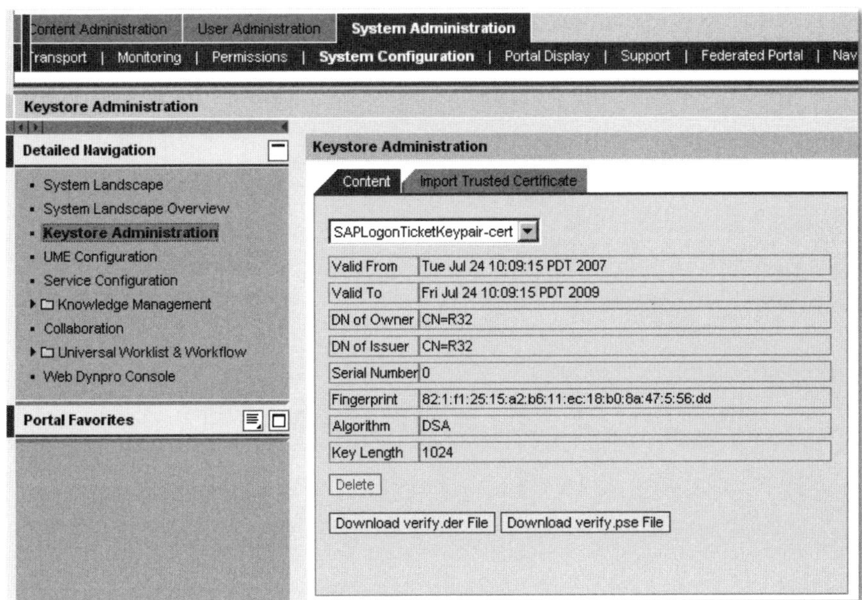

Figure 9.2 Enterprise Portal – Keystore Administration

4. Click the DOWNLOAD VERIFY.DER FILE button. The *verify.der* file contains the portal certificate that you'll import to your SAP NetWeaver Business Warehouse system with the trust manager.

5. Save the file to your local system and unzip it. If necessary, assign the ZIP file extension to the downloaded file and extract the verify.der file from the archive file.
6. Log on to your SAP NetWeaver Business Warehouse system and start Transaction STRUSTSSO2 (see Figure 9.3).

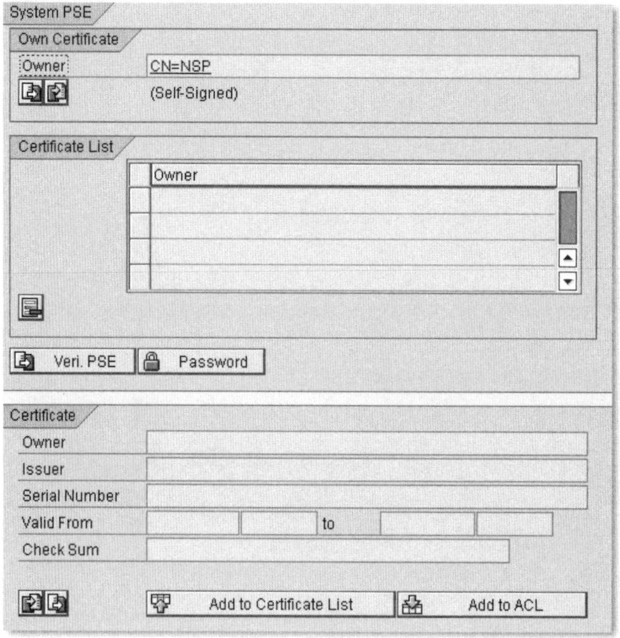

Figure 9.3 Trust Manager

7. Open the *System PSE* folder.
8. Click the IMPORT CERTIFICATE icon in the bottom-left corner (see Figure 9.4).

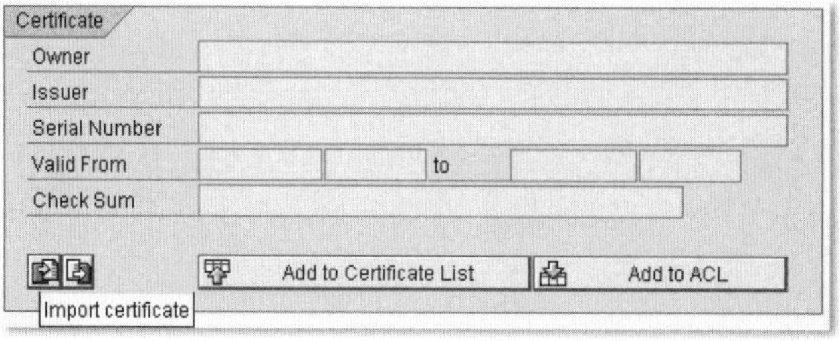

Figure 9.4 Import Certificate

9. When you click the IMPORT CERTIFICATE icon, a new screen will pop up and ask for the path and format of the certificate file (see Figure 9.5). Enter the full path to the portal certificate and select BINARY under FILE FORMAT.

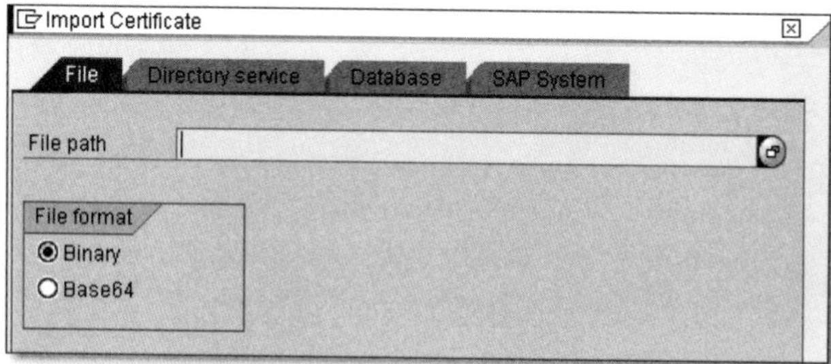

Figure 9.5 File Path and Format for Portal Certificate

10. Click the ADD TO CERTIFICATE LIST button (Figure 9.3) to add the portal certificate to the SAP NetWeaver Business Warehouse system.
11. Then click the ADD TO ACL button, and in the pop-up (see Figure 9.6) enter the system ID from your portal and enter "000" for the client field. Then click OK.

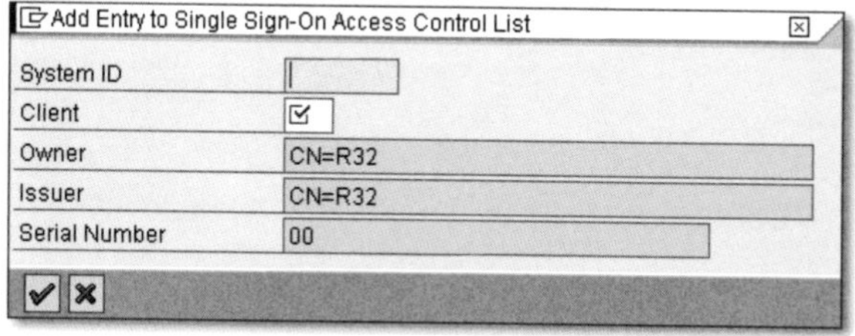

Figure 9.6 Add Entry to Access Control List

You've now exchanged the portal certificate with your SAP system and established trust between these two systems.

Importing the SAP BusinessObjects iView Template

SAP BusinessObjects Integration for SAP Solutions includes an iView template that allows you to create BI-related content from your SAP BusinessObjects Enterprise system in a very easy and simple way. Technically, the iView template generates a URL for you. You could achieve the same goal by using a standard URL iView template, but then you would have to configure each URL yourself.

The iView template is delivered as a Portal archive file as part of the installation of SAP BusinessObjects Integration for SAP solutions. The default path is *\Program Files\Business Objects\BusinessObjects Enterprise 12.0\Web Content\Enterprise12\SAP\iViews\import\ep*, and the filename is *com.BusinessObjects.pct.masteriview.part*.

1. Log on to your SAP NetWeaver Portal system. You need to use a portal user that is part of the system administrator role of your portal.
2. Follow the menu path SYSTEM ADMINISTRATION • SUPPORT (see Figure 9.7).

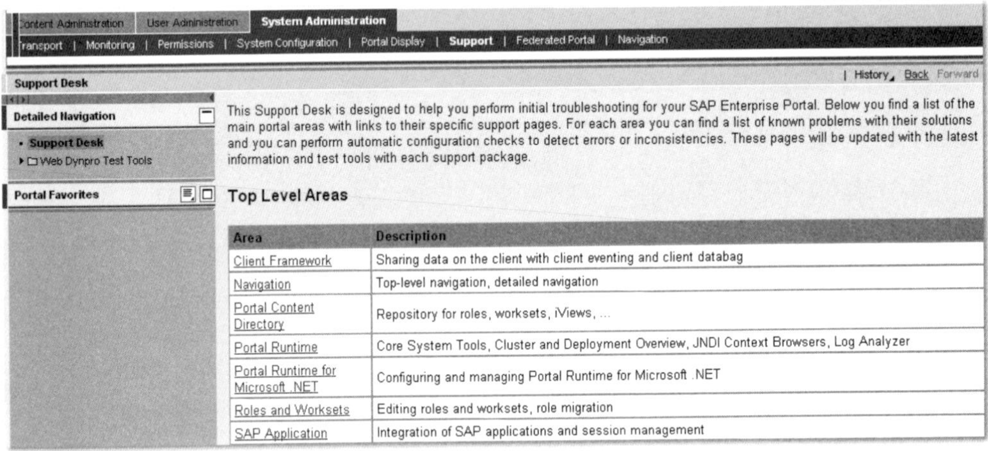

Figure 9.7 Enterprise Portal – Support

3. Select PORTAL RUNTIME from the TOP LEVEL AREAS list to navigate to the next screen (see Figure 9.8).

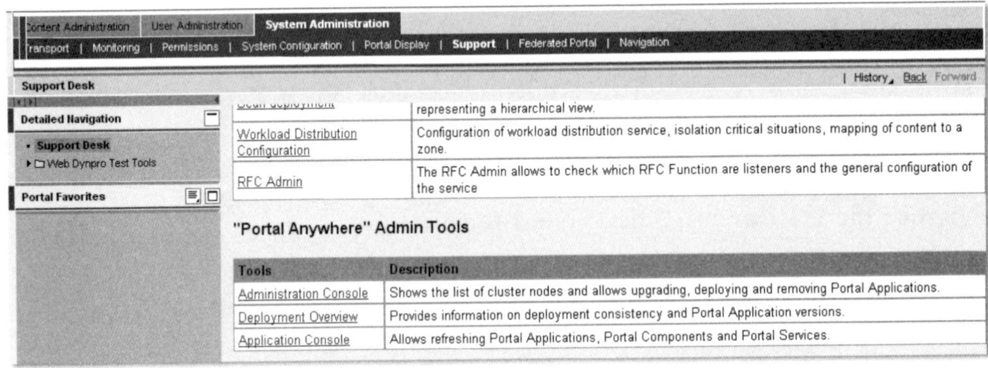

Figure 9.8 Enterprise Portal – Portal Runtime

4. Click ADMINISTRATION CONSOLE under "PORTAL ANYWHERE" ADMIN TOOLS, and you'll be shown the next screen (see Figure 9.9).

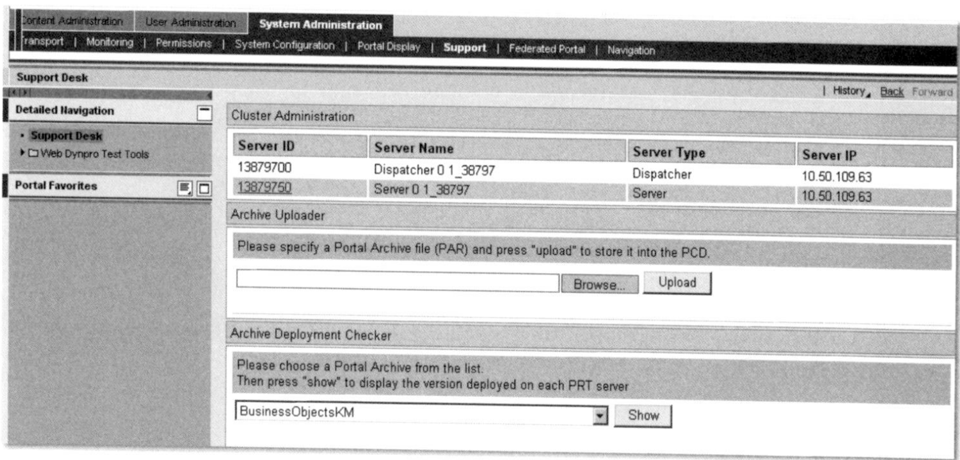

Figure 9.9 Enterprise Portal – Admin Tools

5. Click on the BROWSE button in the ARCHIVE UPLOADER area and select the SAP BusinessObjects iView template portal archive file. You can find the file in the path *Program Files\BusinessObjects Enterprise 12.0\Web Content\Enterprise 12\sap\iviews\import\ep* in case you selected the default installation path.
6. Click UPLOAD.

After you successfully uploaded the portal archive file, the iView template from SAP BusinessObjects Integration for SAP Solutions is available to you, and you can create iView content based on your SAP BusinessObjects system.

Configuring the Portal System Landscape

The iView template you uploaded in the previous section uses values from each system assigned to your iViews. Each system can be configured and created in the Portal system landscape, and in addition to the standard properties, a system also has a set of properties dedicated to integration with your SAP BusinessObjects Enterprise system.

With the following steps we'll create a new system in the portal system landscape and configure those properties, but you can also and configure those properties for your existing systems in your portal landscape.

1. Log on to your SAP NetWeaver Portal system. You need to use a portal user that is part of the system administrator role of your portal.
2. Follow the menu path SYSTEM ADMINISTRATION • SYSTEM CONFIGURATION and select SYSTEM LANDSCAPE in the DETAILED NAVIGATION area (see Figure 9.10).

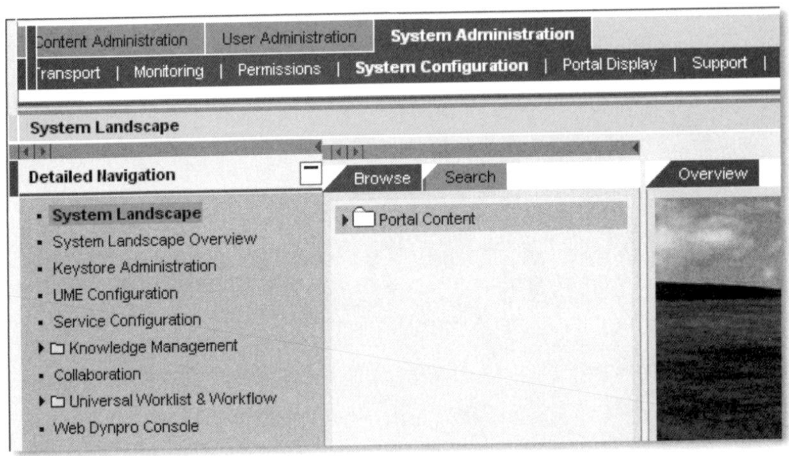

Figure 9.10 Enterprise Portal – System Configuration

3. Right-click PORTAL CONTENT and select the menu NEW • FOLDER to create a new folder in the portal content directory. The reason for creating a new folder is purely for the purpose of organization so that all of the objects you create will be in the same folder.
4. Enter a folder name, folder ID, and folder prefix in the next screen. In our example we enter "SAP BusinessObjects Enterprise" as the folder name and "SAP BusinessObjects_Enterprise" as the folder ID. We can leave the folder prefix empty for now. Click FINISH to close the wizard for creating a new folder.
5. Next navigate to the newly created folder in the Portal Content directory and right-click it.
6. Follow the menu path NEW • SYSTEM (FROM TEMPLATE), and a new screen will show up (see Figure 9.11).
7. Select the template that suits your SAP system best. In our example we'll use the option SAP SYSTEM USING DEDICATED APPLICATION SERVER.
8. Enter a system name, system ID, and system ID prefix (see Figure 9.12). We'll use "SAP_BI_DEMO" as the system name and "SAP_BI_DEMO" as the system ID, and like before, we'll leave the system ID prefix empty for now.

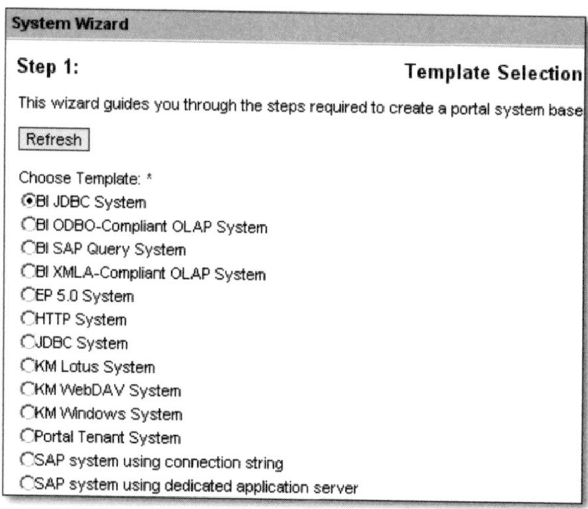

Figure 9.11 System Wizard – Step 1

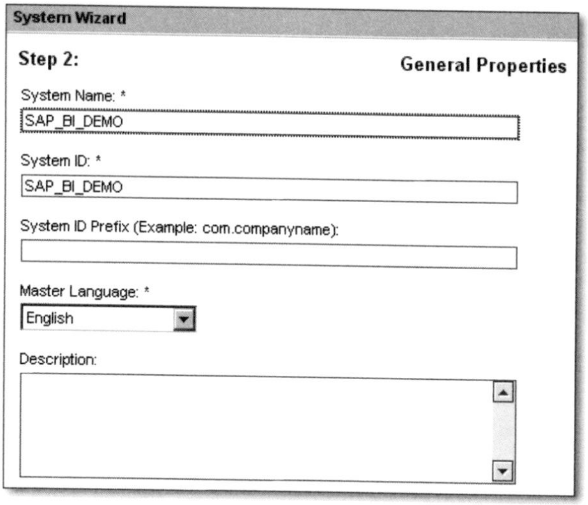

System Wizard

Step 2: General Properties

System Name: *
SAP_BI_DEMO

System ID: *
SAP_BI_DEMO

System ID Prefix (Example: com.companyname):

Master Language: *
English

Description:

Figure 9.12 System Wizard – Step 2

9. Click NEXT to move to the next screen.
10. Click FINISH and select OPEN THE OBJECT FOR EDITING when the wizard closes. You'll be presented a new screen (see Figure 9.13).

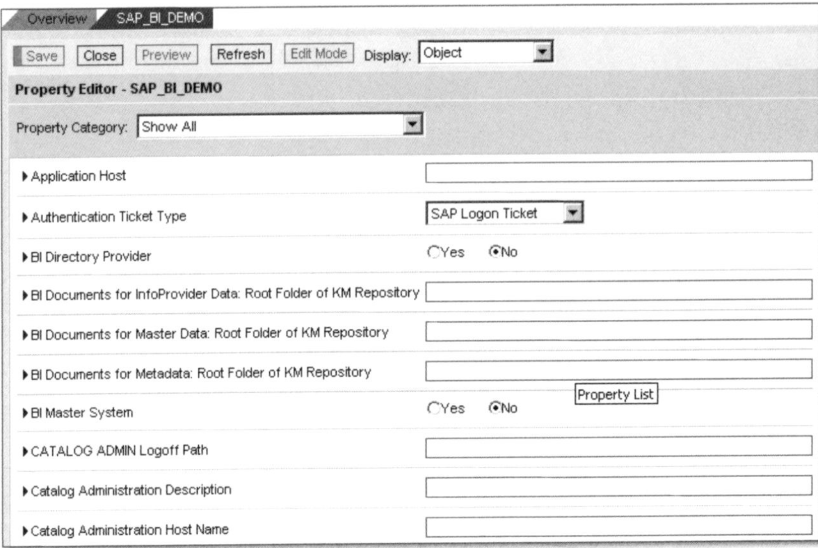

Figure 9.13 System Properties

11. In the Property Category field select Crystal Enterprise Server, and the next screen will come up (see Figure 9.14).

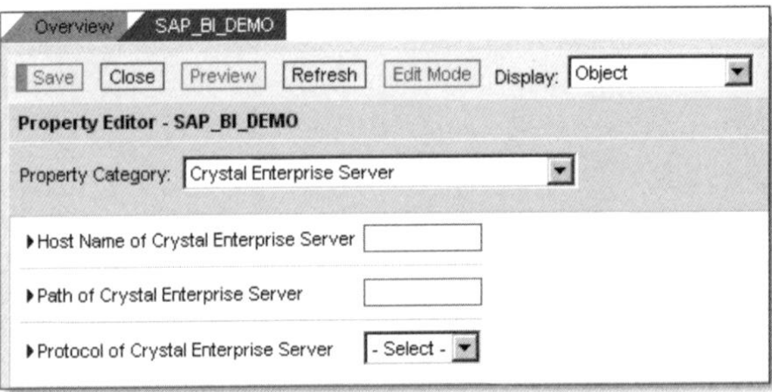

Figure 9.14 Crystal Enterprise Server Properties

12. Enter the full qualified name of your application server from your SAP BusinessObjects Enterprise system, including the port, in the Host Name of Crystal Enterprise Server field. In our example this is "VMWSAP12.WDF. SAP.CORP:8080".
13. Enter "/SAP" in the Path of Crystal Enterprise Server field. This is the default deployment path on the application server for the SAP-specific viewing applications.

14. Select "http" in the Protocol of Crystal Enterprise Server field, unless you configured https.

Property Category – Crystal Enterprise Server

The name "Crystal Enterprise Server" for the property category still uses the name of the predecessor product from SAP BusinessObjects Enterprise but works perfectly with SAP BusinessObjects Enterprise.

15. Select "User Management" in the Property Category field (see Figure 9.15).

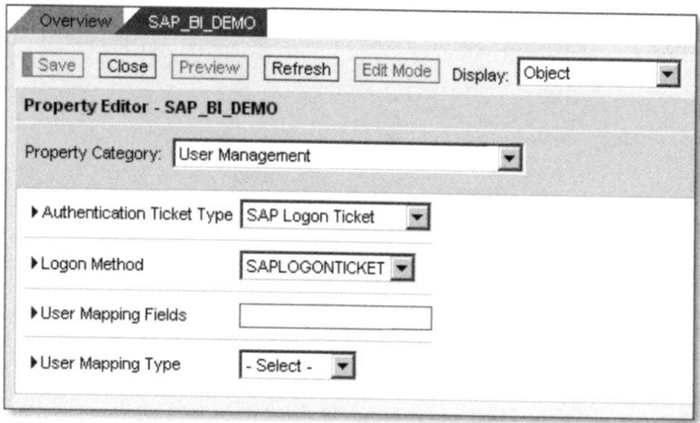

Figure 9.15 User Management

16. Select the value SAPLOGONTICKET in the Logon Method field .
17. In the Authentication Ticket Type field select "SAP Logon Ticket".
18. In the next step, select "Connector" in the Property Category field. The screen will update and show the details for the selected property category.
19. Configure the values for application host, gateway host, gateway service, logical system name, SAP client, SAP system ID (SID), and SAP system number according to your SAP system, and save your changes.
20. Select System Aliases in the Display field (see Figure 9.16).
21. Enter an alias name for your new system. In our example we'll use "SAP_BI".
22. Click the Add button to add the new alias to the list of available aliases.
23. Save your changes and close the properties of your new system.

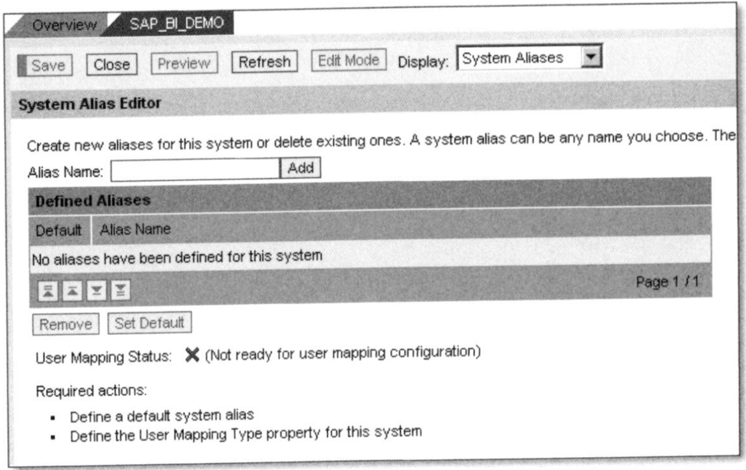

Figure 9.16 System Alias

You have now created a new system in the portal system landscape with the necessary properties for your SAP BusinessObjects Enterprise system. The advantage of this configuration is that you can use the system alias for all of your iViews showing SAP BusinessObjects Enterprise-related content and all of them will read the configuration details from the system definition, instead of entering those details for each iView.

9.1.3 SAP BusinessObjects Enterprise – Configuration Steps

Configuring the Default System for the SAP Authentication

The default system as part of the SAP authentication allows you to configure one SAP system from the list of configured entitled SAP systems in the Central Management Console to set up as the default system. The default system is used as the fallback system when the authentication process does not provide the system details. For example, you could log on to the Universe Designer using the SAP authentication without specifying your username in the complete syntax (SAP System ID ~ SAP Client/Username). In such a situation the SAP BusinessObjects Enterprise system will try to authenticate the user against the configured default system.

In addition to the technical prerequisites mentioned in Section 9.1.1, Technical Prerequisites, you should also ensure that DEFAULT SYSTEM is selected in the OPTIONS tab of the SAP authentication (see also Section 2.4.1, Configuration of

SAP Authentication). The default system is used to validate a logon token when no SAP system is explicitly specified. So in cases where your iView does not specify which configured SAP entitlement system (configured as part of the SAP authentication of your SAP BusinessObjects Enterprise system) should be used, the token will be validated against the default system.

Configuring InfoView for Single Sign-On

If you want to create an iView for integrating InfoView directly into your portal, you need to ensure that InfoView is configured for Single Sign-On.

For the Java version of InfoView (Windows environment) you need to edit the file *web.xml*, which is located (assuming Tomcat is your application server) in the directory *\Program Files\Business Objects\Tomcat55\webapps\InfoViewApp\WEB-INF* for the actual deployment. In addition, you can make the change to the file in the folder *<INSTALLDIR>\BusinessObjects Enterprise12.0\warfiles\WebApps\InfoViewApp\WEB-INF*. The files in the second location are used when you redeploy the web applications with a tool like wdeploy.

For the .Net version of InfoView you need to edit the file *web.config*, which is located in the directory *\Program Files\Business Objects\BusinessObjects Enterprise 12.0\Web Content\InfoViewApp\InfoViewApp*.

You need to change the parameter values according to Table 9.1.

Parameter Name	Configuration Value
authentication.default	secSAPR3
siteminder.enabled	False
sso.enabled	True

Table 9.1 Configuration Parameters for InfoView

Configuring OpenDocument for Single Sign-On

In addition to making the described changes to the files for InfoView, you should also make those changes to the deployment of the OpenDocument application.

For the Java version of OpenDocument (Windows environment) you need to edit the file *web.xml*, which is located (assuming Tomcat is your application server) in the directory *\Program Files\Business Objects\Tomcat55\webapps\OpenDocument\WEB-INF*. In addition, you can make the change to the file in the folder *<INSTALLDIR>\BusinessObjects Enterprise12.0\warfiles\WebApps\OpenDocument\WEB-INF*. The files in the second location are used when you redeploy the web applications with a tool like wdeploy.

For the .Net version of OpenDocument you need to edit the file *web.config*, which is located in the directory *\Program Files\Business Objects\BusinessObjects Enterprise 12.0\Web Content\InfoViewApp\OpenDocument*. You need to change the parameter values according to Table 9.2.

Parameter Name	Configuration Value
opendoc.authentication.default	secSAPR3
opendoc.siteminder.enabled	False
opendoc.sso.enabled	True

Table 9.2 Configuration Parameters for OpenDocument

9.1.4 Create Your First iView

In this section we'll create our first iView showing content from our SAP BusinessObjects Enterprise system.

1. Log on to your SAP NetWeaver Portal and follow the menu path Content Administration • Portal Content.
2. Open the folder Portal Content and navigate to the folder you created in the previous section (in our example "SAP BusinessObjects Enterprise").
3. Right-click the folder and select the New iView tab (see Figure 9.17).

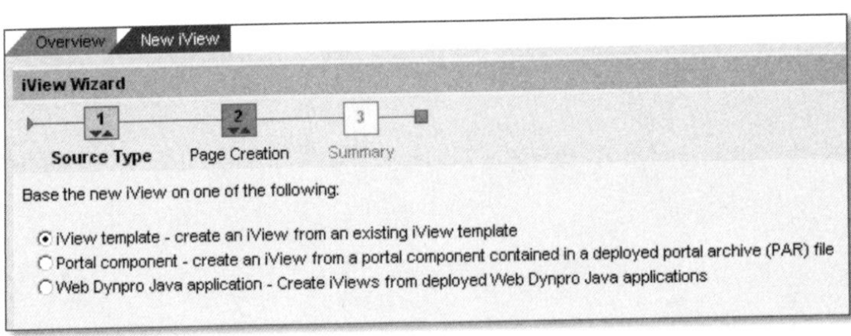

Figure 9.17 iView Wizard

4. Select iVIEW TEMPLATE and go to the next screen (see Figure 9.18, which is the default screen).

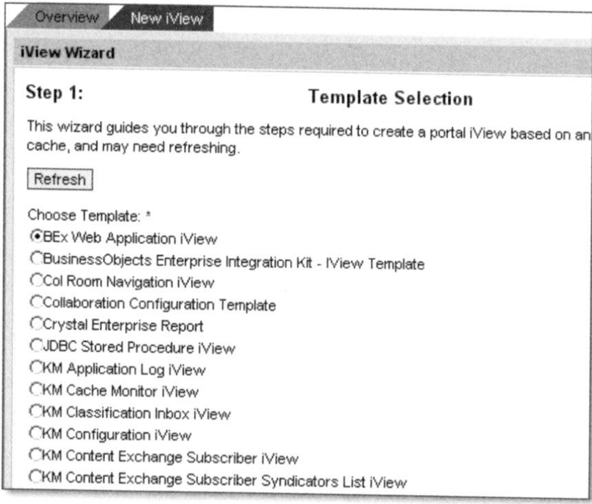

Figure 9.18 iView Templates

5. Select BUSINESSOBJECTS ENTERPRISE INTEGRATION KIT – iVIEW TEMPLATE and click NEXT.
6. Enter an iView name, iView ID, and iView ID prefix. We'll use "BusinessObjects Report 1" as the iView name and "BUSINESSOBJECTS_REPORT_1" as the iView ID, and we'll leave the iView ID prefix empty for now.
7. Click NEXT and you'll be led to step 3 of the wizard (see Figure 9.19).

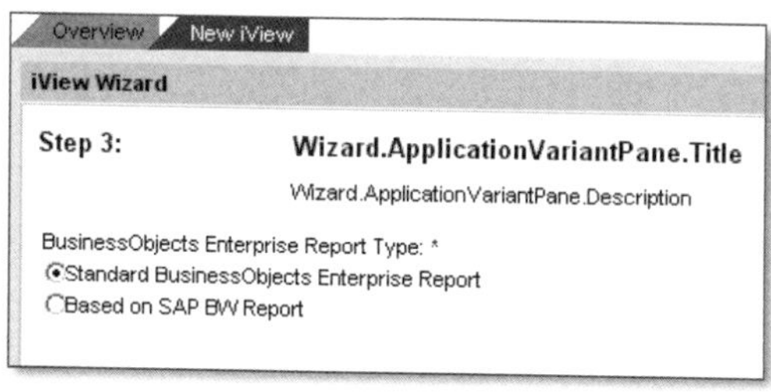

Figure 9.19 Selecting Report Type

In this screen you're asked to select between STANDARD BUSINESSOBJECTS ENTERPRISE REPORT and BASED ON SAP BW REPORT. If you select the STANDARD BUSINESSOBJECTS ENTERPRISE REPORT option, then you need to provide the ID of the report from your SAP BusinessObjects Enterprise system.

If you select the Based on SAP BW Report option, then you need to provide the technical name (which is a GUID) of the Crystal Reports object in SAP NetWeaver Business Warehouse. The option Based on SAP BW Report is only available for Crystal Reports as of now (Release XI 3.1).

For our example we'll select Standard BusinessObjects Enterprise Report and go to the next screen (see Figure 9.20).

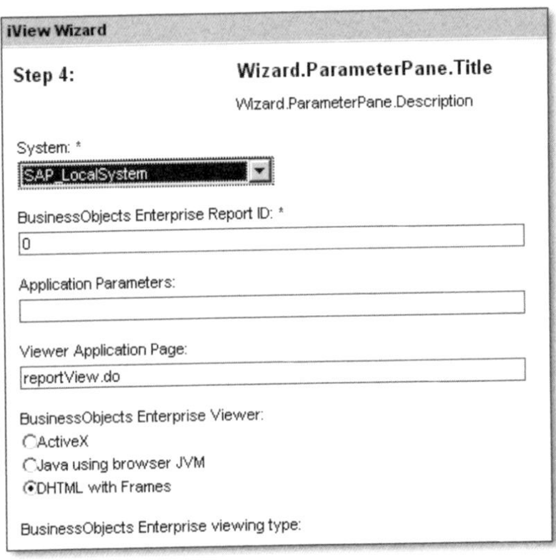

Figure 9.20 SAP BusinessObjects iView Properties

8. Now you need to select your system alias from the previous section from the list of available systems so that the iView will use your SAP BusinessObjects Enterprise system.
9. Enter the report ID of the report you want to show in the portal.
10. Enter the following in the Application Parameters field: "cms_name=<CMS>:<CMS_PORT>," where <CMS> is replaced with the name of your Central Management Server, and <CMS_PORT> is replaced with the port configured for the Central Management Server. In our example this is "cms_name=VMWSAP12:6400".
11. Enter the viewing application in the Viewer Application Page field. For Java deployment the default viewing application is *reportView.do*; for .NET environments the default viewing application is *iviews/report_view.aspx*.
12. Select a BusinessObjects Enterprise viewer and a viewing type.

13. Click NEXT and select OPEN FOR EDITING WHEN WIZARD COMPLETES. Then click the PREVIEW button for your iView.

You have created a new iView showing content from your SAP BusinessObjects Enterprise system. You can now use this iView and integrate it into your standard portal pages, portal worksets, and portal roles.

SAP BusinessObjects Enterprise Object ID

You can find the ID of each object in your SAP BusinessObjects Enterprise system by opening the properties either directly in InfoView or in the Central Management Console. Ensure that you're using the value of the CUID of your object because if you move the objects to a different deployment of SAP BusinessObjects Enterprise, the CUID remains the same, and the ID reference is not corrupted.

Additional Parameter for URL iViews

When you use a URL iView to integrate, for example, InfoView into the portal, or when you use OpenDocument for viewing content, you can add two additional URL parameters:

SAP_SYSID with the value for your SAP system ID (three-digit code) and SAP_CLIENT with the value for your client (three-digit code).

Example:

http://vmwsap12.wdf.sap.corp:8080/InfoViewApp?sap_sysid=CIM&sap_client=003.

By using these additional URL parameters, you can ensure that the authentication is done against the correct SAP system.

SAP BusinessObjects iView Template or URL iViews?

Technically, you can use the URL iView template in your portal to integrate the content from your SAP BusinessObjects Enterprise system, but the advantage of the SAP BusinessObjects iView template is that you can configure your server properties once and reuse them for all iViews. More importantly, you have a single location if you need to make modification. If you use the URL iView, you have to make those changes for each iView.

9.2 BI Content with Knowledge Management

In this section you'll learn how you can use the Knowledge Management technology from your SAP NetWeaver Portal to integrate your SAP BusinessObjects-based content into the SAP NetWeaver Portal and use features that are part of Knowledge Management

9.2.1 Technical Prerequisites

Similar to the integration of SAP BusinessObjects Enterprise content via iViews, the integration into the Knowledge Management component of your SAP NetWeaver Portal has a list of technical prerequisites.

- Your SAP NetWeaver Portal and the SAP NetWeaver Business Warehouse system need to be configured as trusted systems (see Section 9.1.2, SAP NetWeaver Portal – Configuration Steps).
- All involved systems (SAP NetWeaver Portal, SAP NetWeaver Business Warehouse, and SAP BusinessObjects Enterprise) need to be in the same domain; otherwise, Single Sign-On based on a token or ticket will fail.
- All involved URLs should always use the full qualified domain names of the involved systems.
- SAP authentication is configured on your SAP BusinessObjects Enterprise system (see Section 2.4.1, Configuration of SAP Authentication), and SAP roles and users have been imported for your SAP NetWeaver BusinessWarehouse system.
- Your SAP NetWeaver BusinessWarehouse system should accept Single Sign-On logon tickets (see Section 2.3.4, Single Sign-On).
- The Web services need to be deployed for your SAP BusinessObjects Enterprise system on your application server.

SAP J2EE and SAP BusinessObjects Web Services

At this time the XI 3.1 release of SAP BusinessObjects Enterprise does not support Web service deployment on SAP J2EE as the application server. This might change in a future service pack or a future release, so you should look at the latest list of supported platforms at *http://service.sap.com.bosap-support*.

9.2.2 SAP NetWeaver Portal – Configuration Steps

The SAP BusinessObjects Integration for SAP Solutions delivers Knowledge Management integration as a portal archive file, which you need to upload to your portal server.

1. Log on to your SAP NetWeaver Portal system. You need to use a portal user that is part of the system administrator role of your portal.
2. Follow the menu path SYSTEM ADMINISTRATION • SUPPORT.
3. Select PORTAL RUNTIME from the list of top level areas.
4. Click ADMINISTRATION CONSOLE in the list "PORTAL ANYWHERE" ADMIN TOOLS.
5. Click the BROWSE button in the Archive Uploader and select the SAP BusinessObjects KM portal archive file. In a default installation you'll find the portal archive file in the path *\Program Files\Business Objects\BusinessObjects Enterprise 12.0\java\applications* and the file name is *BusinessObjectsKM.par.*
6. Click UPLOAD.

After you uploaded the portal archive file, you can proceed with the following steps to verify the installation.

1. Log on to your SAP NetWeaver Portal.
2. Follow the menu path SYSTEM ADMINISTRATION • SYSTEM CONFIGURATION (see Figure 9.21).

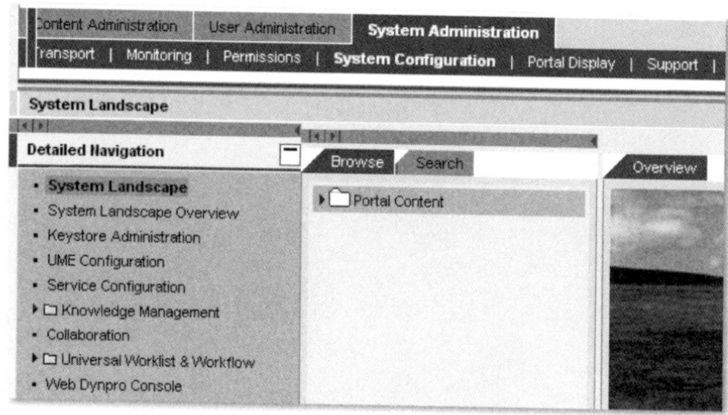

Figure 9.21 Enterprise Portal System Configuration

3. Click KNOWLEDGE MANAGEMENT in the DETAILED NAVIGATION area.
4. Select CONTENT MANAGEMENT from the drop-down menu, and a new screen will open (see Figure 9.22).
5. Select REPOSITORY MANAGERS, and in the following screen, select BUSINESS OBJECTS REPOSITORY.

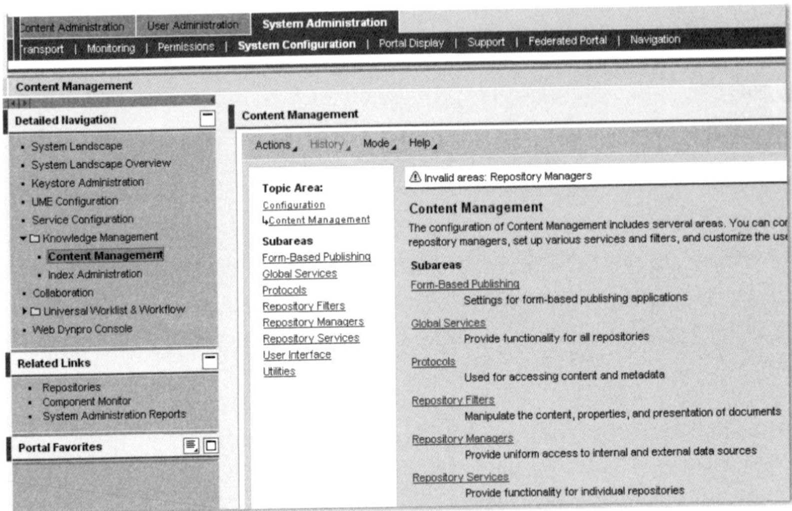

Figure 9.22 Enterprise Portal – Content Management

6. Click NEW. You should now see a definition similar to Figure 9.23. We'll use this template in the next section to configure the repository manager to connect to your SAP BusinessObjects Enterprise system.

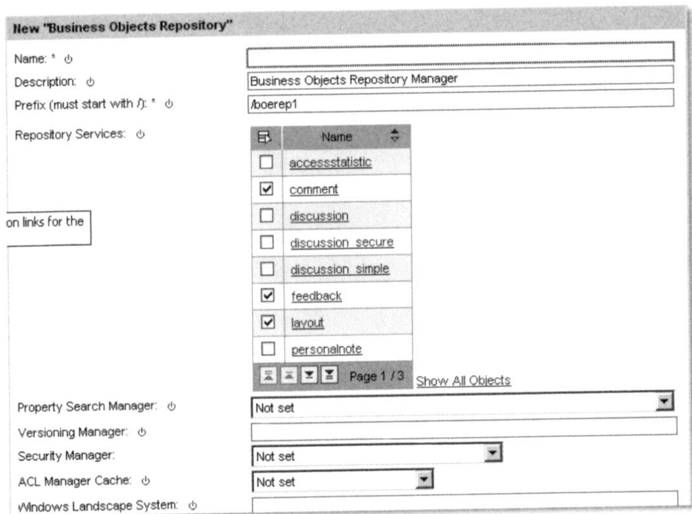

Figure 9.23 Business Objects Repository

9.2.3 SAP BusinessObjects Enterprise – Configuration Steps

In addition to the previously listed technical prerequisites, you need to configure the OpenDocument application for integration with the repository manager.

For the Java version of OpenDocument (Windows environment) you need to edit the file *web.xml*, which is located (assuming Tomcat is used as the application server) in the directory *\Program Files\Business Objects\Tomcat55\webapps\OpenDocument\WEB-INF*. You can also make the change to the file in the folder *<INSTALLDIR>\BusinessObjects Enterprise12.0\warfiles\WebApps\OpenDocument\WEB-INF*. The files in the second location are used when you redeploy the web applications with a tool like wdeploy.

For the .Net version of OpenDocument you need to edit the file *web.config*, which is located in the directory *\Program Files\Business Objects\BusinessObjects Enterprise 12.0\Web Content\InfoViewApp\OpenDocument*. You need to change the parameter values according to Table 9.3.

Parameter Name	Configuration Value
opendoc.authentication.default	secSAPR3
opendoc.siteminder.enabled	False
opendoc.sso.enabled	True

Table 9.3 Configuration Parameters for OpenDocument

9.2.4 Setting Up Your Repository

In this section we'll use the template that you imported via the portal archive file and set up a repository manager that will use your SAP BusinessObjects Enterprise system.

1. Log on to your SAP NetWeaver Portal system.
2. Follow the menu path System Administration • System configuration.
3. Click Knowledge Management in the Detailed Navigation area.
4. Select Content Management.
5. Select Repository Managers.
6. Select Business Objects Repository.

7. Click NEW to start creating a new entry. The system will create a new repository manager entry with several placeholders for you to fill in (see Figure 9.24).

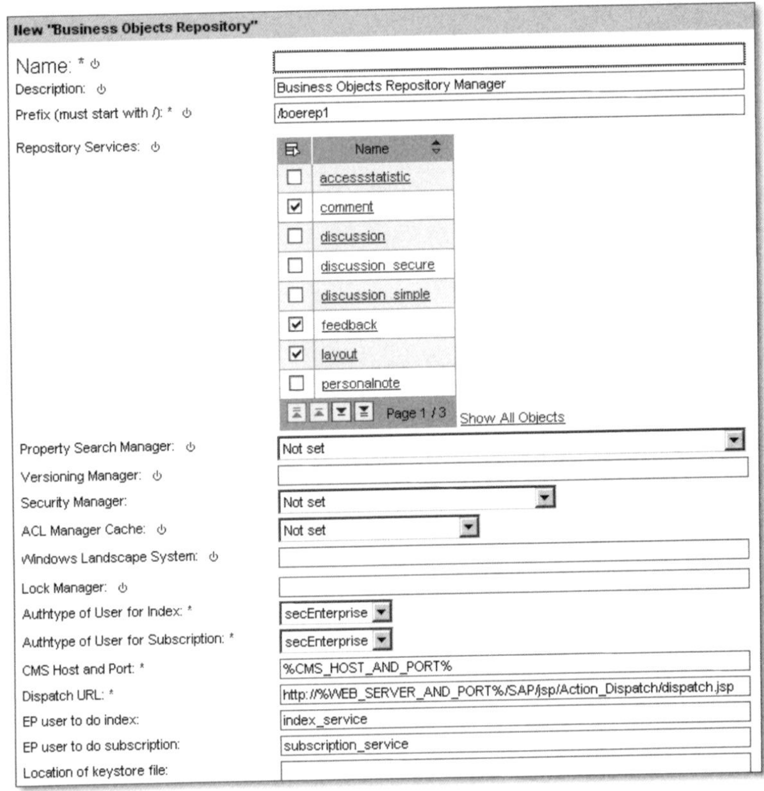

Figure 9.24 Business Objects Repository Template

8. Enter a name, description, and prefix for your repository. In our example we'll use "VMWSAP12" as the name, "BusinessObjects Enterprise" as the description, and "/VMWSAP12" as the prefix. The prefix is used in the Knowledge Management component when multiple repositories are shown in a browser to identify your repository.
9. Next select REPOSITORY SERVICES. Select at least the repository service layout, but if you're not sure which repository services you want to use, you can select them all.
10. Enter the other values for the existing placeholders according to Table 9.4.

Setting	Value
Property Search Manager	Ensure that the value is set to "Not Set". There have been cases where the property search manager prevents the Business Objects Repository manager from working properly.
CMS Host and Port	The full qualified name of your Central Management Server and the port number. Example: vmwsap12.wdf.sap.corp:6400
Dispatch URL	Replace the placeholder %WEB_SERVER_AND_PORT% with the value of your application server and port number. Example: vmwsap12.wdf.sap.corp:8080
OpenDoc URL	Replace the placeholder %WEB_SERVER_AND_PORT% with the value of your application server and port number. Example: vmwsap12.wdf.sap.corp:8080
SAP Client	The client number of your SAP system. Example: 003
SAP System ID	The system ID of your SAP system. Example: CIM
Log Off URL	Replace the placeholder %WEB_SERVER_AND_PORT% with the value of your application server and port number. Example: vmwsap12.wdf.sap.corp:8080
Web Service URL	Replace the placeholder %WEB_SERVER_AND_PORT% with the value of your application server and port number. Example: vmwsap12.wdf.sap.corp:8080
Starting Folder ID	Here you can enter the ID for the folder in your SAP BusinessObjects Enterprise system that should be used as the root folder for your repository. You can receive the ID via the properties of the folders in the Central Management Console.

Table 9.4 Repository Manager Properties

11. Save your changes, and your repository should now appear in the list of available repositories.
12. For the SAP BusinessObjects Enterprise-specific commands to be available for your repository, you need to configure a layout set for your repository.
13. Follow the menu path CONTENT ADMINISTRATION • KM CONTENT and select KM CONTENT in the DETAILED NAVIGATION area (see Figure 9.25).

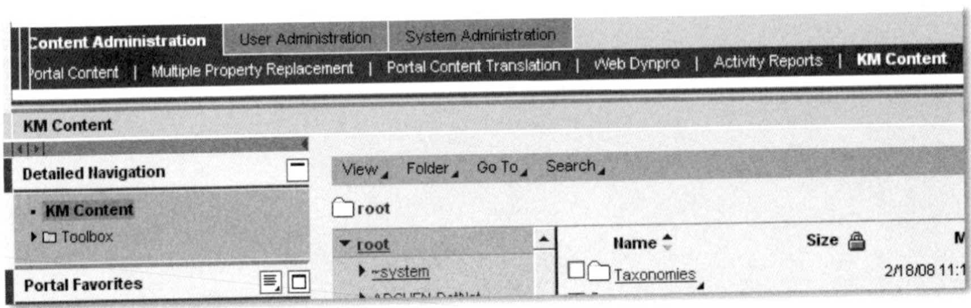

Figure 9.25 Knowledge Management

14. You should, based on the prefix defined (in our example /VMWSAP12), now be able to see your repository in the list in the middle of the screen (see Figure 9.26).
15. Click the little triangle in the bottom-right corner of your repository folder.

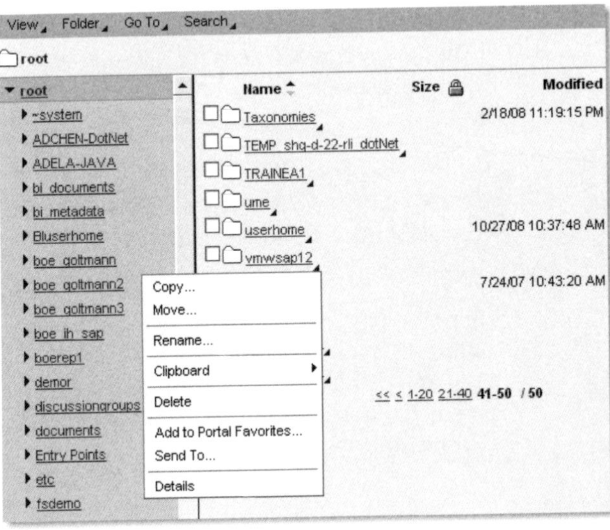

Figure 9.26 Business Objects Repository Folder

16. Select DETAILS, and another screen will be presented (see Figure 9.27).

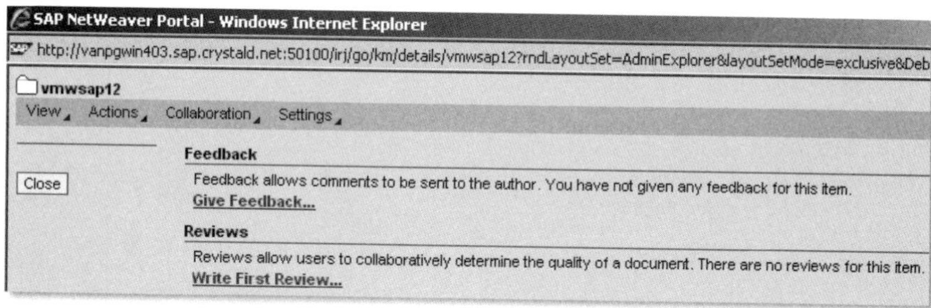

Figure 9.27 Details for the Repository

17. Follow the menu path SETTINGS • PRESENTATION, and in the new screen you can determine how the folder will be presented for all users and personalize its layout (see Figure 9.28). Click on the SELECT PROFILE button on the SETTINGS FOR ALL USERS tab.

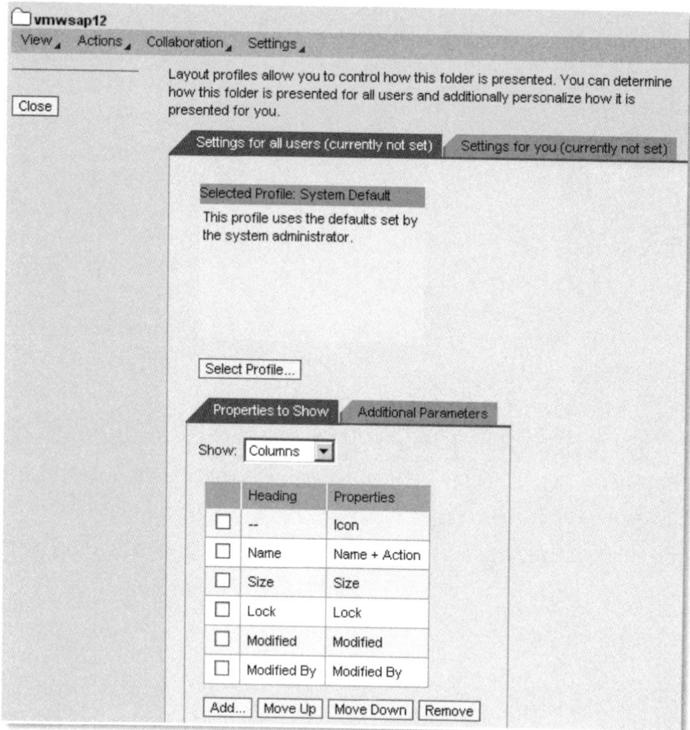

Figure 9.28 Presentation Settings

18. In the next screen (Figure 9.29) you'll be presented with different profile settings. Select LAYOUT SET and select the value "BOBJELayout" from the drop-down list. This layout set has been imported as part of the KM portal archive file that you imported previously.

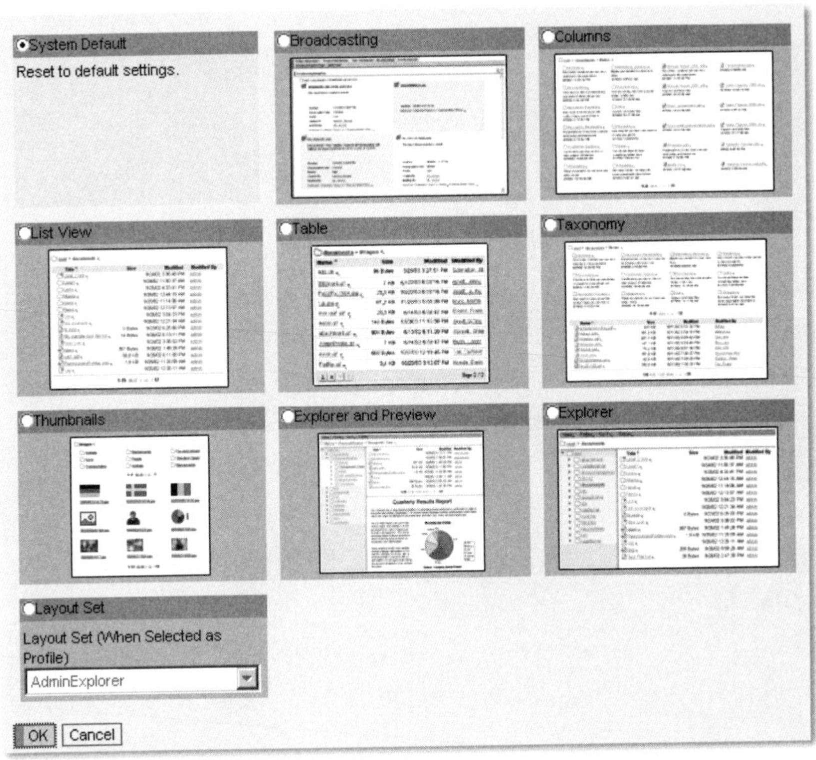

Figure 9.29 Profile Settings

19. Click OK to move to the next screen (see Figure 9.30).
20. Select APPLY SETTINGS TO ALL SUBFOLDERS to ensure that the layout is applied to all folders in the repository. You can also select the USE SETTINGS FOR ALL IVIEWS checkbox to ensure that any iView based on the repository will use the layout.
21. Click SAVE and close the screen.

You have now configured your repository to offer SAP BusinessObjects Enterprise specific commands such as View History, View Latest Instance, and InfoView.

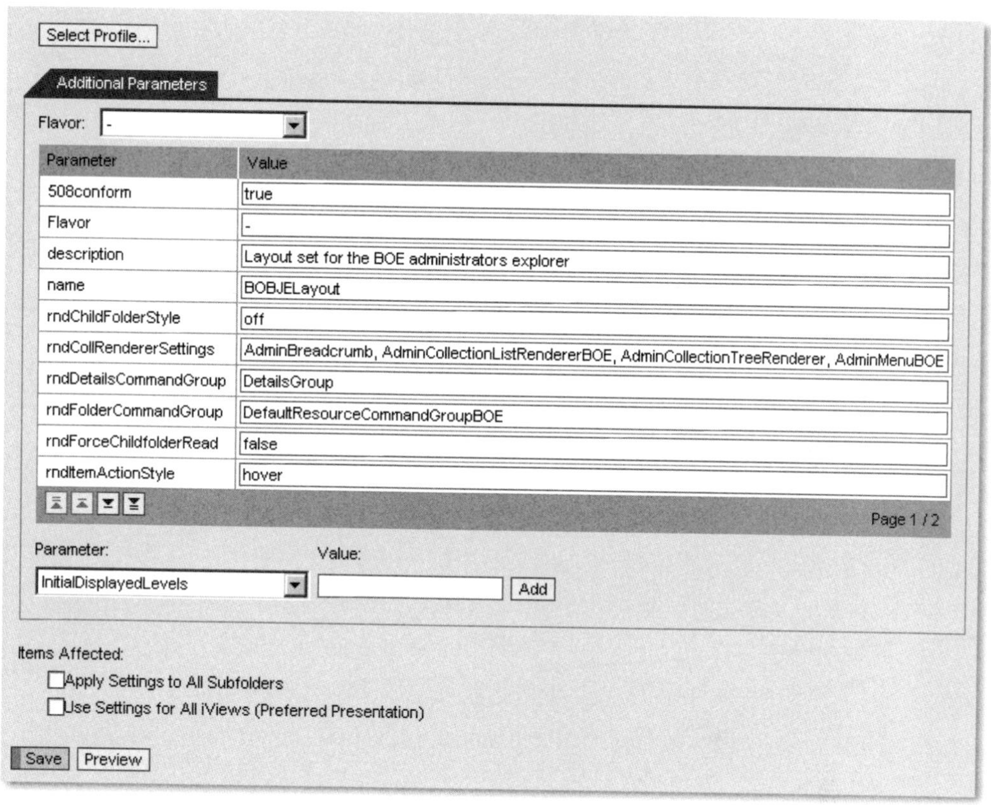

Figure 9.30 Applying Profile Settings

9.2.5 Using the Repository Manager

This section shows some of the common functions of the newly created repository manager.

1. Follow the menu path Content Administration • KM Content and select KM Content in the Detailed Navigation area.
2. Your repository should appear in the list based on the configured prefix.
3. Select the repository you previously configured from the list, and you'll see another screen (see Figure 9.31).
4. The configured starting folder ID (a property you can set as part of the configuration) is used here, and any folder below is shown on the right-hand side. You also can see the SAP BusinessObjects-specific menus.

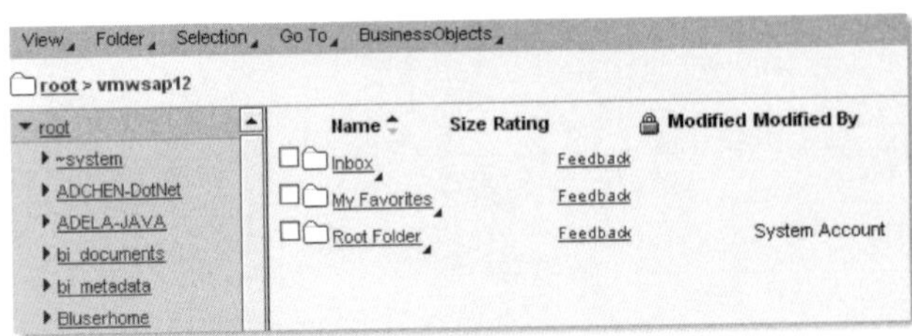

Figure 9.31 KM Repository View

5. Click VIEW in the menu bar to switch between a view by folders or by category.
6. The menu item FOLDER allows you to create new documents (see Figure 9.32).

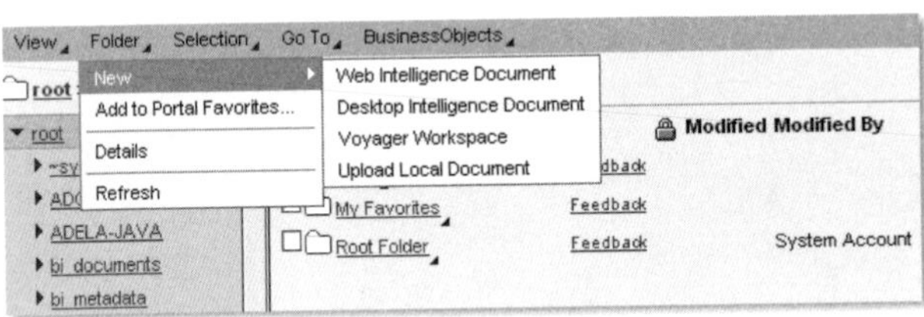

Figure 9.32 Menu "Folder"

7. Click SELECTION in the menu bar to copy, move, or delete objects in your repository.
8. Click GO TO to directly navigate to InfoView (see Figure 9.33).

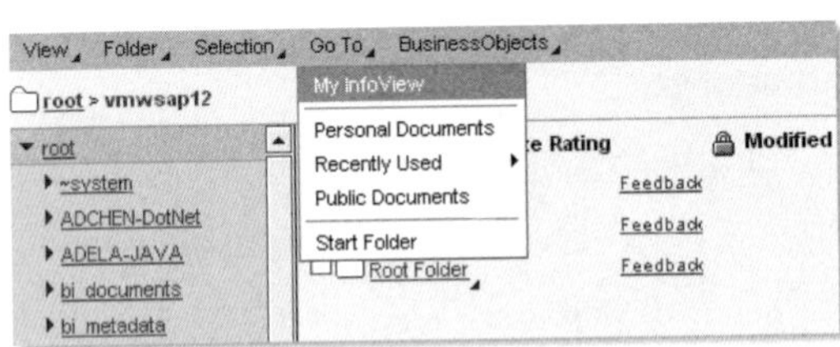

Figure 9.33 Menu "Go To"

9. The menu item BUSINESSOBJECTS allows you to switch to the view by category, navigate to InfoView, and log off from the repository.
10. Navigate down to the folder for the role from your SAP NetWeaver Business Warehouse system that you used to publish the Crystal Reports content (Figure 9.34). Each object in the repository offers a context menu (bottom-right triangle symbol). Open the context menu of the Crystal Reports object.

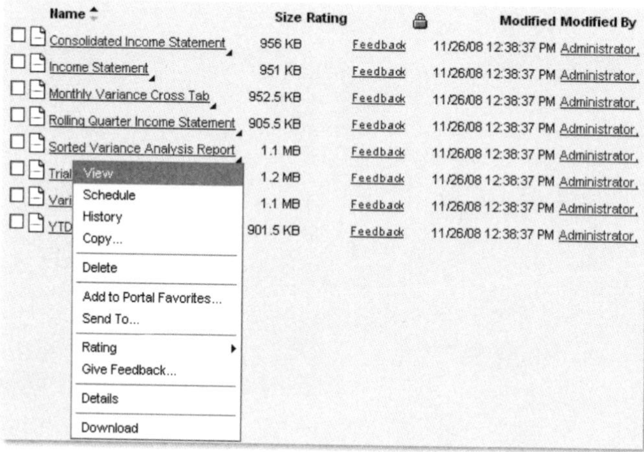

Figure 9.34 Context Menu

As you can see, the context menu offers SAP BusinessObjects-specific menu items such as VIEW, SCHEDULE, and HISTORY. It offers Knowledge Management-specific menu items such as RATING and DETAILS.

11. Select the DETAILS, and you'll be presented with a new screen (see Figure 9.35).

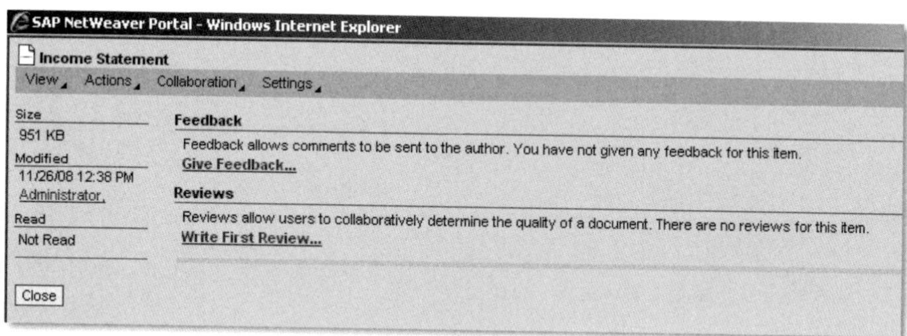

Figure 9.35 Details

12. In the details you can provide feedback, provide reviews, and rank the document. These elements are part of the Knowledge Management component.

In this chapter you learned how you can integrate the content from your SAP BusinessObjects system into your SAP NetWeaver Portal system. You learned how to integrate the content via iViews and how to configure the integration with the Knowledge Management component.

In this chapter you will learn some of the steps you can use to troubleshoot some common scenarios of your deployment and you can follow these steps to collect more details in case you are facing issues with the software.

10 Troubleshooting and Tips

In the following sections I'll present information and steps you can use to troubleshoot issues you might face and some tips on particular topics that will help improve your solutions. Some of the information provided here might require you to look for further details in the SAP documentation because it is beyond the scope of this book.

Registry Files on Unix Platforms

To set up the traces on a Unix platform you can follow Note 1235111, which explains where and how to create the *.registry* file on your Unix platform.

The explanation in the note is based on the SAP BusinessObjects Voyager/SAP BusinessObjects Web Intelligence connectivity, but you can follow the steps for other registry entries as well.

10.1 Data Connectivity

In this section we'll focus on how you can verify the connectivity you're using in the SAP BusinessObjects client tools and which tools are available to you for troubleshooting.

10.1.1 Steps to Validate the Configuration

Before we go into the details of tracing the connectivity and verifying the derived metadata from your underlying SAP system, the following is a list of steps you can take to verify your configuration:

- Have all required ABAP transports been imported correctly to your SAP system? You can use Transaction STMS to verify the transports.

- Does the user have enough authorizations to perform the required task? You can use Transaction ST01 to create an authorization trace that will show you any missing authorizations.
- For InfoSet connectivity you should verify with the help of Transactions SQ01, SQ02, and SQ03 that the InfoSet is assigned to the global or local environment and that the InfoSet is assigned to a user group.
- For SAP NetWeaver Business Warehouse connectivity you should verify if the underlying BW query has been marked for external access in the SAP Business Explorer (BEx) Query Designer by setting the property Allow external access.

10.1.2 Tracing

For tracing the data connectivity you can use the registry (on a Windows environment). All of the Crystal Reports connectivity can be found in the registry key *HKEY_LOCAL_MACHINE\SOFTWARE\Business Objects\Suite 12.0\SAP*, listed based on the name of the connectivity (see Figure 10.1).

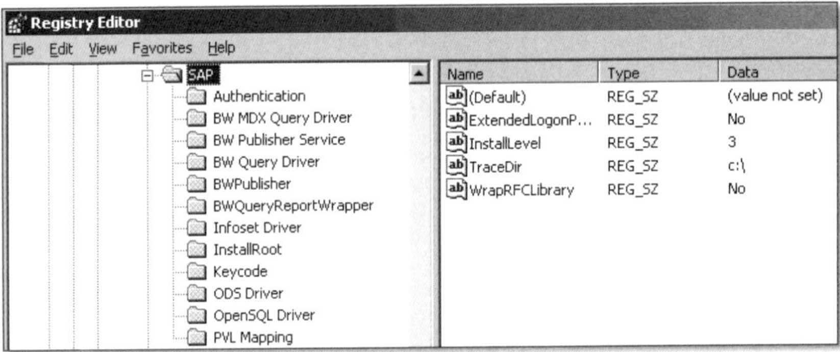

Figure 10.1 Registry Settings

Each of Crystal Reports connectivity has a registry key `Trace`, which is a simple Yes or No value. The location of the trace files can be configured by the registry key called `TraceDir` in the registry folder *HKEY_LOCAL_MACHINE\SOFTWARE\Business Objects\Suite 12.0\SAP*, which points to the folder for the logfiles.

For SAP BusinessObjects Web Intelligence you need to set the registry keys and values according to Table 10.1.

Registry Branch	Registry Key	Value
HKEY_LOCAL_MACHINE\SOFTWARE\Business Objects\Suite 12.0\MDA\Log\Modules\SAP-MODULE	Verbosity	A decimal value from 0 (no tracing) to 10 (most details)
HKEY_LOCAL_MACHINE\SOFTWARE\Business Objects\Suite 12.0\MDA\Log\Modules\SAP-MODULE	MDX Query Log	Path to the MDX logfile
HKEY_LOCAL_MACHINE\SOFTWARE\Business Objects\Suite 12.0\MDA\Log	LogFile	Path to the general logfile Example: *C:\SAP_SOFA.log*

Table 10.1 Registry Settings for SAP BusinessObjects Web Intelligence

Some of these registry branches, keys, and values are not part of the installation routine, so you have to create them manually.

The resulting traces provide you with a high level of detail, and in the first step you want to look at those traces for common error messages that might not have occurred in the actual software. You can go through those traces and see every step that was performed using the software.

These traces also contain information about the metadata that has been retrieved, the statement that was used for data retrieval, and in some cases the actual data that has been retrieved.

In addition to the traces on the SAP BusinessObjects side, there is a set of tools you can use on your SAP system:

- You can use Transaction ST01 to create several kinds of traces. Most importantly, you can use Transaction ST01 to create authorization traces.
- You can use Transaction ST05 to create remote function call (RFC) and Structured Query Language (SQL) traces, which are especially helpful for the connectivity with the SAP ERP system.
- You can use Transactions RSTT and RSRTRACE to generate an OLAP trace, which can be repeated at any time.

10.1.3 Validating Metadata

You can validate the metadata that you retrieved in the client tools such as Crystal Reports, SAP BusinessObjects Web Intelligence, and Universe Designer by using a set of SAP tools:

- For the InfoSet connectivity you can use Transaction SQ02 to validate the metadata that you received with the actual InfoSet in your SAP system.
- For the Open SQL connectivity providing access to tables, views, and ABAP functions, you can use Transaction SE11 and Transaction SE37 to compare the metadata from your SAP system with the metadata in your SAP NetWeaver BusinessWarehouse system.
- For the BW connectivity you can use Transaction SE37 and call the BAPI functions manually to retrieve the metadata. You can then compare the result in Transaction SE37 with the metadata in Crystal Reports or the Universe Designer.

OLAP BAPI Function	Metadata Being Retrieved
BAPI_MDPROVIDER_GET_CATALOGS	List of cubes
BAPI_MDPROVIDER_GET_CUBES	List of queries
BAPI_MDPROVIDER_GET_DIMENSIONS	List of dimensions
BAPI_MDPROVIDER_GET_HIERARCHYS	List of hierarchies
BAPI_MDPROVIDER_GET_LEVELS	List of levels for hierarchies
BAPI_MDPROVIDER_GET_MEASURES	List of key figures
BAPI_MDPROVIDER_GET_PROPERTIES	List of display attributes

Table 10.2 OLAP BAPI Functions

The BAPI functions listed in Table 10.2 are the basis for the metadata retrieval in an SAP NetWeaver Business Warehouse scenario. You can use those functions in Transaction SE37 to retrieve the metadata directly from the SAP NetWeaver Business Warehouse system without any additional software. Most of these functions require input values such as the name of the cube or query that you want to use; those input values have to be provided as technical names.

Further information can be found in the ADDITIONAL DEVELOPMENT TECHNIQUES area of the SAP NetWeaver Business Warehouse documentation (*http://help.sap.com*).

10.1.4 Validating the Results

If you need to validate the actual data being retrieved, there is a set of tools that you can use.

- For the InfoSet connectivity for Crystal Reports you can easily create a query on top of your InfoSet using Transaction SQ01 and simulate the connectivity without any additional software being involved.
- For the connectivity with tables for Crystal Reports you can use the Quick-Viewer (Transaction SQVI) to create the linkage between the tables and see the actual result set. In addition, you can use Transaction ST05 to enable an RFC and SQL trace on your SAP system to see further details.
- If you're using connectivity with your SAP NetWeaver Business Warehouse system, you can use Transaction MDXTEST to validate the result set. The MDX (*Multidimensional Expressions*, a query language for OLAP databases) that is being sent from the client tools or from your SAP BusinessObjects Enterprise system is part of the trace files (see Section 10.3.2, Tracing).
- Other options to validate the data are to execute the underlying BW query with the SAP BEx toolset or to execute the query in Transaction RSRT.

10.2 Single Sign-On and Authentication

In this section we'll focus on steps and tools you can use to verify the steps of the user authentication in your landscape with SAP NetWeaver and SAP BusinessObjects Enterprise.

10.2.1 Steps to Validate the Configuration

The following is a list of steps to verify your configuration in regard to Single Sign-On and the SAP authentication.

- Ensure that the SAP authentication is enabled in the Central Management Console and verify that the SAP entitlement system for your SAP system is not disabled.
- Ensure that the SAP system is configured properly and that the necessary SAP roles have been imported to your SAP BusinessObjects system (see Section 2.4.1, Configuration of SAP Authentication).
- Ensure that the underlying SAP system can create and accept logon tickets (see Section 2.3.4, Single Sign-On).
- Ensure that all systems are in the same domain and all machine names are always fully qualified.
- If you're missing features and functions on your SAP BusinessObjects system, ensure that the imported SAP roles received the necessary authorizations in your SAP BusinessObjects system to perform the task.
- Ensure that the *web.xml* file has been configured properly if you're using OpenDocument or InfoView inside the SAP NetWeaver Portal (see Section 9.1.3, SAP BusinessObjects Enterprise – Configuration Steps).
- Ensure that the roles you want to import into your SAP BusinessObjects Enterprise system have users assigned to them, because the SAP authentication will only list roles with users assigned to them.
- If you're using the SAP NetWeaver Portal as an entry point, ensure that your portal system and your SAP system are configured as trusted systems by exchanging certificates (see section 9.1.2, SAP NetWeaver Portal – Configuration Steps).
- Ensure the imported users and the user type based on the SAP roles match your licensing type. You can verify that on the OPTIONS tab of the SAP authentication, where you can configure the user type for the import. In addition, you can select the menu item SETTINGS and look at the global metrics to verify the user type of the logged-on accounts.

10.2.2 Tracing

You can use the registry key `Trace` in the registry branch *HKEY_LOCAL_MACHINE\SOFTWARE\Business Objects\Suite 12.0\SAP\Authentication* to enable the tracing for the SAP authentication. The trace file will be located based on the path of the registry key `TraceDir` in the branch *HKEY_LOCAL_MACHINE\SOFTWARE\Business Objects\Suite 12.0\SAP*.

10.3 Publishing Crystal Reports

In this section we'll focus on the publishing integration of Crystal Reports with SAP NetWeaver Business Warehouse, steps you can use to ensure a proper configuration, and steps you can use to troubleshoot this area of the integration of your SAP system with SAP BusinessObjects Enterprise.

10.3.1 Steps to Validate the Configuration

Similar to the previous sections, the following is a list of items for you to check if you're having trouble with the publishing integration of Crystal Reports with SAP NetWeaver Business Warehouse.

- Ensure that the role you're trying to use on the SAP NetWeaver Business Warehouse side has been imported to your SAP BusinessObjects Enterprise system and has been assigned in Transaction /CRYSTAL/RPTADMIN as the role to your SAP BusinessObjects server definition (see Section 2.4.2, Setting up the Publishing Process for Crystal Reports).
- Ensure that the role has a valid description in all languages you want to use. This can be done in Transaction PFCG.
- Ensure that your RFC destination in Transaction SM59 is working properly (see Section 2.4.2).
- Ensure that the user publishing a report has all of the necessary rights in the SAP BusinessObjects system (see Section 2.4.2).
- Ensure that the imported users and the user type based on the SAP roles match your licensing type. You can verify that on the OPTIONS tab of the SAP authentication, where you can configure the user type for the import. In addition, you can select the menu item SETTINGS and look at the global metrics to verify the user type of the logged-on accounts.
- You can use Transaction SMGW to look for error messages from the SAP Gateway.

10.3.2 Tracing

The publishing integration can use either an SAP Gateway or the SAP NetWeaver Business Warehouse publishing service. If you're using the publishing service, you can trace the activity of the publishing service by setting the key `Trace` in the registry branch *HKEY_LOCAL_MACHINE\SOFTWARE\Business Objects\Suite 12.0\SAP\BW Publisher Service* to the value "Yes". The path for the trace files has been configured by the registry key `TraceDir` in the registry branch *HKEY_LOCAL_MACHINE\SOFTWARE\Business Objects\Suite 12.0\SAP*.

The SAP NetWeaver Business Warehouse Publisher itself can be traced by setting the key `Trace` in the branch *HKEY_LOCAL_MACHINE\SOFTWARE\Business Objects\Suite 12.0\SAP\BWPublisher* to "Yes".

10.4 Publications

In this section we'll focus on the publication process and the tools you can use to validate your configuration and to trace the publication process if you're facing some issues in your system landscape.

10.4.1 Steps to Validate the Configuration

If you're facing issues with a publication process, there are several areas that you should validate in your configuration. Based on the complexity of the configuration, the best step is to go back to the starting point and ensure that all necessary configuration steps have been taken and have been entered correctly (see Chapter 8, Publications with SAP Security).

However, there are some steps you can use before going through the complete configuration:

- A good starting point is always the automatically generated logfile for the publication itself. If your publication fails, you can click the status FAILED, and you'll receive more details; more importantly, you'll receive a VIEW LOG FILE option that provides you with the logfile of your publication.
- Ensure that you always entered the correct Distinguished Name for your SAP and SAP BusinessObjects systems. Keep in mind that the values are case sensitive.
- Ensure that the Distinguished Name is entered with the prefix "p:" in Transaction SNCO and in the Central Management Console for the SAP authentication (see Sections 8.3.4, SNC Access Control List, and 8.3.8, SNC Options in the Central Management Console).

- Ensure that your SAP BusinessObjects services are running under an account that has access to the PSE files (see Section 8.3.7, SAP BusinessObjects Services).
- Ensure that the user groups you are using as enterprise recipients contain a user. If you're using imported SAP roles, ensure that the assigned SAP users have been imported as well. On the OPTIONS tab of the SAP authentication, you can select FORCE USER SYNCHRONIZATION and then click the UPDATE button on the ROLE IMPORT tab.
- Ensure that you can view the reports that you use for a publication by using the SAP authentication in InfoView without being prompted for your SAP credentials during viewtime.
- Ensure that the user groups you're using as enterprise recipients have the necessary rights assigned in your SAP BusinessObjects Enterprise system to view the public folders and to view the reports.

10.4.2 Tracing

Tracing the details of a publication means tracing the underlying data connectivity of the Crystal Reports object or the Web Intelligence objects that you're using. You can use the details in Section 10.1.2, Tracing, for tracing the connectivity.

When you trace the data connectivity for your publication, you should be able to see the text shown in Listing 10.1, which is similar for your SAP system as part of the logfile:

```
Logon string: CLIENT=003 LANG=EN ASHOST="cimtdc00.wdf.sap.corp"
SYSNR=00 SNC_MODE=1 SNC_QOP=1
SNC_LIB="C:\Program Files\SAP\CRYPTO\sapcrypto.dll"
SNC_PARTNERNAME="p:CN=CIM, OU=PM, O=SAP, C=CA"
SNC_MYNAME="p:CN=BOESERVER,OU=PM,O=SAP,C=CA"
EXTIDDATA=USER_A EXTIDTYPE=UN
```

Listing 10.1 Example for Connectivity Trace

The trace needs to include the proper EXTIDTYPE=UN for the user name, and the EXTIDDATA needs to include the user name of the recipient.

10.5 Performance

In this section we'll outline some common options that you can use to ensure that you're getting the best performance possible from your system.

In general, any knowledge you have about performance improvement and performance tuning for your SAP NetWeaver Business Warehouse system applies to the usage of the SAP BusinessObjects software on top of the SAP NetWeaver Business Warehouse system.

10.5.1 General Performance Considerations

The following are some general recommendations in regard to the performance of your SAP NetWeaver Business Warehouse system. Covering SAP NetWeaver Business Warehouse performance tuning completely would be beyond the scope, and resources are available on the SAP Developer Network (*http://sdn.sap.com*) and the SAP NetWeaver documentation (*http://help.sap.com*) explaining this topic to a much deeper extent. The items listed here are the most common items we have come across so far.

- Use your BW statistics to identify the most used but also the slowest-performing BW queries and to identify the reasons for the performance results.
- Use Transaction ST03 to evaluate the need for aggregation of the BW queries that you're using for reporting. Pay particular attention to the overall time spent on the database and the ratio between the database selected records and the transferred records. An indicator of missing aggregates would be a ratio higher than 10 for the records and a 30 % or higher database time compared to the overall time.
- You can use Transaction RSRT to execute a single BW query in a debug mode and receive a lot of information about several aspects of performance such as aggregates and technical information for the selected query.
- You can use Transaction RSTT/RSRTRACE to trace and analyze the execution of a BW query or the execution of an SAP BusinessObjects report on top of SAP NetWeaver Business Warehouse for a single user and even go into debug mode for the execution of the trace.

10.5.2 BW Query Design

The following recommendations concern BW query design:

- When your query contains several restricted keyfigures and calculated keyfigures, you should select USE SELECTION OF STRUCTURE ELEMENTS. You can select this option per BW query in Transaction RSRT by opening the properties of the BW query. By setting this property, you ensure that the structure elements such as a restricted keyfigure are sent down to the database for processing.
- A common approach (and also a common mistake) is to create a single BW query per InfoProvider, which then is used with Crystal Reports or SAP BusinessObjects Web Intelligence. It is correct that Crystal Reports and SAP BusinessObjects Web Intelligence are able to explicitly ask for specific elements (see Section 10.5.4, Report Documents and Data Retrieval) of a BW query and retrieve the data for those elements, but the number of elements in your BW query can have a significant impact on the performance, and there is no need to create a single BW query for every single Crystal Reports or SAP BusinessObjects Web Intelligence object.

  Therefore, it is recommended that you create BW queries that represent the common denominator. You should try to break down the requirements for your BW environment into groups of characteristics and keyfigures that represent a high commonality but also represent a manageable number of BW queries. If you're not sure if the BW queries that you create are becoming to large in terms of number of elements, you can easily use the available tools to trace the runtime of your BW queries and then take the necessary steps to make the necessary changes.

BW Query Design and Performance

The impact of the BW query design on the overall performance when using the SAP BusinessObjects client tools can be significantly improved by applying the correction notes listed in Section 12.2, Important Correction Notes from SAP, and the available fix packs from SAP BusinessObjects. This does not mean there is no impact at all, but you'll see major improvements.

10.5.3 Universes

The XI 3.1 release of the SAP BusinessObjects software includes several enhancements to the OLAP Universe integration with SAP NetWeaver Business Warehouse that you can use to enhance the overall performance for your end users:

- You can use a delegated search feature for the prompt objects (resulting in SAP variables) in your universe. This feature allows you to provide search functionality to your users for the list of values when being asked to provide a value for a prompt. A great side effect of this feature is that the list of values is not loaded automatically. To activate this functionality you need to navigate to the properties of the List of Values (LOV) object for the dimension objects in your universe (normally this resides in the same class in the universe) and select the property DELEGATE SEARCH.
- Optional and mandatory variables are treated differently in OLAP Universes in regard to one major item that can impact overall performance. A mandatory variable results in a mandatory prompt that will always automatically load a list of values from which the user can select. An optional variable results in an optional prompt that can be left blank, so the list of values is not loaded at all unless the user explicitly refreshes the list of values. You might want to consider having more optional variables in your underlying BW queries or to activate the delegate search (see above) for the mandatory variables.

10.5.4 Report Documents and Data Retrieval

This section will explain the differences between the data that is used for your report and the data that is retrieved from the underlying system.

- Crystal Reports only asks for data for characteristics and keyfigures that are being used in the actual report. You can always verify that yourself by following the menu path DATABASE • SHOW SQL QUERY in the Crystal Reports Designer. For SAP NetWeaver Business Warehouse, this means that even though your BW query has 10 characteristics and 10 keyfigures and your Crystal Reports object has 2 characteristics and 2 keyfigures, Crystal Reports will send an MDX statement asking for 2 characteristics and 2 keyfigures.
- For SAP BusinessObjects Web Intelligence you have an additional step compared to Crystal Reports. The SAP BusinessObjects Web Intelligence report is based on an SAP BusinessObjects Web Intelligence query, which is based on the OLAP Universe. Each time you refresh the SAP BusinessObjects Web Intelligence report, the definition that you created in the query panel is used for data retrieval. This is not necessarily a bad idea because SAP BusinessObjects Web Intelligence provides your users an ad hoc reporting environment, and the initial large query definition results in a large data volume being available

to your users, but it is something to consider for the overall performance. In the SAP BusinessObjects Web Intelligence scenario, the report itself does not decide which data is being retrieved, but instead the objects used in the query panel are those that will be use for data retrieval.

- When the needed information is available as a display attribute and as a navigational attribute, you might want to consider using the display attribute because the usage of navigational attributes leads to additional table joins in the database schema on the SAP NetWeaver Business Warehouse side.
- When using SAP BusinessObjects Web Intelligence, you should make sure the option USE QUERY DRILL in the document properties is activated. This is especially helpful when working with hierarchies and allowing your end-users to drill down from a higher level into more details.

  Even though Crystal Reports and SAP BusinessObjects Web Intelligence are capable of sending explicit statements for data retrieval based on large BW queries, the query design has an impact on the overall performance.

10.5.5 Caching, Scheduling, and Publication

The following items refer to ways of precalculating either the data or the actual report so that there is no need for direct on-demand access anymore. Especially in cases where you need to share either a very large data volume or you need to share a report with a very large set of users, you might want to consider those options:

- For scenarios where most of the navigations and variable selections of your users are predictable, you can use the information broadcasting functionality to cache those query results in the SAP NetWeaver Business Warehouse system.
- You can give each of your end users the right to schedule a report for themselves and thus create a report with saved data in the SAP BusinessObjects Enterprise system. You can set the proper rights for your users in the SAP BusinessObjects Enterprise system to allow the usage of scheduling.
- When you're providing reports to a large set of users, but those reports can be scheduled based on the data validity, you should consider setting up a publication for the report and use the imported SAP roles as enterprise recipients.

- Especially in cases where you want to provide dashboards with Xcelsius to a large set of users, you should consider using a combination of a publication (using a Crystal Report or SAP BusinessObjects Web Intelligence document) and SAP BusinessObjects Live Office to provide the data to Xcelsius. In that way you can prepare the data and provide a good performance for your dashboard by keeping the data-level security configured in your SAP system intact.
- In addition to the items mentioned above, Crystal Reports 2008 offers a feature that allows you to create selections on top of saved data. By following the menu path Report • Select export • Saved data you can set up a selection for your Crystal Report object that will be used on top of saved data. This is a great feature in combination with the publications described previously. By combining a publication process and the functionality to apply a selection on top of saved data in a report, you can set up a scheduling process for a larger data volume but keep the data-level security intact, and then offer your users additional selection criteria on top of the saved data in your report. This is especially useful when you want to provide data with additional selections to Xcelsius via SAP BusinessObjects Live Office.

In this chapter you will receive a short overview of some upcoming topics that might be of interest for an integrated deployment of SAP Business-Objects and SAP software.

11 Integration Outlook

When I was starting to write this book (November 2008), the integration work of the SAP and SAP BusinessObjects teams was in full progress but because of the schedule for this book, I wasn't able to include some of the upcoming integration capabilities here. The next couple of paragraphs outline some upcoming items for the SAP BusinessObjects XI 3.x platform, which are also mentioned on the road-map from SAP and SAP BusinessObjects.

Xcelsius

The major enhancement for the Xcelsius integration is a direct connectivity on top of SAP NetWeaver Business Warehouse, which will allow you to directly consume BW queries inside your Xcelsius dashboard, without the need for several layers.

This will be a great enhancement for the dashboarding area, and it provides you with a direct connectivity toward SAP NetWeaver Business Warehouse in addition to the existing capabilities of using Crystal Reports and SAP BusinessObjects Web Intelligence in combination with publications.

Data Federator

Data Federator is a product that allows you to combine multiple data sources into a virtual view so that you can use the combination of these sources in the SAP BusinessObjects BI tools. Part of the current integration roadmap is an SQL interface on an InfoProvider level for Data Federator. By using this new capability you'll be able to use relational data access on top of SAP NetWeaver Business Warehouse. More importantly you'll be able to use Data Federator to combine

SAP and non-SAP data and use the combined view in the SAP BusinessObjects toolset.

SAP BusinessObjects Polestar

SAP BusinessObjects Polestar is a product that allows you to search, explore, and analyze data in a very unique and simple to use UI. As part of the integration roadmap, SAP BusinessObjects Polestar can use the scalability of BW Accelerator and in that way provide search and explore capabilities on already indexed InfoCubes.

Product Roadmap Disclaimer

The above descriptions of future functionality are the author's interpretation of the public available product integration roadmap. These items are subject to change at any time without any notice, and the author does not provide any warranty on these statements.

A regular updated product integration roadmap is available on the SAP Developer Network (*http://sdn.sap.com*).

Appendices

A Using SNC for Authentication

In Chapter 8, Publications with SAP Security, you learned how to use the SAP Cryptographic Library to implement server-side trust between the SAP BusinessObjects Enterprise system and your SAP system by configuring a Secure Network Communication (SNC) communication. You also use SNC to configure a client authentication. In the next couple of steps you'll learn how to set up your SAP BusinessObjects Enterprise system and your SAP system to use client-side authentication via SNC. We'll configure the systems to use a Windows active directory (AD) account as the primary account for SAP BusinessObjects Enterprise with an alias assigned to it, which is the SAP account. In addition to the steps outlined here, you need to make sure that your SAP system is configured for SNC (see also Section 8.2, Configuring Your SAP Server), that your SAP BusinessObjects Enterprise system is prepared for SNC, and that the SNC library is deployed on the system.

To configure SAP BusinessObjects Enterprise to use SNC, you must complete the following tasks:

- Configure SAP BusinessObjects Enterprise servers to start and run under an appropriate user account.
- Configure the SAP system to trust your SAP BusinessObjects Enterprise system.
- Configure the SNC settings in the Central Management Console of SAP BusinessObjects Enterprise.
- Map SAP users as aliases to Windows AD users.

In the following steps, we'll use the Microsoft NTLM implementation for SNC. Some of the outlined steps might require different values depending on the SNC implementation you use.

Technical Prerequisites

To be able to configure SNC for client authentication, your SAP server needs to be set up for SNC (see Section 8.2, Configuring Your SAP Server), and the SNC library needs to be deployed on your SAP BusinessObjects system (Section 8.3.1, SAP Cryptographic Library). Please remember that these examples are done with the SAP Cryptographic Library or the Microsoft NTLM implementation of SNC and that you can use other implementations, but you then have to ensure that you're using the proper files and file names in the configuration dialogs.

Configuring SAP BusinessObjects Enterprise

For client SNC to work properly in your SAP BusinessObjects Enterprise system, some services of your landscape need to be started with a user account that is configured for SNC. This is similar to the steps outlined in Section 8.3.7, SAP BusinessObjects Services. For client SNC, your application server, your Central Management Server, and your processing tier (for example Crystal Reports job server and Crystal Reports processing server) need to use the SNC account. The processing tier is not a necessity for a client SNC configuration to work, but when you want to use the full functionality of your SAP BusinessObjects platform, the processing tier needs to be configured to use the established trust between your SAP and SAP BusinessObjects systems.

To set up those services to leverage the SNC account, there are different options (see Section 8.3.7 for further details). In the following example we'll use a single Server Intelligence Agent and configure it to use the SNC account. The SNC account that you set up needs to be a domain user.

1. Start the Central Configuration Manager of your SAP BusinessObjects Enterprise system (START • PROGRAMS • BUSINESSOBJECTS XI RELEASE 3.1 • BUSINESSOBJECTS ENTERPRISE • CENTRAL CONFIGURATION MANAGER).
2. Select your Server Intelligence Agent (SIA) and stop the service.
3. Select the Server Intelligence Agent and click PROPERTIES.
4. Unselect the LOG ON AS SYSTEM ACCOUNT checkbox (see Figure A.1) and enter the SNC account in the syntax DOMAIN\USER. In our example we'll use the user IHILGEFORT from the domain SAP_ALL.
5. Click OK and start the Server Intelligence Agent service.
6. Now you need to follow the same steps to configure your application server to use the SNC account. In our example the application server is Tomcat.
7. Select TOMCAT in the Central Configuration Manager and stop the service.
8. Click PROPERTIES.
9. Unselect the LOG ON AS SYSTEM ACCOUNT checkbox and enter the SNC account.
10. Click OK and start your application service.

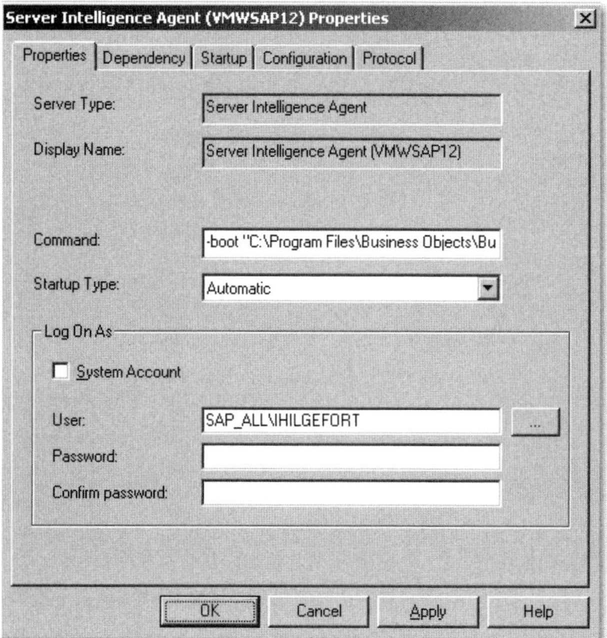

Figure A.1 Server Intelligence Agent Properties

Configuring Trust

Similar to Section 8.3.4, SNC Access Control List, you now need to create a system ID in Transaction SNCO and configure it with your SNC account.

1. Log on to your SAP system and start Transaction SNCO.
2. Click the New Entries button.
3. Enter the name of your SAP BusinessObjects system as the System ID, in our example VMWSAP12.
4. Enter the SNC account with the prefix "p:" in the SNC name field.
5. Select the Entry for RFC activated and Entry for ext ID activated checkboxes (see Figure A.2).
6. Click Save.

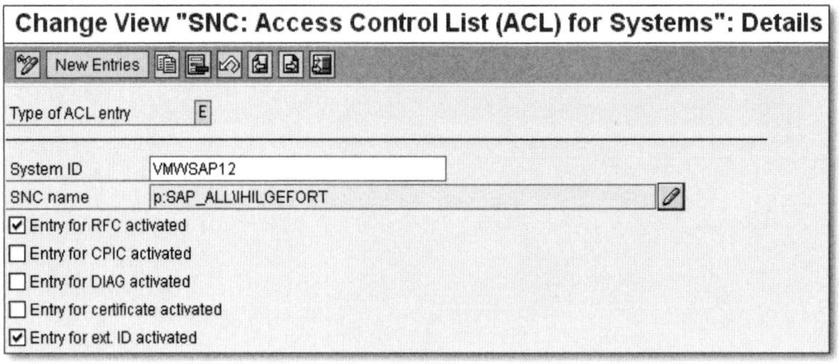

Figure A.2 Transaction SNCO

Configuring SNC Options

Before you can configure the SNC option in the Central Management Console, you need to configure the user you'll use to set up the SAP entitlement system (see also Section 2.4.1, Configuration of SAP Authentication) for SNC.

1. Start Transaction SU01 on your SAP system (see Figure A.3).

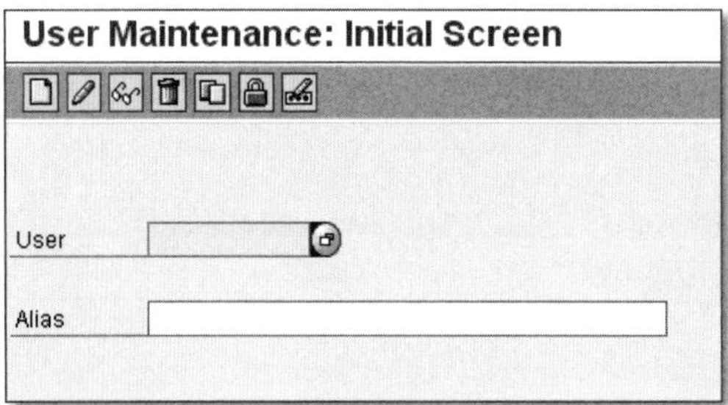

Figure A.3 User Maintenance

2. Enter the user name of the SAP account that you're going to use to set up the SAP entitlement system.
3. Follow the menu path USERS • CHANGE.
4. Select the SNC tab (see Figure A.4).
5. Enter the SNC account that you used to start the SAP BusinessObjects services (with the prefix "p:") in the SNC NAME field. In our example it would be p:SAP_ALL\IHILGEFORT.
6. Save your changes.

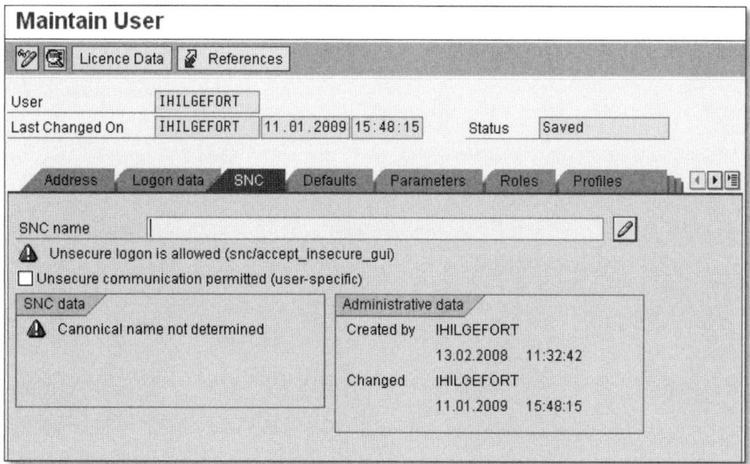

Figure A.4 User Maintenance – SNC Tab

With these steps you have configured the SAP account used to authenticate against the SAP system. Now you need to navigate to the SNC options of your SAP entitlement system in the Central Management Console to finish the SNC configuration.

1. Log on to the Central Management Console of your SAP BusinessObjects Enterprise system.
2. Navigate to the Authentication area and select the SAP authentication.
3. Navigate to the SNC Options tab and ensure that your SAP system is the one that is selected in the Logical system name field (see Figure A.5).
4. Select the Enable Secure Network Communication [SNC] checkbox.
5. Select Authentication in the Quality of protection area.
6. Enter the full path including the filename to the SNC library in the SNC library path field.
7. Enter the Distinguished Name of your SAP system in the Mutual authentication settings field. In this case you need to add the prefix "p:".
8. Navigate to the Entitlement Systems tab (see Figure A.6).
9. Enter the SNC account name in the SNC name field without any password. All other values should already be filled with the values you entered during the initial configuration.

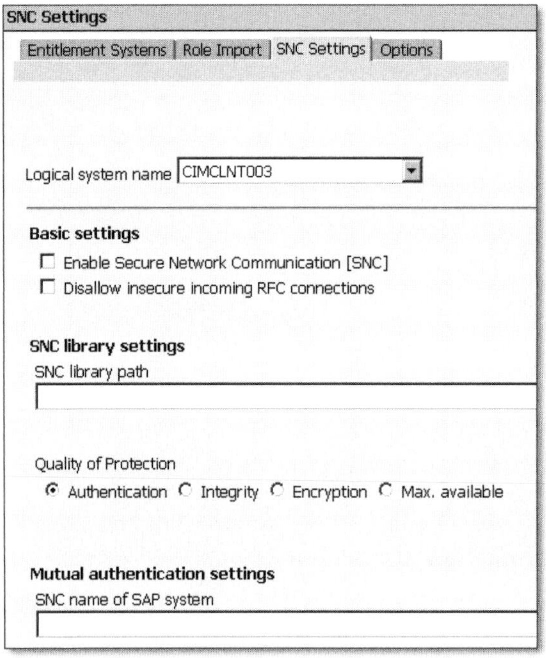

Figure A.5 SNC Options in the Central Management Console

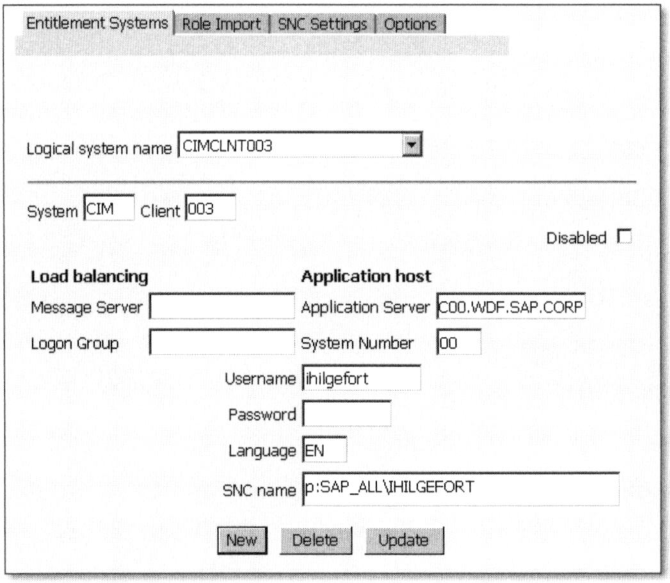

Figure A.6 Entitlement System

Mapping SAP Users

Now that you've configured the SNC options for your SAP entitlement system, you need to map the SAP credentials to your Windows AD credentials. The Windows AD user will become the primary account, and the SAP account will act as secondary account.

1. Log on to the Central Management Console of your SAP BusinessObjects Enterprise system.
2. Navigate to the Users and Groups area.
3. Click User List.
4. Click on the Windows AD user that will be configured with an SAP alias account.
5. Follow the menu path Manage • Properties (see Figure A.7).

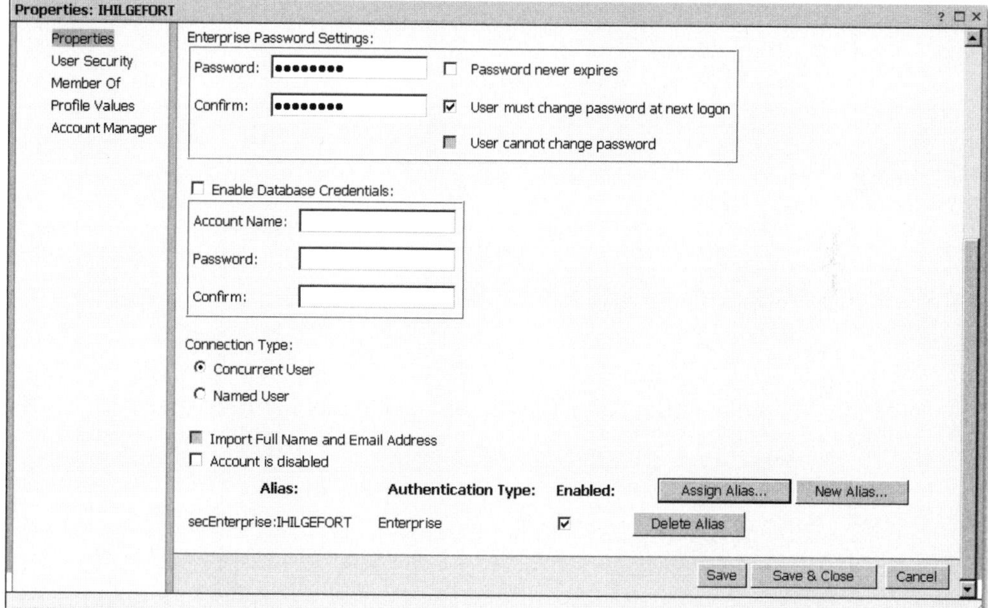

Figure A.7 User Properties

6. Click the Assign Alias button.
7. Select the SAP user from your entitlement system and add the user as the alias to the Windows AD credentials.

8. Click OK.
9. Click the SAVE & CLOSE button.

You can add multiple SAP users as an alias to the Windows AD account and in that way achieve Single Sign-on to multiple SAP systems with a single account.

Now you should be able to log on with these Windows AD credentials to your SAP BusinessObjects Enterprise system and still achieve Single Sign-On for content objects in your system.

B Important Correction Notes from SAP

The notes shown in Table B.1 are major changes in the integration of SAP BusinessObjects tools into the SAP NetWeaver landscape. I highly recommend that you use these notes to increase the performance of your deployment. A large set of these notes require SAP NetWeaver 7.01 SP2 to be installed.

Note Number	Note Title
1007048	MDX: Filtering of variables in the hierarchy display
1125433	MDX: Incorrect VALUE_TYPE entry in table CELL_DATA
1164552	Performance improvement if zero suppression is active
1161911	OLE DB for OLAP: Many read accesses to table RSRREPDIR
1162349	OLE DB for OLAP: Restriction on text and performance
1162416	OLE DB for OLAP: Restriction on MEMBER_CAPTION
1168013	MDX: Not enough data for GENERATE and NON EMPTY
1169205	MDX: Filter transfer in the case of cross join
1170323	MDX: Performance when filtering on hierarchy node
1172076	Performance improvement in special situation
1230303	MDX: Buffering of hierarchy metadata
1230712	MDX: Implementing the unorder function
1235608	MDX: Optimized memory consumption for flattening access
1237104	Performance problems occur when reading the master data
1238661	Slight performance improvement in internal business volume
1240165	Performance optimization for hierarchy authorizations
1241650	MDX: API for flattening access based on basXML
1248806	MDX: Access to [LEVEL00] using flattening
1250186	OLE DB for OLAP: Short length spec. for compounded members
1250242	Memory Leak in librfc32(u).dll when Threads Terminate

Table B.1 Important SAP Notes

Note Number	Note Title
1252370	MDX: Runtime error GETWA_NOT_ASSIGNED for cell properties
1254205	OLE DB for OLAP: Data type for properties
1254300	MDX: No values for property DESCRIPTION
1255918	MDX: Integrating statistics and tracing for basXML API
1257923	MDX: Error "Division by zero" with CROSSJOIN function
1257723	OLE DB for OLAP: Short length specified for MEMBER_CAPTION

Table B.1 Important SAP Notes (cont.)

Be sure to look at the note text, because some of the notes require a manual activity.

C The Author

Ingo started with Crystal Decisions in Frankfurt, Germany, in 1999 as a trainer and consultant for Crystal Reports and Crystal Enterprise. In 2001 he became part of a small team working at SAP headquarters in Walldorf for Crystal Decisions as a program manager. During this time Ingo worked closely with the SAP BW development group and helped design and shape the first integration of Crystal Reports with SAP BW, which then became an OEM relationship between SAP and Crystal Decisions. With the acquisition of Crystal Decisions by SAP BusinessObjects, he moved into the product management role for the integration between the SAP BusinessObjects product portfolio and SAP. In 2004 Ingo moved to Vancouver, which is one of the main development sites for SAP BusinessObjects.

In addition to his experience in product management and engineering roles, Ingo has been involved in architecting and delivering deployments of SAP BusinessObjects software in combination with SAP software for a number of worldwide customers. He also has been recognized by the SDN and SAP BusinessObjects communities as an SDN mentor for SAP BusinessObjects and SAP integration-related topics.

Recently Ingo has been focusing on the topic of embedded analytics, on which he is working with members of the BusinessSuite team to integrate the SAP BusinessObjects portfolio into the business processes of SAP applications.

Index

D

E

F

G

H

I

T

U

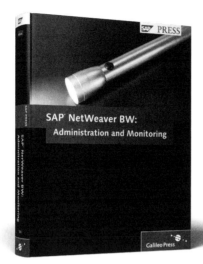

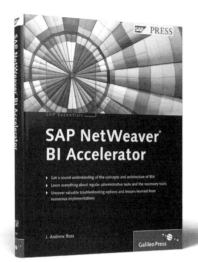

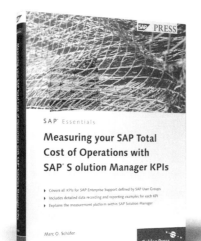

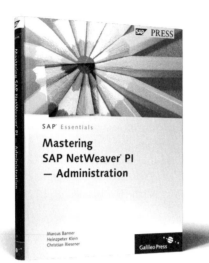

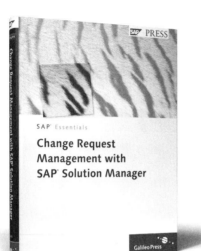